NATIONALISM AND
THE BODY POLITIC

NEW INTERNATIONAL LIBRARY OF GROUP ANALYSIS

Series Editor: Earl Hopper

Other titles in the Series

Contributions of Self Psychology to Group Psychotherapy: Selected Papers
  by Walter N. Stone

Difficult Topics in Group Psychotherapy: My Journey from Shame to Courage
  by Jerome S. Gans

Resistance, Rebellion and Refusal in Groups: The 3 Rs
  by Richard M. Billow

The Social Unconscious in Persons, Groups, and Societies.
Volume 1: Mainly Theory
  edited by Earl Hopper and Haim Weinberg

The Social Nature of Persons: One Person is No Person
  by A. P. Tom Ormay

Trauma and Organizations
  edited by Earl Hopper

Small, Large, and Median Groups: The Work of Patrick de Maré
  edited by Rachel Lenn and Karen Stefano

The Dialogues in and of the Group: Lacanian Perspectives on the
Psychoanalytic Group
  Macario Giraldo

From Psychoanalysis to Group Analysis: The Pioneering Work of
Trigant Burrow
  edited by Edi Gatti Pertegato and Giorgio Orghe Pertegato

The One and the Many: Relational Psychoanalysis and Group Analysis
  by Juan Tubert-Oklander

Listening with the Fourth Ear: Unconscious Dynamics in Analytic
Group Therapy
  by Leonard Horwitz

Forensic Group Psychotherapy: The Portman Clinic Approach
  edited by John Woods and Andrew Williams (joint publication
  with Portman)

NATIONALISM AND THE BODY POLITIC

Psychoanalysis and the Rise of Ethnocentrism and Xenophobia

Edited by

Lene Auestad

KARNAC

First published in 2014 by
Karnac Books Ltd
118 Finchley Road, London NW3 5HT

British Library Cataloguing in Publication Data

A C.I.P. for this book is available from the British Library

ISBN 978 1 78049 102 8

Edited, designed and produced by The Studio Publishing Services Ltd
www.publishingservicesuk.co.uk
e-mail: studio@publishingservicesuk.co.uk

Printed in Great Britain

www.karnacbooks.com

CONTENTS

ABOUT THE EDITOR AND CONTRIBUTORS   viii

NEW INTERNATIONAL LIBRARY OF GROUP
ANALYSIS FOREWORD by Earl Hopper   xii

INTRODUCTION by Lene Auestad   xv

PART I: BODIES AND BOUNDARIES:
XENOPHOBIC IMAGININGS

Editor's introduction to Chapter One   3

CHAPTER ONE
Fortress hypochondria: health and safety   5
Julia Borossa and Caroline Rooney

Editor's introduction to Chapter Two   21

CHAPTER TWO
"Budapest, the capital of Hungarians": rhetoric, images,   23
and symbols of the Hungarian extreme right movements
Ferenc Erős

Editor's introduction to Chapter Three   39

CHAPTER THREE
Idealised sameness and orchestrated hatred: extreme and   41
mainstream nationalism in Norway
    Lene Auestad

PART II: CONSTELLATIONS OF NATIONALISM

Editor's introduction to Chapter Four   63

CHAPTER FOUR
Funeral policy: the case of mourning populism in Poland   65
    Szymon Wróbel

Editor's introduction to Chapter Five   85

CHAPTER FIVE
The theory of Incohesion: Aggregation/Massification   87
as the fourth basic assumption in the unconscious life
of groups and group-like social systems
    Earl Hopper

Editor's introduction to Chapter Six   107

CHAPTER SIX
The schizoanalysis of Gilles Deleuze and Félix Guattari,   109
or the political between schizophrenia and paranoia
    Audronė Žukauskaitė

Editor's introduction to Chapter Seven   127

CHAPTER SEVEN
Fundamentalism, Nazism, and inferiority   129
    Haakon Flemmen

PART III: HISTORY, LONGING, IDENTIFICATION

Editor's introduction to Chapter Eight   143

CHAPTER EIGHT
The Mexican: phantasy, trauma, and history   145
    Jonathan Davidoff

Editor's introduction to Chapter Nine 161

CHAPTER NINE
Psychoanalysis and peace: Erich Fromm on history, 163
politics, and the nation
Martyn Housden

Editor's introduction to Chapter Ten 185

CHAPTER TEN
The making of the isotype character in the panoptic 187
system and its relation to globalised nationalism
Svein Tjelta

PART IV: THE "I" AND MOURNING

Editor's introduction to Chapter Eleven 207

CHAPTER ELEVEN
The evil I retreat from in myself: nationalism and *das Ding* 209
Calum Neill

Editor's introduction to Chapter Twelve 223

CHAPTER TWELVE
Between fantasy and melancholia: lack, otherness, 225
and violence
Margarita Palacios

APPENDIX
Introducing Psychoanalysis and Politics: a conversation 247
with Lene Auestad and Jonathan Davidoff
Conducted and edited by Steffen Krüger

INDEX 267

ABOUT THE EDITOR AND CONTRIBUTORS

Lene Auestad, PhD, is research fellow in philosophy, University of Oslo, affiliated with the Centre for Studies of the Holocaust and Religious Minorities, Oslo. She moved to the UK to pursue her long-standing interest in British psychoanalysis. She founded and co-ordinates the conference series Psychoanalysis and Politics. Working at the interface of psychoanalytic thinking and ethics/political theory, her writing has focused on the themes of emotions, prejudice, and minority rights. She is the editor of *Psychoanalysis and Politics. Exclusion and the Politics of Representation* (Karnac, 2012) and has co-edited a book on Hannah Arendt in Norwegian (Akademika, 2011).

Julia Borossa is director of the research centre and of the programmes in psychoanalysis at Middlesex University. She is the editor of *Sandor Ferenczi: Selected Writings* (1999) and (with Ivan Ward) of *Psychoanalysis, Fascism, Fundamentalism* (2009), and the author of *Hysteria* (2001). Her work on the histories and politics of psychoanalysis has appeared in edited collections and journals, including the *Oxford Literary Review*, the *Journal of European Studies*, and the *Journal of Postcolonial Writing*.

Jonathan Davidoff trained as a psychotherapist at the Tavistock Centre in London and works as an honorary psychotherapist at Middlesex University Hospital in London. He is a research psychologist working in the private sector and PhD candidate at the Psychoanalysis Unit of University College London. He has been one of the co-ordinators of Psychoanalysis and Politics since 2010. His research aims to combine psychoanalytic theory, philosophy, literature, and historiography to understand social and individual phenomena. He has publications on the topics of exclusion, social and individual representations, and Lacanian psychoanalytic theory.

Ferenc Erős is senior research fellow at the Research Institute for Cognitive Neurosciences and Psychology at the Research Center for Natural Sciences of the Hungarian Academy of Sciences, and Professor of Social Psychology at the Faculty of Humanities of the University of Pécs, where he directs a postgraduate programme in psychoanalytic theory. His main research areas include history and theory of psychoanalysis, and social psychology of prejudice and discrimination. In these fields he has several publications in Hungarian, English, and German.

Haakon Flemmen is a journalist, writer, and historian of ideas. He is culture editor of the Norwegian national daily newspaper *Klassekampen* and is among the editors of *Arr – The Norwegian Journal of the History of Ideas*. His research interests include Norwegian intellectual history, pre-war history of Norwegian philosophy, and the history of psychoanalysis.

Earl Hopper, PhD, CGP, FAGPA, is a psychoanalyst, group analyst and organisational consultant in private practice in London. He is a supervisor and training analyst for the Institute of Group Analysis, the British Association of Psychotherapists, and the London Centre for Psychotherapy, a Fellow of the British Psychoanalytical Society, and a member of the Group Analytic Society. He is an Honorary Tutor at the Tavistock and Portman NHS Trust and a member of the Faculty of the Post-Doctoral Program at Adelphi University, New York. He is also a Fellow of the American Group Psychotherapy Association, a former President of the International Association for Group Psychotherapy and Group Processes, a former Chairman of the Association of

Independent Psychoanalysts of the British Psychoanalytical Society, and a former member of the Executive Committee of the Group Analytic Society (London).

Martyn Housden is Reader in Modern History at the University of Bradford. His main research interests are German history 1918–1945, the history of European national minorities during the interwar period, the humanitarian work of the League of Nations (particularly concerning refugee history), and the history of ideas.

Steffen Krüger, PhD, is an independent scholar, university lecturer and a researcher in residence at the Institute for Media and Communication at Oslo University. He is a contributing editor of the journal *American Imago*, founded by Sigmund Freud and Hanns Sachs in 1939. His research interests are in the fields of media aesthetics and media communication from a psychoanalytic/psychosocial perspective. He has done extensive research on the "applied" psychoanalytic works of Ernst Kris (1900–1957). Recently, he has turned his attention to Alfred Lorenzer and the depth hermeneutic method of scenic understanding. His latest publications in English: "Fresh brains—Jacques Lacan's critique of Ernst Kris's psychoanalytic method in the context of Kris's theoretical writings" (*American Imago*, 04/2012); "How far can I make my fingers stretch—a response to Vivian Sobchack's 'What my fingers knew' from a depth-hermeneutic perspective" (*Free Associations*, 04/2013).

Calum Neill, PhD, is lecturer in critical psychology and discourse analysis at Edinburgh Napier University, Scotland. His main research interests are ethics, politics, and subjectivity. He is the author of *Lacanian Ethics and the Assumption of Subjectivity* (Palgrave, 2011) and *Ethics and Psychology: Beyond Codes of Practice* (Routledge, 2012).

Margarita Palacios is Senior Lecturer in the Department of Psychosocial Studies, Birkbeck College, University of London, UK. Her research interests include the study of the intersections of social and psychoanalytic theory, continental philosophy, gender, and postcoloniality. She is the author of *Fantasy and Political Violence: The Meaning of Anti-Communism in Chile* (2009) and *Radical Sociality: On Disobedience, Violence and Belonging* (2013).

Caroline Rooney is Professor of African and Middle Eastern Studies at the University of Kent, UK. From 2009–2012, she held an ESRC/ AHRC Global Uncertainties fellowship with a research programme entitled Radical Distrust. She is currently a Global Uncertainties Leadership Fellow, conducting a programme that examines the roles played by utopian thinking and arts activism in the imagining of a common ground. Her books include: *African Literature, Animism and Politics* (Routledge, 2000) and *Decolonising Gender: Literature and a Poetics of the Real* (Routledge, 2007).

Svein Tjelta is a specialist in clinical psychology in Bergen, Norway. He is a group analyst and a psychoanalytic psychotherapist, a training therapist at IFP, Institute for Psychotherapy, and IGA Norway. He has published a book on projective identification and a number of articles.

Szymon Wróbel is professor of philosophy at the Institute of Philosophy and Sociology of the Polish Academy of Sciences and at the Faculty of Artes Liberales, Warsaw University. He is a psychologist and philosopher interested in contemporary social and political theory and philosophy of language. He has several publications in these fields in English and Polish. His latest book, *Deferring the Self*, has been published this year in English by Peter Lang.

Audronė Žukauskaitė is senior researcher at the Lithuanian Culture Research Institute and Vilnius University, and is President of the Association of Lithuanian Philosophers. Her main research areas include contemporary philosophy, psychoanalysis, visual and cultural studies. Her recent publications include a monograph *Gilles Deleuze and Félix Guattari's Philosophy: The Logic of Multiplicity*, Vilnius: Baltos lankos, 2011, and an edited volume *Intensities and Flows: Gilles Deleuze's Philosophy in the Context of Contemporary Art and Politics*, Vilnius: LKTI, 2011. She also co-edited (with Steve Wilmer) *Interrogating Antigone in Postmodern Philosophy and Criticism*, Oxford: Oxford University Press, 2010.

NEW INTERNATIONAL LIBRARY OF GROUP ANALYSIS
FOREWORD

Psychoanalysis, sociology, and group dynamics are the three pillars that support group analysis. Perhaps a better metaphor is that they are the taproots through which group analysis draws its nourishment in seeking to understand our patients in the context of the dynamic matrices of groups within the foundation matrices of wider societies. However, we have comparatively few examples of attempts to integrate these intellectual traditions characterised by sustained argument and by empirical and clinical illustration. We especially lack work which is informed by the ideas of Freud, Klein, and the members of the Group of Independent Psychoanalysts in the UK, as well as the revisionists and neo-revisionists, including Fromm, Lacan, Kristeva, and other contemporary scholars who are prepared to challenge the orthodoxy of the establishments in psychoanalysis and group analysis. Moreover, it is unfortunate that nowadays psychoanalysis is not informed by developments in group analysis, and *vice versa*.

It is, therefore, with great pleasure that I am able to include in the New International Library of Group Analysis *Nationalism and the Body Politic*, edited by Dr Lene Auestad. This is the second volume derived from a continuing series of annual conferences and seminars concerned with the general theme of "psychoanalysis and politics". These events are themselves a contribution to the culture of psychoanalysis and group analysis, and perhaps to the intellectual and political culture of Europe. They have fostered the international and interdisciplinary study of the pathogenesis of European societies and the pathologies of their peoples. The pursuit of knowledge and understanding of such topics is best explored in the context of international and interdisciplinary events, in which students become aware of, and take as problematic, the structures and processes of their own societies, cultures, and political realities, and, thus, gain insight into their social unconscious and its influence on their styles of thinking, and what they are able to accept as problematic (Hopper & Weinberg, 2011).

Originally from Norway, but now living and studying in London, Dr Auestad has undertaken academic training in psychoanalysis, philosophy, and the social sciences. We are fortunate to be able to include in this book a special "conversation" between Lene Auestad and her associate, Jonathan Davidoff, conducted and edited by Steffen Krüger, telling the fuller story of their project and the development of these books. It is a remarkable story of the commitment of two so-called "young people" to the development of both a deeper and a wider view of psychoanalysis, and their attempts to understand the social context of personality and the personal context of society. They have gathered together a network of scholars and clinicians who share their highly ethical and passionate commitment to understanding the nature of social injustice.

In so far as the contributions to this book form a single whole, I am reminded of the saying, perhaps to be credited to Heine, "There is nothing as whole as a broken heart". *Nationalism and the Body Politic* is the story of Europe and its multiplicity of peoples who constantly create one another and, at the same time, are driven to annihilate one another, while constantly refusing to mourn their mutual losses, yet simultaneously developing brilliant theories and new schema for understanding the human condition.

My one reservation, to be debated in future volumes, is the implicit use of organismic homologies in the application of psychoanalytical ideas to the study of societal social systems. This problem is endemic in applied psychoanalysis. It remains a challenge to the basic theory of group analysis. It is possible that the new developments in relational psychoanalysis and group analysis will facilitate our increased understanding of the social as well as the biological nature of how persons organise their power relations while simultaneously coping with their fears of powerlessness in the context of traumatogenic processes.

I look forward to the next volume of papers, which is already in preparation, and to the next Conference in Budapest in May 2014. I hope that this book and these seminars will provide space for the expanding network of psychoanalysts, social scientists, and group analysts for the development of their theories and the refinement of their clinical work.

Earl Hopper, PhD
Series Editor

Reference

Hopper, E., & Weinberg, H. (Eds) (2011). *The Social Unconscious in Persons, Groups, and Societies. Volume I: Mainly Theory*. London: Karnac.

Introduction

Lene Auestad

"But the great nations themselves, it might have been supposed, would have acquired so much comprehension of what they had in common, and so much tolerance for their differences, that 'foreigner' and 'enemy' could no longer be merged, as they still were in classical antiquity, into a single concept"

(Freud, 1915b, p. 277)

Multiculturalism has failed utterly, declared Angela Merkel in a speech to her Christian Democratic Union party, adding that the idea of people from different cultural backgrounds living happily "side by side" did not work. This was after the former central banker Thilo Sarrazin had published a highly controversial book in which he accused Muslim immigrants of lowering the intelligence of German society (Weaver, 2010). Merkel's speech received a standing ovation, and it was echoed by conservative political leaders in countries across Europe, among them the outgoing Belgian prime minister Yves Leterme, Dutch deputy prime minister Maxine Verhagen, Danish Liberal Party immigration minister Søren Pind, and British prime minister David Cameron. If you do not want to accept "to melt into a single community, which is the national community" stated the French president, Nicolas Sarkozy, "you cannot be welcome in France" (Fekete, 2011, pp. 40–41).

This volume aims to question the recent revival of neo-nationalist policies in the light of the many fantasies involved in these developments. It examines both recent movements of right-wing extremism and the way in which rearticulated neo-ethnic ideas have been adopted by mainstream politicians and in mainstream public discourse. As Marianne Gullestad argued in *Plausible Prejudice* (2006), politicians from other than the right-wing populist parties have resisted specific ways of talking that are considered too extremist, rather than their underlying frame of interpretation. Thus, new forms of ethnic nationalism are being normalised and presented as self-evident. When the then UK Home Secretary David Blunkett advocated the idea of a British citizenship test, the British Nationalist Party (BNP) "with some justification, pointed out that questions of language and culture were at the core of long-standing BNP policies that had been 'stolen' by New Labour" (Banks, 2006, p. 57). Similar tendencies can be observed in other countries; in Fekete's words,

> It would seem that the centre-right is responding to the greater coordination of the European anti-immigrant, anti-Muslim electoral forces in preparation for the 2014 European Parliament elections by embracing their arguments. This mirrors the way Margaret Thatcher stole the clothes of National Front in January 1978 in her notorious "swamping" speech. It is no exaggeration, therefore, to say that the centre-right and the extreme-right are simultaneously building on the anti-immigration, anti-cultural pluralism and anti-anti racism legacy of Powell and the New Right. (Fekete, 2011, pp. 43–44).

Gullestad described how, within a nation-state, the elites of the population defines racism and xenophobia as properties belonging to "others", to layers of the population perceived as "below" themselves, so as to exempt their own contributions from self-reflection:

> In order to make sense of the many diverse opinions in the debates on immigration, large sections of the political and cultural elite now discursively limit xenophobia and racism to an imagined part of the population. They see themselves as decent and characterize this part of the population using metaphors such as the 'undercurrents' and

'the dregs of the depths of the popular masses'. . . . Discrimination is
safely assigned to the 'dregs' from which one explicitly distances
oneself. This social model makes it possible for elite people to avoid
reflecting on their own frames of interpretation. (Gullestad, 2006,
pp. 185, 187)

However, she argues, the cultural and political elite is active in formulating, promoting, and legitimising frames of interpretation that
produce and reproduce discrimination (p. 189). These are frameworks
wherein notions of history, descent, religion, and morality are inter-
twined, and these are largely exempt from critical reflection. In other
words, they are socially shared and pre- or unconscious, not yet
thought on the basis of habitual ways of conceiving of one's life-
world, and/or "maintained through a series of protective defences
against the experience of painful anxieties that would follow from the
recognition of certain social phenomena" (Hopper & Weinberg, 2011,
pp. xxxiv–xxxv).

  "What makes recent memories hang together", wrote Halbwachs
(1992, p. 52) "is not that they are contiguous in time: it is rather that
they are part of a totality of thoughts common to a group, the group
of people with whom we have a relation". Nationalism can be thought
of as such a way of making memories hang together, lending them a
teleology, a link to a larger purpose. When we say, *Something happened
because* . . ., we can mean both that it happened because of a pre-exist-
ing cause that effected it and that it happened for the sake of something that was going to happen later on: because it served a purpose.
The agent is conceived both as being pushed forward from behind
and as stretching towards a future aim. The past and the future tense
influence one another; the question of *Who was I?* or *Who were we?* is
not independent of the question of *Who do I or we want to be?* A nation,
in Anderson's words, is an imagined political community, conceived
of as limited and sovereign. "It is imagined because the members of
even the smallest nation will never know most of their fellow-
members, meet them, or even hear of them, yet in the minds of each
lives the image of their communion" (2006, p. 6). The idea of a nation,
of national identity, of who does and does not belong, is not so much
supported by direct experience as culturally fabricated or construed.
Nationalist imaginaries are taught to children in schools and distrib-
uted to the population via modern mass media. A national school

system and national media both contribute to the standardisation of language. "A language is a dialect backed by an army", writes Eriksen (2002, p. 103), who uses the example of how Danish, Swedish, and Norwegian would be referred to as one language rather than three if it had not been for nationalism. We might also think of how Serbo-Croatian, after the dissolution of Yugoslavia, was turned into distinct languages applying to each nation-state, "cleansed" of some of the words that had recently become "foreign". The education system and the media also spread and endorse, make normative, a nationalist reading of history and a national focus on what is "newsworthy" in the present, thus being central in creating "a totality of thoughts common to a group" (Halbwachs, 1992) where the "group" is imagined rather than directly experienced. Both systems, furthermore, tend to give priority to a nation's own culture; literature, in particular, is conceived of and promoted as "national". The idea of the nation is frequently staged in sports events, where, whether it is teams or individuals competing, these are most often construed as representatives of nations, combating other nations. The winners are celebrated with flags and national anthems, thus their nationality, rather than any other characteristic, is emphasised. The use of such symbols mobilises emotions, even forceful passions, for something that, in itself, might seem abstract and remote. Anderson emphasises this abstract and peculiarly modern character of nationalism in reference to the example of the tombs of Unknown Soldiers. In these, nothing remains of the individuals who have died; only the idea of the nation is successfully commemorated:

> No more arresting emblems of the modern culture of nationalism exist than cenotaphs and tombs of Unknown Soldiers. The public ceremonial reverence accorded these monuments precisely *because* they are either deliberately empty or no one knows who lies inside them, has no true precedents in earlier times. . . . Yet void as these tombs are of identifiable mortal remains or immortal souls, they are nonetheless saturated with ghostly *national* imaginings. (Anderson, 2006, p. 9, original italics)

This commemoration could be read as failing to make sense of these persons' deaths in postulating an abstract, idealised cause while failing to make a link to human experience. Suggesting that social traumas operate analogously to individual traumas, and making use of Masud Khan's proposal that Freud's protective barrier be understood not as a "stimulus barrier", but as the relationship of a helpless baby with its carer, Young-Bruehl (2013) argued that the events of the Second World War became a shared cumulative trauma. A breach in the protective shield repeats or reactivates earlier breaches, and "a society provides the individuals who constitute it with a protective shield or shields, and there are traumas that breach these shields of existential belonging and social care or service and political union" (2013, pp. 46–47). Her example of the USA as reacting to the trauma of the Second World War illustrates her use of this model of thought:

> America became a "Never again!" society: being resolute about never being traumatised again was as close as the society came to acknowledging that it had been traumatised, even though it had been victorious in the war and had emerged "a superpower". There were many facets of this rigidity: assertions of territorial and military invulnerability; assertions of moral rectitude . . . rejection of anything that could be called "appeasement" in foreign affairs, assertions of "exceptionalism"; celebrations of American individualism (often gendered as "rugged individualism" and thus indistinguishable from *machismo*); and triumphalism (particularly as the Cold War was "won"). These social defences became so normal that individuals with these forms of narcissistic character armour could not recognise them as such. (Young-Bruehl, 2013, pp. 48–49)

The last sentence cited reveals a value of the microcosm/macrocosm thinking involved; stating that some individuals' characters were like that of the large-scale social system enables one to conceive of social groupings, units, or movements as sharing some of the same features as individual neuroses or psychoses. Processes that would be regarded as pathological when encountered on an individual level commonly occur on a collective level without being thought of as abnormal, as Freud emphasised in his *Group Psychology and the Analysis of the Ego* (1921b, p. 142) and in *Totem and Taboo* (1912–1913, p. 74). "Normality" is changeable, which is apparent from the tendencies referred to in the beginning of this introduction; hostility towards immigrants and refugees and people conceived of as "others" is no longer restricted to extremists, but taken up and endorsed by large swathes of the political centre. In Young-Bruehl's terms, some social defences have become so "normal" as to have become unnoticeable to many. Or, one might say, some fantasies have become so normal as to be socially accepted as real. Fantasies might be thought of as psychical façades which bar the way to memories, or as ways of re-elaborating and, thus, partly recognising repressed occurrences. In relation to the Wolf Man's fantasies, where the passive role he had played towards his sister had been envisioned as reversed, Freud (1918b, p. 20) wrote that they "corresponded exactly to the legends by means of which a nation that has become great and proud tries to conceal the insignificance and failure of its beginnings". This example informs us of the Wolf Man's fantasy, and compares it to the nationalist legends encouraged by states; where the sister had, in reality, undressed and seduced him, his fantasy transformed the event into its opposite. Such a fantasy becomes social or political in so far as it is shared, in so far as its members take part in the love and worship of common ideals, in enforcement of collective defences, in avoidance of common taboos. Yet, importantly, what the micro-/macrocosm thinking exemplified by Young-Bruehl covers up, and what the example of the Wolf Man's phantasy hints at but does not render explicit, is the potential asymmetry involved in unconscious alliances. As René Kaës points out, "The secret is established between two or more persons vis-à-vis a third party who is excluded from it" (2007, p. 110). The promoters of the secret are protected by keeping the unconscious contents in the dark, while the individual who is excluded from the secret, but included in the alliance, is left to carry the intolerable thoughts and affects. In terms of such a distinction between asymmetrical and symmetrical unconscious alliances, the fantasies linked with nationalism are asymmetrical in so far as nationalism explicitly or implicitly links ethnicity with the state. Thus, nationalisms can be defined as

> ethnic ideologies which hold that their group should dominate a state. A nation-state, therefore, is a state dominated by an ethnic group, whose markers of identity (such as language or religion) are frequently embedded in its official symbolism and legislation. (Eriksen 2002, p. 98)

Its legitimacy depends on convincing the popular masses that it actually represents its population, conceived as a cultural unit.

As Corell points out (2010, pp. 30–31), there is no obvious connection between the "we" of today and the "them" of the past; thus, it is

of interest to ask to what extent historians present an earlier population as part of today's "we". The question of the construction of the
"we" is related to questions about the heroes, or protagonists, and
villains, or antagonists, of the text, and of who is afforded agency;

> Active and passive verbs reveal who the grammatical agents of the
> text are, who is doing something, and who has something being done
> to them. . . . Passive constructions and the use of large and abstract
> substantives remove the focus from singular actors, for instance
> Norwegian policemen's participation in the arrest of the Norwegian
> Jews [in the autumn of 1942]. A number of events are compressed into
> one large unit. . . . words such as "arrest" and "deportation" can
> conceal the materiality of the past, since they encompass a number of
> physical bodies and human destinies, both as victims and perpetra-
> tors. (Corell, 2010, pp. 32–33, translated for this edition)

This historian's example draws attention to the processes and
distortions involved in the construction of the "we" and of the corre-
sponding "them" as to who is presented as acting and afforded
responsibility, who is rendered visible and invisible, who are
described as individuals, and who are compressed into masses.
Similar selections are made in relation to which events are singled out
for remembrance and which can be forgotten. The example above
illustrates historians' usage of condensation so as to blur or suppress
the responsibility of the perpetrators as well as the fate of the victims.
Condensation also operates in the construction of the "we" on which
"the body politic" in the title plays. The fantasy of the nation as a body
(Koenigsberg, 1977; Reich 1970[1933]), could be seen to draw on fantasies of fusion or "imagined sameness" (Gullestad, 2006). The nation
is conceived of as a living organism. Via considerations of purity, this
organism is perceived as suffering from a disease, the source of which
is a category of people internal to the body of this organism. The solution, necessary to "save the nation" may be to "remove" this category
of people from the body of the nation (Koenigsberg, 1977, p. 15). The
metaphor of the nation as a body is echoed in Money-Kyrle's (1939, p.
218) characterisation of "group hypochondria" in connection with the
burning of witches and heretics: "The Church, and State united to it,
could tolerate no foreign body within itself, and turned ferociously
upon any that it found". The analogy might call to mind fantasies of
scooping out, sucking dry, of poisoning, or of the other's supreme

enjoyment. Where "the foreign body" in Freud's formulation designates the memory of the trauma, they admit that the analogy breaks down in that the resistance is what infiltrates the ego and that the treatment consists in "enabling the circulation to make its way into a region that has hitherto been cut off" (1895d). Thus, conversely, one might think, along the lines of Butler's (2004) reflections on the obituary as an act of nation-building, when the national public sphere is constituted on the basis of a prohibition on certain forms of public grieving, certain forms of remembering, how one might allow for narration, or representation of the hitherto cut-off region.

The nation is often imagined as a mother or a father. "Never forget that your country is the mother of your life" declared Joseph Goebbels, and Angriff stated, "*The idea of 'Mother'* is inseparable from the idea of 'being German'. Is there anything which can lead us closer together than our mutual honouring of the mother?" (Reich, 1970[1933], p. 91). Note how separate mothers have merged into one abstract idea, again merged with the idea of the nation. Add on the idea of a threat, and the image turns violent; "If someone cracks a whip across your mother's face, would you say to him, Thank you! Is he a man too?! One who does such a thing is not a man – he is a brute!" (Goebbels, cited by Reich 1970[1933], p. 93). Nationalism might begin as new nations claim their independence from other states, regarded, more or less legitimately, as oppressors, and draw on rhetorics of freedom from a larger state in legitimising themselves. They might then, in the next instance, go on to oppress others, and perceive hostile aggressors where none exists. This is clearly the case where the metaphor of invading forces is applied to refugees or immigrants; the other as a real historical adversary has been made an enemy within. The abstract community postulated by nationalism is conceived of in terms of kinship and likened to a kin group. In times when the social importance of kinship is weakened, nationalism tends to appear, promising security and stability at a time when people are being uprooted; its ideology aims to re-create a sense of wholeness and continuity with the past (Eriksen, 2002, p. 104). Of course, this sentiment of wholeness is imagined, the continuity construed based on selective history telling, and the fantasised kinship is not like real, close relations. At the same time, it is socially instituted so as to make people feel they are part of a nation—and so as to make others feel they are not. In reference to the aftermath of 9/11, which marked a shift towards greater stereotyping of people who, because of their religion or ethnicity, "looked like they might be terrorists", Phillips states:

> Only a few days after the collapse of the Twin Towers, I sat in my New York classroom facing my undergraduates. . . . I gestured to the whole room. 'Who in here feels one hundred per cent comfortable with describing themselves as a citizen of the United States of America? . . . Not a single non-white student raised a hand. (Phillips, 2011, pp. 29–30)

This relates to an underlying question of how we conceive of belonging, and whom we refer to as "we". Is belonging best seen as based on a force of habit (Hume, 1985[1739–1740]), or as a product of the workings of the pleasure principle? Since identities are imposed on individuals from without, though, they are socio-political as well as personal, and often far from merely pleasurable. Representatives of the "them" tend to be seen as more homogenous than representatives of the "we", though probing the category of the "we" leads to its fragmentation:

> Thus, when one says "I am a vegetarian" (or Christian or whatever), one cannot actually look directly at these terms, or look within them. One cannot probe them. For identity to work, the internal space "knowing who I am" must not be tested. . . . The place one stands on, one's identity, is often enough illusory—a reification. (Dalal, 2012, p. 92)

Collective and personal identities are reifications. Nationalism reifies history into a selective and celebratory identity narrative. It might be that there is a temptation, when engaged in the activity of making sense of something, to make, so to say, hyper-sense: to master the material so thoroughly that nothing is left to chance, to contingency, or spontaneity, but this pull or temptation to make too much sense, to a full narrative closure, is also problematic. Thus, Arendt wrote about her first main work that it "does not really deal with the 'origins' of totalitarianism", instead, it "gives a historical account of the elements which crystallized into totalitarianism" (1994[1953], p. 403). This is why she was accused of being "unscientific"—she did not present a unified tale of why everything had to happen the way it did, because her claim is that it did not. "All historiography", she stated, "is necessarily salvation and frequently justification" (1994 [1953], p. 402), while in writing about something one does not wish to conserve but, rather, to destroy, it is important to preserve the thought that it could have been otherwise—by not eliminating one's human reactions to the situation, and by resisting an urge or demand to close all the gaps.

This book was inspired by a conference titled "Nationalism and the Body Politic" that took place in the rooms of the Norwegian Psychoanalytic Society in Oslo, 25–27 March 2011, the second in the series Psychoanalysis and Politics. This is a conference series that aims to address how crucial contemporary political issues may be fruitfully analysed through psychoanalytic theory and vice versa—how political phenomena may reflect back on psychoanalytic thinking. The series is interdisciplinary and welcomes perspectives from different psychoanalytic schools. Thus, the contributors to this volume represent different academic fields and different psychoanalytical directions, based on the belief that, through such encounters, dogmatism is avoided, and new and surprising connections are made, allowing for fresh developments of thought.

While the first symposium discussed acts of social exclusion, denigration, and demonisation (see Auestad, 2012), the next one was centred on the reverse side of such acts, specifically: idealisation and the idealised, pure object, addressing the revival of neo-nationalist policies in different countries, and the fantasies connected with them. When the thought of the symposium was conceived, in the autumn of 2010, there were frightening signs of such developments in many countries, and there were also resistances, in the planning and in the aftermath, to raising and reflecting on such issues. Curiously, as we know now, Breivik's terrorist attacks in Oslo and on Utøya took place only a few months afterwards. Upon reflection, we have experienced enactments on a smaller scale of some of the cultural–political conflicts we were analysing on a larger scale in the realm of national and international politics. One of the participants, who was positive about the conference, wrote afterwards, in describing what he had learnt from it, that it took place on the 9th of April. As mentioned, it was held in March, but the date he remembered is not just any date; it marks the day when German soldiers invaded Norway, as well as Denmark, in 1940. Thus, the slogan "Never again 9th of April" is known to everyone in both these countries. The participant appeared to express that, while appreciating these reflections, he also unconsciously experienced them as an attack on a good (or idealised) object, that there were pains associated with questioning these relationships. In later symposia, we have included a group reflection session, a space for presenters and participants to think about their own relationships and reactions to the themes presented and evoked.

This book is divided into four parts. Part I, "Bodies and boundaries: xenophobic imaginings", gathers together three chapters that discuss fantasies centred on the body in relation to xenophobia and nationalism. The first contribution introduces the notion of "the foreign body", or "the body as foreign", to question the formation of racism in relation to social anxieties around health and safety. The second examines the iconography of anti-Semitic propaganda in relation to the Hungarian extreme-right party Jobbik, drawing on Imre Hermann's analogy between the urge to eliminate parasites from the skin, the "delousing" practices, and the "epidemics" of persecutions of Jews. The third contribution explores the continuity between more and less extreme varieties of xenophobia, examining the concept of "imagined sameness" and sexualised fantasies of merging in Norwegian nationalism.

The second part of this volume, "Constellations of nationalism", contains four contributions with more of a structural focus on phenomena linked with nationalism. The first discusses populism as a discourse in which the logic of equivalence operates unchallenged; the image of society resembles that of a "crowd" or a "mass", and refers to the recent post-communist history of Poland. The second contribution examines the fourth basic assumption in the unconscious life of groups which the author has termed "Incohesion: aggregation/massification" or (ba) "I:A/M", arguing that the massification of traumatised societies is dominated by processes of fatal purification. The third interprets Deleuze and Guattari's concepts of the schizophrenic and paranoid poles of political economy in relation to the Lithuanian political scene, where the revolutionary drives of 1990 were replaced by reactionary nationalist forces. The author argues that the increasing outbursts against ethnic and sexual minorities reveal the deep connections between the paranoid form of the psyche and the nation state. The fourth contribution examines the history of the concept of fundamentalism and scholars who aimed to explore the psychology of the fundamentalist and apply it to an understanding of Nazism, discussing the Adlerian Ingjald Nissen's analysis of the creation of feelings of inferiority in the masses that were fed with compensatory ideology.

Part III, "History, longing, identification", contains three contributions which, in different ways, discuss the problem of history and nostalgia in relation to nationalist fantasies. The first contributor argues that the phantasy of the primal scene is at the basis of the repetition compulsion of Mexican history and the destructive cycle in which Mexican historicity is caught up, and then turns to a discussion of the historical causes of this fantasy. The second discusses Erich Fromm's ideas on Nazism, history, politics, and the nation, and highlights the lasting value of his analyses. The third contribution addresses regulation of society by standardisation, based on increasing demands for more control, and suggests that the ideology of nationalism can be seen as a regressive reaction of primary identification with the local group in the face of threats caused by globalisation.

The fourth and final part of this book, "The 'I' and mourning", is made up of two contributions that relate the phenomenon of nationalism to the ontology of the "I" and to the nature of finished or unfinished mourning. The first contribution considers the encounter with the other and the role of identification, discussing the gravitation towards assigning an evil character to the unknown in the other in the light of identification and national identity. The final chapter explores fantasy and melancholia in relation to political and social violence. In fantasy that accompanies episodes of political violence and of nationalist hatreds, it is argued, there is an overproduction of meaning and the enjoyment of the exclusion of the feminised other who appears as a threat to the possibility of "fullness" of the national identity. In the case of melancholia, which accompanies some expressions of current social violence, on the other hand, there is inclusion without recognition of the other, the death drive not being projected into an exterior other, but instead on to the self or community.

The contributors to this volume do not present us with one unified view of the causes and essence of nationalism, or of the recently revived tendency towards ethnocentrism and xenophobia. There are differences of opinion as well as differences of emphasis. It is to be hoped that these differences will stimulate the reader to further independent reflection, as the encounter between the participants at the conference is replaced by the encounter between the texts and their readers and as the social and political realities that occasioned these thoughts are followed by a range of new phenomena.

References

Anderson, B. (2006). *Imagined Communities. Reflections on the Origin and Spread of Nationalism* (revised edn). London: Verso.

Arendt, H. (1994)[1953]. A reply to Eric Voegelin. In: H. Arendt & J. Kohn (Eds.), *Essays in Understanding* (pp. 401–408). New York: Schocken.

Auestad, L. (Ed.) (2012). *Psychoanalysis and Politics. Exclusion and the Politics of Representation.* London: Karnac.

Butler, J. (2004). *Precarious Life. The Powers of Mourning and Violence.* London: Verso.

Corell, S. (2010). *Krigens ettertid. Okkupasjonshistorien i norske historiebøker.* Oslo: Scandinavian Academic Press.

Dalal, F. (2012). *Thought Paralysis. The Virtues of Discrimination.* London: Karnac.

Eriksen, T. H. (2002). *Ethnicity and Nationalism* (2nd edn). London: Pluto Press.

Fekete, L. (2011). Understanding the European-wide assault on multiculturalism. In: H. Mahamdallie (Ed.), *Defending Multiculturalism* (pp. 38–52). London: Bookmarks.

Freud, S. (1895d). *Studies on Hysteria. S.E., 2.* London: Hogarth.

Freud, S. (1912–1913). *Totem and Taboo. S.E., 13*: 1–161. London: Hogarth.

Freud, S. (1915b). Thoughts for the times on war and death. *S.E., 14*: 275–300. London: Hogarth.

Freud, S. (1918b). *From the History of an Infantile Neurosis. S.E., 17*: 7–122. London: Hogarth.

Freud, S. (1921c). *Group Psychology and the Analysis of the Ego. S.E., 18*: 67–143. London: Hogarth.

Gullestad, M. (2006). *Plausible Prejudice.* Oslo: Universitetsforlaget.

Halbwachs, M. (1992). *On Collective Memory.* Chicago, IL: University of Chicago Press.

Hopper, E., & Weinberg, H. (2011). Introduction. In E. Hopper & H. Weinberg (Eds.), *The Social Unconscious in Persons, Groups, and Societies. Vol. 1: Mainly Theory.* London: Karnac.

Hume, D. (1985)[1739–1740]. *A Treatise of Human Nature.* London: Penguin Classics.

Kaës, R. (2007). The question of the unconscious in common and shared psychic spaces. In: J. C. Calich & H. Hinz (Eds.), *The Unconscious. Further Reflections* (pp. 93–119). London: International Psychoanalytical Association.

Koenigsberg, R. A. (1977). *The Psychoanalysis of Racism, Revolution and Nationalism*. New York: Library of Social Science.

Money-Kyrle, R. (1939). Varieties of group formation. In: D. Meltzer & E. O'Shaughnessy (Eds.), *The Collected Papers of Roger Money-Kyrle* (pp. 210–228). Strathtay, Perthshire: Clunie Press, 1978.

Phillips, C. (2011). *Colour Me English. Selected Essays*. London: Harvill Secker.

Psychoanalysis and Politics www.psa-pol.org.

Reich, W. (1970)[1933]. *The Mass Psychology of Fascism*. London: Penguin.

Weaver, M. (2010). Angela Merkel: German multiculturalism has 'utterly failed'. *Guardian*, Sunday 17 October.

Young-Bruehl, E. (2013). Civilisation and its dream of contentment: reflections on the unity of humankind. In: *The Clinic and the Context. Historical Essays*. London: Karnac.

PART I

BODIES AND BOUNDARIES: XENOPHOBIC IMAGININGS

Editor's introduction to Chapter One

T
he chapter addresses the imaginary malady, or malady of the
imagination, called hypochondria through its relation to questions of safety. Its title refers to one of Ferenczi's patients, an
artist who attempted to construct a total system to serve as his own
invulnerable world, a familial "fortress hypochondria". In hypochondria, as in paranoia, there is an understanding that the self is under
threat, though this is not a case of being persecuted by hostile others,
but of a hostile something. The authors argue that hypochondria is not
only an individual phenomenon, but also one in which something like
a socially maintained superego seeks to supervise not so much the
realm of ethics as the realm of the ontological. Ours is a culture of
contempt for the body, where a desire for perfection is linked with
demands to eliminate physical diversity and signs of lived life. It
effects a pressure to sustain an invulnerable body, requiring an ever-
ready obligation of vigilant defence in a world emptied of trust. The
hypochondriac takes the body to be potentially his or her worst
enemy, being neither quite self nor as sufficiently other, wishing to
protect the body out of self-love while also feeling it is the body that
has turned against him or her. The authors raise the notion of "the
foreign body, the body as foreign" to question the formation of

racism, how a paranoid form of collective hypochondria might be mobilised. Our fears around disease can be made to serve a politics of separatism; while we take our own bodily habits for granted and cease to notice them, the presence of the bodily manifests itself to us through the body of the other as a disturbance. They argue in favour of de-pathologising the pathological through a deconstruction of the dichotomy of health and illness. We all inhabit degrees of un-health, and no one is free or immune from physical suffering; "We are all vermin". One cure for hypochondria, the authors suggest, might be forms of activism on behalf of suffering others, helping each other to bear the unbearable.

CHAPTER ONE

Fortress hypochondria: health and safety

Julia Borossa and Caroline Rooney

A s our title indicates, we wish to address the question of nationalism somewhat obliquely, invoking the imaginary malady, or malady of the imagination, that is called hypochondria and exploring its relation to security. We will begin this enquiry through attending to the personal dimensions of anxieties around health and safety and then extend our considerations to what may be termed a biopolitics of hypochondria, which is a question of whether or not hypochondria has the potential to manifest itself as a group psychology. In researching this collaborative paper, we have found that any attempt to make definitive statements about hypochondria tends quite frequently to give rise to counter-assertions. We have made use of this perplexity to structure our paper dialectically, as a dialogue of sorts, bouncing back and forth in the manner of "on the one hand . . . and on the other hand". It is as if not only the condition of hypochondria but the very concept of it serves to resist diagnosis.

On the one hand, then, it would be possible to suggest that the condition arises through an empathetic response to illness. With reference to case histories of hypochondriacs, including those assembled in Dillon's exemplary book, *Tormented Hope: Nine Hypochondriac Lives* (2009), it seemed especially striking to us that quite frequently the onset of morbid attention to one's own health is triggered by the serious illness or death of a close relative or friend. As Dillon writes,

> it comes as no surprise . . . to discover in the literature on hypochondria that a child who grows up in close proximity to illness or death is considerably more likely to develop hypochondriacal tendencies as a young adult. (2009, p. 4)

This may be corroborated by Baur's observation that many instances of early onset hypochondria involve "the irrational sense of vulnerability that may be impressed upon a child through his observation of another's pain and death" (Baur, 1988, p. 61). In other words, in such cases, the real and frightening helplessness of being faced with the sufferings of loved others leads to a heightened consciousness of ontological insecurity. It might also be that this empathy we speak of is bound up with feelings of survivor's guilt. It is as if a penance were being exacted from the survivor for not being able to save their loved ones from the horror of serious illness. Culturally, empathy is valued, but what does it actually mean to take on the physical and emotional suffering of others?

While hypochondria is certainly bound up with questions of empathy, on the other hand, it belies what empathy is commonly understood to mean, in so far as it is a form of suffering that appears to be intensely self-preoccupied. A consequence of hypochondria is that it can lead to a reclusive shunning of contact with others and the external world in the obsessive pursuit of safety. Famously reclusive, both Marcel Proust and Howard Hughes suffered from forms of hypochondria, or we could say, fortress hypochondria, an inverse quarantining of the well from sources of illness in the outer world (Dillon, 2009). It is our conjecture that hypochondria, while quite possibly originating as an empathy for stricken others, most often plays itself out as an empathy turned round upon the self, or, in other words, turned inwards.

What might classical psychoanalysis have to say about this? As a matter of fact, surprisingly little. Here, psychoanalysis could seem to share the discomfort or impatience of the medical profession on being confronted with the persistent demand of hypochondria, the insistence on an illness that can never be located or addressed with sufficient authoritativeness. It is a demand that is baffling in that it seems to have recourse to an excess of any given response, and it is from the fact that it cannot be satisfied that the persistence of the demand derives. More specifically, it could be said that the hypochondriac resists the correction of their delusion that they are ill, calling into question the reliability of medical knowledge. Here, what is agreed on as knowledge might be said to depend on a complex inter-relationship between power, expertise, mutuality, and trust that play themselves out differently in the respective spheres of psychoanalysis and medicine.

On the one hand the hypochondriac goes to the doctor in search of an expertise superior to their own, to have their doubts assuaged. On the other hand, the hypochondriac refuses from the outset to trust the one from whom he or she seeks certainty. The hypochondriac may be said to maintain a fascinated distrust of the medical profession. Given this, such a particular patient and their doctor seem bound to play out their relationship in an irresolvable one-upmanship around questions of knowledge and trust. But knowledge of what exactly?

"Trust me, I know I am ill," says the hypochondriac.

"Trust me, I know that you are not," says the doctor. The circularity of such exchanges can miss the true nature of the demand. Would a psychoanalyst fare better? After all psychoanalysts are aware that knowledge is always deferred by the unconscious, that as professionals their only certainty is knowing that they do not know. However, this suspension of final certainty will not satisfy the hypochondriac, whose demand in some ways challenges the very premise of psycho-analysis. Whereas the psychoanalyst might wish to insist "It's all in the mind", the hypochondriac replies "It certainly is not". It is almost as though the hypochondriac is asking for a form of total knowledge that would serve to eradicate the difference between mind–body, self–other, and, in the arena of knowledge, between subject and object of expertise.

Returning to our earlier line of analysis, the self-involvement of the hypochondriac is a paradoxical one, for it might derive from an empathy for the suffering of others. In one of his few references to hypochondria, Freud in his essay "On narcissism", describes it as a complaint of ego libido rather than object libido (Freud, 1914c). We would add to this that what might be at stake could be a paradoxical case of narcissistic empathy, self-empathy, or auto-empathy. Freud's recourse to the term "ego libido" possibly owes itself to Jung's attempts to differentiate psychoses from neuroses, where Jung maintains that in psychotic illness the libido withdraws itself from objects or others and is instead absorbed by the ego. Both hypochondria and paranoia may be understood to be based on the inward turn of feelings and desires that are supposed to be, or should be, directed outwards. A certain sociality is being refused here, a consideration that we will go on to discuss.

As Leader (2004) points out, there is certainly a connection between hypochondria, paranoia, narcissism, and the seeking out of absolute knowledge, which can readily observed in psychoanalytic texts from the early twentieth century. For instance, Ferenczi, in "Some clinical observations on paranoia and paraphrenia" (1952) written shortly after Freud's work on the paranoid Schreber (Freud, 1911c), traces the case history of a young artist who, having read a treatise on tuberculosis, convinced himself that he had it, even undergoing treatment for it after his results were negative. His condition worsened after an encounter with a doctor whom he felt had not taken him seriously enough. His response was to develop a whole cosmography expressing his search for absolute knowledge, and this coincided with his belief that in order to achieve this, he must withdraw his energy from the world. He also declined to have his sexual needs met in the outer world and tried to persuade his sister (who he had already conscripted as his nurse) to follow what he called the "energetic imperative" (Ferenczi, 1952, p. 286). That is, he encouraged her to devote her life to him in helping him to conserve his energies to the extent that she was asked to become his sexual partner to save him from unnecessary expenditure in the pursuit of women. What is striking about the young artist's imaginary architecture is that it shows him trying to construct a total system that would serve as his own invulnerable world, one that would be completed by a kind of fusion of himself and his sister. We could call this his attempt to construct a little familial fortress hypochondria.

More generally, in psychoanalytic terms, the withdrawal of libido from the world occurs not only in instances of hypochondria and paranoia, but also as far as melancholia or depression is concerned. While these may thus constitute a family of mental illnesses or disturbances, in the subjective withdrawal of energy, markedly different psychic states are concerned. So what, then, is special about hypochondria? First, as a point of differentiation, the melancholic notably experiences a loss of self-esteem along with loss of interest in the outer world. If the hypochondriac lives in fear of illness, the melancholic often feels that it is as if they had died while still alive, and—unlike the hypochondriac—might wish that they were actually dead. That is, the difference here is that the hypochondriac may be said to value their own life intensely, whereas for the melancholic it is perhaps only the life of the lost yet encrypted other that has value, not the self. However, as we have begun to explore, the value that the hypochondriac accords his or her own life could be the site of a mournful transference. The hypochondriac conveys the impression of mourning the passing and demise of their own lives while still alive, as if the mourning process had been transferred from others to the self.

Conversely, what hypochondria and paranoia may be said to share is a delusion of being under attack, and what paranoia in particular enables us to entertain is that the persecution in question is a form of self-persecution. This is to suggest that while the paranoid person thinks he is being preyed on by others, it is actually a part of his own libido that has become foreign, despicable, and malign to him. It might be said that the paranoid are the poets of the libidinally real, giving hallucinatory mental representations—in the forms of voices and personae—to what are, in effect, somatic or biological states. In hypochondria, there is a somewhat more rational understanding that if the self is under threat, this is not a case of being persecuted by hostile others but of a hostile something that pertains to the body's own biological vicissitudes.

While those who are depressed turn hostility against the ego, and those who are paranoid set up imagined hostile others that may threaten them or those they love, the hypochondriac occupies a middle ground in this respect. That is, hypochondriacs take the body to be potentially the worst enemy: as neither quite self nor as sufficiently other. More precisely, the hypochondriac wishes to protect the body out of self-love at the same time that they feel it is the body that has turned against them. This splitting entails an ambivalent love–hate towards the body: on the one hand, intense concern for the body, and, on the other hand, a hatred for it as a source of potentially vast and uncontrollable malfunctionings.

Lucy Ellmann, in her novel *Doctors and Nurses* (2006), lists at great length all the alarming ways in which our bodies can GO WRONG, stating:

Without bodies we would no longer be subject to:

Mono syndrome
Myalgia
Arthralgia
Thrombocytopenia
Ascites
. . .
CAT-SCRATCH disease
Grunting
Rectal tenesmus
Subacute endocacarditis
Poverty of thought content
Increased libido
lid lag
bone erosion
low Apgar scores
hangovers
. . .
bird flu
BINGO WINGS. (Ellman, 2006, pp. 55–66)

And so on, and so on. This is but a small selection of the list of possible ailments: in the novel, it continues for pages.

The sense of outrage expressed in Ellman's work is not against the fragile body as such; rather we are encouraged to take the side of the body, to sympathise with it in its being subjected to regimes of anxiety. For it is our bodies that are made to bear the weight of social expectations and the policing morality of ideals concerning how it—the body—should feel and how it should look and how it should behave. Hypochondria is more than an individual experience, for it is also ideologically conditioned in that societies have punitive attitudes towards the supposedly freakish, the deviant, the uncontrollable. As such, hypochondria, as a socially conditioned narcissism, may be considered to share tangents with anorexia and obsessions with cosmetic surgery

The culture of contempt for the body would seem to depend on a desire for perfection. When this is a matter of outer appearance, it is actually treated as almost normal in a world of standardising commodification: no flab, no wrinkles, no outward signs of our human diversity and our ravaged passages through the course of life.

Lucy Ellmann confronts our hypochondriac fears with an affirmation of the body, writing:

> She was tired of hating herself (REALLY tired of it). EVERYBODY gets to have a body. Not just the BEAUTIFUL, not just those in FIRST CLASS. EVERY BODY is a legitimate example of the species! Not fair to treat a single one with disdain – not even JEN's. The body is where all the LIFE is! Even sick bodies, old bodies. They're ALIVE. Every defect, every illness springs from LIFE. (Ellman, 2006, p. 133)

A culture in which we are continually pressured to take care of our bodies, to keep them in shape, is actually one in which there is little compassion for the failings of the body. With hypochondria, while the body might look fine, it is its hidden imperfections that are most feared. In fact, we could say that it involves a terror of the invisible, the unlocatable, the unknown. In particular, preoccupations with the narcissism of appearance merely serve to screen off or disavow the truth of what the hypochondriac is certain of: that "our beautiful worlds" are diseased and death infested and no keeping up of appearances can mitigate this. There is a kind of honesty in hypochondria in this respect. Yet, on the other hand, with this very conviction, the hypochondriac would seem to cling to the anxious fantasy of keeping their worlds safe from disease and death.

We would interpolate here that this anxious fantasy of illness deferred might sometimes be not merely one's own, but directly transmitted by identifiable sources. In particular, for example, parents who are fearful of the safety of their children might seek to inculcate hypochondriacal dispositions in them, constantly insisting that they take care. The psychoanalyst Anzieu writes the following of his experience as a child subjected to over-protective parenting:

> I was not allowed to risk myself in the outside air without being smothered under several layers of clothing: sweater, overcoat, beret and scarf. The envelopes of care, concern and warmth with which my parents surrounded me, one upon another, did not part from me even when I left home. I carried their load with me on my back. My vitality was hidden at the heart of an onion under several outer coverings. (Anzieu, 1990, pp. 4–5)

Anzieu, in his later professional life, sublimated his swaddled beginnings in developing his theories of the skin ego and psychic envelopes, which brought him international recognition. What is particularly striking, in this context, about Anzieu's particular elaboration of psychoanalytic theory is the way that it maintains that the earliest formation of the ego is through the anxious establishment of a body ego informed by awareness of contact and separation.

The fragility of the body ego is not only spatially experienced in terms of contact and separation but also in relation to time. Copjec points out that Kierkegaard maintains that the formula of anxiety is not "my God, my God, why has thou forsaken me", but, rather, captured by the entreaty "what you are going do to me do quickly" (Copjec, 2009, p. 170). While the anxiety of the hypochondriac might take this form in pressing for the dreaded diagnosis, it can also take the form of "I know something awful is going to happen, but please not yet."

Therefore, as we are beginning to show, hypochondria is not only an individual phenomenon, but one in which something like a socially maintained superego seeks to supervise not so much the realm of ethics as the realm of the ontological. That is to say, the regulatory pressure bears on sustaining an invulnerable body, an impossibility. What is required, therefore, is an ever-ready obligation of vigilant defence in a world emptied of trust. A work by Tracey Emin captures the outrage that might be felt faced with such a demand. This artwork's blazon or embedded text is "Don't try to sell me your fucking fear", and it figures an advert for gas masks. We both remembered this image as discussed in an article on Emin that appeared in the Tate Modern's magazine some years ago (McGrath, 2003). However, we both happened also to misremember it. Misled by a vivid yet mistaken visual memory, we began searching for what we called "that piece by Emin that depicts a figure wearing a gas mask". However, as we traced the actual work, we realised that in fact it contained no visual image of gas masks or anyone wearing one, but, rather, represented an advertisement for gas masks. Strikingly, the mere verbal suggestion of gas masks had lead us to hallucinate a world peopled by those intimidated into actually wearing them. This, of course, is how hypochondria functions. The suggestibility of a threat to life becomes performatively concretised. This is precisely the outrage expressed in Emin's piece, "Don't try to sell me your fucking fear". Although Emin is addressing weapons, not diseases, the point we wish to make is that fear of contagion can become a contagious fear.

Significantly, the aforementioned work by Emin was produced in the context of the aftermath of September 11, and the war on terror, and it leads us to consider how certain socio-political agendas may be said to thrive on and exploit the fear of contagion that is a contagious fear. This concerns a biopolitics in which the social body has to defend its health from the fear of proximate but different bodies, which is also to say, defend it from the otherness of the body (including our own bodies) that can never be properly known. This notion of "the foreign body, the body as foreign" is raised to broach questions of the formation of racism, and what we will go on to address is how a paranoid form of collective hypochondria may be mobilised. This would play itself out differently from our individual experiences of hypochondria, but concerns the ways in which our fears around disease might be made to serve a politics of separatism that we will come to define as pathological. However, it is important in this respect to avoid getting caught up in the infectious demonisation of pathology.

In a quotidian sense, racism might arise from the differences in the material culture of ourselves and others. What is at stake is how we take what is habitual for ourselves to be normal and neutral, whereas the habits of others might, conversely, impress themselves on us with an unwanted physicality. Imagine yourself sharing a building with an immigrant neighbour. Their cooking smells intrude as not the right cooking smells; their footfalls on your ceiling are too pounding at odd hours; their attempts to greet you over-emphatically, or perhaps conspicuously to avoid you, jar your sensibilities of shared social space. They wear the wrong clothes for the weather. While our own bodily habits are something we cease to notice and take for granted, the presence of the bodily is brought back to us through the body of the other as a disturbance. In other words, the body manifests itself as precisely a body through its occasions of foreignness, and it is the body of the other that is the fantasmatic carrier of a certain unease and potential disease.

Dillon draws attention to Canetti's reading of Schreber, the paranoid hypochondriac whose autobiography became the basis of Freud's famous case history, as rehearsing "the resentment, fear and appalling ambition of Adolf Hitler", commenting further of Schreber, or Canetti's Schreber, "His body and his book incarnate forces in the German soul, and in the politics of modern Europe, that neither country nor continent can yet recognize in themselves" (Dillon, 2009,

p. 180). Loosely speaking, Schreber sees his own bodily state as having a cosmic significance in which he is specially chosen for the messianic destiny of creating a race of God's children. The anticipation of Nazism that Canetti and others detect might, therefore, be a question of saving the life force from dissipation in the role of acting as its guardian. Certainly the ideology of Nazism concerns exhortations with respect to the healthy body and the preservation of its vital forces, and this is clearly accompanied by a paranoid fear of contaminating otherness. It is this contagious fear of the fear of contagion that is projected on to the body of the Jew. Vikram Seth writes, in *Two Lives* (2005), his autobiographical exploration of the persecution of the Jews, of how the German desire to separate the Jews from the social body had recourse to biomedical imagery. He writes,

> These were the first of many laws passed not with any regularity but in fits and starts over the following years. All this was accompanied by propaganda comparing Jews to germs or vermin, dangerous to the health of a resurgent nation – or indeed any nation. The Nazi party and those who helped them sought to separate Jews from their fellow Germans in every possible sphere – work, friendship, marriage, cultural life, leisure – in order both to immiserise them financially and to exclude them socially. (p. 90)

Of course, the pathologisation of the Jews has a much longer and wider history. Gilman writes the following of a nineteenth century discourse linking the Jews with disease:

> The Jews' disease is written on the skin. The appearance, the skin color, the external manifestations of Jews mark them as different. They have the skin color of 'Kaffers', of blacks. But black skin also had medical significance. The Enlightenment Jewish physician Eclan Isaac Wolf saw the 'black-yellow' skin color of the Jew as a pathognomonic sign of disease. By the close of the nineteenth century this image of the black skin of the Jews as a sign of their inherent illness came to be associated with their inherent 'racial' character. (Gilman, 1993, 20–21)

Gilman further explores how the Jews came to be associated with systemic diseases such as syphilis and cancer. Moreover, he draws attention to a late nineteenth century counter-discourse in which Jews are considered to be the guardians of the best health. Here he quotes Rabbi Josph Krauskopf informing his Reform congregation that

> Eminent physicians and statisticians have amply confirmed the truth
> that the marvelous preservation of Israel, despite all the efforts to blot
> them out from the face of the earth, their comparative freedom from a
> number of diseases, which cause frightful ravages among the non-
> Jewish people, was largely due to their close adherence to their excel-
> lent Sanitary Laws. Health was the coat of their mail, it was their
> magic shield that caught, and warded off, every thrust aimed at their
> heart. Vitality was their birthright . . . (Gilman, 1993, p. 180)

The reported health of the Jews is here said to be their very fortress in
ways that serve to anticipate a certain Zionist celebration of Israel's
fortitude.

This very discourse of "health and safety" is paradoxically inseparable from the virulence of racism, and the racialising of health and
illness to serve a political cause has now become widespread in Israel
in the paranoid reactions of Zionist extremists to their Palestinian
neighbours. The performative concretisation of this discourse is to be
found in the wall called "the security fence", the "cordon sanitaire"
that constitutes the quarantining of the Palestinians at the same time
that it constitutes a form of self-imprisoning on the part of their Israeli
neighbours. Bowman (2009) has spoken of the wall in terms of a logic
of encystation, a term referring to cysts of diseased matter that are
isolated from the body they are a part of. "Encystation" is a term that
Bowman chooses to emphasise, in accordance with what he identifies
as "a bodily metaphorics of disease and generation that resonates with
a bio-politics deeply embedded in Israeli concepts of nation and
nationhood" (2009, p. 302, n.6). For instance, Palestinians are regularly
described as a virus, a cancer, and the like, as well as in terms of
disease-carrying vermin. In an article for Z Net, Liat Weingart, a Jew
well aware of the history of anti-Semitism, recalls a chilling visit to a
family friend. In the context of a discussion of American foreign
policy which she believes should be more supportive of Palestinian
rights, her friend says,

> [Supportive] In what way? So that the Arabs will throw the Jews into
> the sea? . . . Look what I have to say isn't pretty but I am not afraid.
> I'm going to say it anyway. The Palestinians are nothing but vermin.
> They make trouble in every country they live in. Even the other Arab
> countries don't want them.

Weingart's response to this is, "I take a deep breath. Then I realise, I have heard that sentence only with 'Jews' instead of 'Palestinians'" (Weingart, 2004). The sentence she has heard before is, of course, "Jews are vermin."

It is not only the Palestinians in this context that are routinely marked out through this rhetoric as vermin and the carriers of disease; it is also those Israelis who find themselves unable to support the right-wing extremism of Fortress Israel. A very recent case of this concerns university professor Neve Gordon, a long time peace activist and Israeli citizen, who, worried that his children were growing up in an apartheid state, called for massive international pressure to be applied on the state of Israel towards a resolution of the conflict. He was denounced by Israeli politicians in the press and, according to Sydney Levy, "hundreds of angry readers called Gordon a traitor, a virus, cancerous, and have threatened to expel him from Israel" (Jewish Voices for Peace, via Academics for Justice).

What is at stake in this right-wing Israeli discourse of radical distrust and the desperate need for endless vigilance and security? Might an analysis of paranoid hypochondria throw any light on this situation? If our own line of analysis has any pertinence, would it be possible to regard Zionist extremism in terms of an empathy turned inwards, a form of narcissistic auto-empathy. Certainly, the Jewish experience of the Holocaust is one to which an immense compassion is due. Here, for the Jewish people, the difficulty would be one of being thrown into a certain space of inward-turning auto-empathy through historical circumstance. The fact that this leads to the separatism and sense of radical distrust that may be found in Israeli discourse and politics should not lead us into the anti-Semitic trap of pathologising the Israelis for their racism, for then the racist curse would return to sender. This point is well made by Szasz in a letter to the editor of *Commentary*, when he comments on an article by the historian, Paul Johnson, titled "The anti-Semitic disease". Szasz states,

> Though Paul Johnson is an historian with a special interest in the tragedies of our age, he seems unaware of how closely the language with which he condemns anti-Semitism resembles the language of its foremost practitioners in Nazi Germany. Mr Johnson asserts that anti-Semitism is "an intellectual disease, a disease of the mind, extremely infectious and massively destructive". (Szasz, 2005)

That is, the same rhetoric of disease used to denounce the Jews is now being used to denounce anti-Semitism. Therefore, the biopolitical deployment of a fear of disease is not something that should be fearfully pathologised in turn, as it would have the effect of participating in an inward spiral that isolates the pure and the healthy from the contaminating.

What is really at stake in this question of an adequate response is the need to de-pathologise the pathological through a deconstruction of the dichotomy of health and illness. One way to look at it would be to consider that we all inhabit degrees of un-health and that no one is free or immune from physical suffering. We are all vermin, we all carry germs. As Dillon observes in the concluding essay of his book, one dedicated to Andy Warhol,

> The hypochondriac's historical mistake is to imagine a condition of bodily being that is physically or psychically null or neutral, a state of simultaneous (therefore impossible) vigour and inertia. According to this fantasy nothing happens inside the body and yet it continues to function becoming in fact more energetic, more efficient, even as it aspires to dessication and stasis. It does not occur to the hypochondriac that the state he or she describes is a state of living death. (Dillon, 2009, p. 265)

Significantly, he goes on to conclude "our bodies are not alone, but trailed by the sickened and the dying, and by those who merely thought they were sickened and dying, that have gone before us" (2009, p. 266). That is to say, there is a sociality of the facts of illness and dying, including the fears that are generated by them, which needs to be, in the end, confronted head on. The ethical obligation then becomes one of helping each other to bear the unbearable. So, one cure for hypochondria could well be forms of activism on behalf of suffering others, and Dillon's careful readings of hyphondriac lives, readings that are full of care, could be regarded as one form of activist cure for the condition. That is, it is a work that encourages us to sympathise with, and not demonise, our fellow hypochondriacs.

While an analysis of hypochondria might enable us to understand something more of the political deployment of a language of health and safety, might the converse also be applicable? Can political regimes of separatism throw any light on our understanding of hypochondria? First, there is an important distinction to be made here. The political deployment of a discourse of contagious disease concerns a performative use of language that entails a literalisation of the metaphorical: the metaphor linking disease and the foreign neighbour is literalised. For the hypochondriac, diseases are *diseases*, not metaphors: the hypochondriac refuses to accept the disease as a figure of speech, hence their suspicion of the inevitable gap between our linguistic formulations of disease and disease itself. That is to say, the hypochondriac seeks to close the gap between a discourse of disease and its actuality, this being a matter of the search for absolute knowledge and certainty. That said, the socio-political condition of a separatist distrust of others does have a bearing on hypochondria. If hypochondria entails a mourning process that is not straightforward, this could be because the loss of loved others makes the outer world seem an untrustworthy place. The need for trust and forms of loyalty would, therefore, be transferred to the inner world of the body and generate intense preoccupations with the anguished question of its trustworthiness. The loss of sociality with respect to the outside world is not a simple matter of excluding others so much as the desire to have them as close as possible to the self. Here, we might recall the young man analysed by Ferenczi whose love object was his own sister, and recall, too, that one of Schreber's desires was to be his own woman: the ultimate sociality on the inside. So, our diagnosis, if one could be risked, is that hypochondria concerns a libidinal internalisation of our bonds with others, an internalisation of an anxious need for trust and fidelity. However, this might not be so in all cases of hypochondria and, honestly speaking, hypochondria would seem to be that which cannot simply be explained away; rather, it encourages ways in which it can be accommodated.

Let us then, in conclusion, stage two mini-dialogues. The first is between a melancholic and his doctor. The doctor says, "I have some extraordinary news for you. You are in such good health you could live forever!" The melancholic's response is, "Oh no, what will I do, this wretched life will never end!" The second dialogue takes place between the hypochondriac and her doctor. The doctor says, "You know, let's admit it and face the truth. You are *right*, you are most certainly going to die. If you are lucky, it will be instant, in an accident, but most probably it will be from a disease or some other form of bodily degeneracy. We just don't know which one as of yet. But, don't worry, we shall keep on looking."

References

Anzieu, D. (1990). *A Skin for Thought: Interviews with Gilbert Tarrab*. London: Karnac.

Baur, S. (1988). *Hypochondria: Woeful Imaginings*. Berkeley, CA: University of California Press.

Bowman, G. (2009). Israel's wall and the logic of encystation. Sovereign exception or wild sovereignity? In: B. Kapferer & B. E. Bertelsen (Eds.), *Crisis of the State: War and Social Upheaval* (pp. 292–304). New York: Berghagn Books.

Copjec, J. (2009). The censorship of interiority. *Umbr(a) Islam Special Issue*: 165–186.

Dillon, B. (2009). *Tormented Hope: Nine Hypochondriac Lives*. Dublin: Penguin.

Ellman, L. (2006). *Doctors and Nurses*. London: Bloomsbury.

Ferenczi, S. (1952). Some clinical observations on paranoia and paraphrenia. In: *First Contributions to Psychoanalysis* (pp. 181–194). London: Hogarth.

Freud, S. (1911c). *Psycho-Analytic Notes on an Autobiographical Account of a Case of Paranoia*. *S.E.*, *12*: 3–82. London: Hogarth.

Freud, S. (1914c). On narcissism: an introduction. *S.E.*, *14*: 67–102. London: Hogarth.

Gilman, S. (1993). *Freud, Race and Gender*. Princeton, NJ: Princeton University Press.

Leader, D. (2004). Hypochondria. *Journal of the Centre for Freudian Analysis and Research*, *14*: 18–26.

McGrath, M. (2003). Something's wrong. *Tate Magazine*, 1.

Seth, V. (2005). *Two Lives*. London: Little, Brown.

Szasz, T. (2005). Anti-Semitism. *Commentary*, October 2005. www.commentarymagazine.com/articlw/anti-semitism.

Weingart, L. (2004). The wrath of the Jews. *ZNet*. November 29, 2004. www.zcommunications.org/the-wrath-of-the-jews-by-liat-weingart.

Editor's introduction to Chapter Two

The chapter is concerned with the rhetoric and symbols of the Hungarian extreme right movements, inspired by two posters from a municipal election campaign in Budapest in the autumn of 2010 by the most influential extreme right wing party, Jobbik. The inscription on the first picture says, "Budapest is the capital of the Hungarians". By means of a simple rhetorical trick, the sentence implies the exclusion of others, the non-ethnic Hungarian citizens, such as Romani and Jews, who are, by the force of this definition, "foreign occupants". According to the ethno-nationalist, populist, right-wing views, Budapest is a town ruled by "strangers", the city is a "foreign body in the heart of the nation". The text on the second poster reads, "Do you really want to stop parasitism? If yes, you are a Jobbik voter!" The slogan, accompanied by a picture of a mosquito, opens a vast space of imagery; the iconography of anti-Semitic propaganda is full of bloodsucking insects, vermin, lice, spiders, rats, and other repelling animals. Our "skin ego" (Anzieu, 1989) is, a psychological shield that defends against penetrations that endanger our integrity or self-identity. The main function of the biological skin is *abjection*: eliminating impure, toxic, undesirable substances and bodily products. A similar function, it is argued, can be attributed to the psychological and social "skin". The author discusses Imre Hermann's arguments from *The Psychology of Anti-Semitism*, where Hermann applies his concepts of "clinging", "going-in-search", and "separation" to understanding the roots of anti-Semitism. He evaluates these interpretations in the light of present psychoanalytic and social psychological approaches and recent political developments, especially the rapid success of the Jobbik party that culminated at the European election in 2009.

CHAPTER TWO

"Budapest, the capital of Hungarians": rhetoric, images, and symbols of the Hungarian extreme right movements

Ferenc Erős

This chapter is a revised version of the paper I presented at the "Nationalism and the body politic" winter symposium in Oslo, March 25–27, 2011,* four months before the Breivik massacre. This tragic event has justified again the urgent need to examine right wing extremism from psychoanalytic and social psychological viewpoints (see Auestad, 2012 for inspirational ideas on this topic). My contribution deals with the rhetoric and symbols of the Hungarian extreme right movements, and was originally inspired by two posters from a municipal election campaign in Budapest in the autumn of 2010. These posters had been made visible for a couple of weeks all over in the streets of Budapest, advertised by the most influential extreme right wing party "Jobbik – The Movement for a Better Hungary". (In Hungarian the word *Jobbik* literally means both "the Right" and "the better".)

The inscription on the first picture reads Budapest *is the capital of the Hungarians* (Image 1). At first sight it seems to be a completely

---

*The original paper was published in 2012 in the Norwegian journal *Impuls*, 2(65): 95–101.

Image 1.

harmless declaration. Who would deny that, for example, *Oslo is the capital of the Norwegians*? However, there is a simple rhetoric trick in it: instead of saying that "Budapest is the capital of *Hungary*", which is an obvious geographical and administrative fact, the statement on the poster presupposes that if Budapest is the capital of the *Hungarians*, it cannot be the capital of *other peoples*. The sentence implies the exclusion of others, the non-ethnic Hungarian citizens, such as Romani and Jews, who are, by the force of this definition, "foreign occupants".

The slogan "Budapest is the capital of the Hungarians" is a performative utterance which invokes tacit assumptions and age-old stereotypes. According to these, Budapest exists under the occupation by foreign forces since centuries. In the 1930s, a well-known "populist" writer, Gyula Illyés declared: "Budapest is not in Hungary. Above, under or beyond, only the good God knows where it is". According to the ethno-nationalist, populist, rightist views, Budapest is a town ruled by "strangers", a city that is a "foreign body in the heart of the nation"; "a sinful city", a cosmopolitan city full of parasites, infected by a

degenerate, alien culture. This kind of anti-urbanism contrasts superficial, alienated city life with a rural life that exists in organic unity
with land, blood, and soil (*Blut und Boden*).

Anti-urban ideology is, of course, not a special Hungarian invention. The French psychoanalyst Chasseguet-Smirgel (1990, pp. 167–
176) refers in her article "Reflections of a psychoanalyst upon the Nazi
biocracy" to Walter Darré, who was one the expounders of the theory
of *Blut und Boden*. Darré later became Minister of Agriculture in
Hitler's Nazi government. He wrote a book under the title *The
Peasantry: Vital Source of the Nordic Race* (1928). As Chasseguet-Smirgel
interprets Darré's ideas,

> Racist ideology is based upon the idea of a symbiosis between the
> subject and Mother Nature. The city dweller is unable to attain this
> symbiosis with the Mother: he is too far removed from Nature. It is an
> idea found in all Utopias, where the city is felt to be an essentially
> hostile element. It is always (implicitly or explicitly) experienced as
> 'Babylon, the great whore', that is unless it obeys certain rules and
> follows an architectural plan which makes it an Ideal City, the
> Heavenly Jerusalem. But what distinguishes the cult of "Blut und
> Boden" from other Utopias, is the overtly biological nature of the link
> which binds the peasant to the earth. (p. 169)

The text on the second poster (Image 2) reads, "Do you really want
to stop parasitism? If yes, you *are* a Jobbik voter!" The slogan does not

Image 2.

call any particular target group or person by name, which can, or should, be metaphorised as "mosquitoes". It opens, however, a vast field of imagination and fantasies in the mind of the recipients of its message. The mosquito in the centre of a traffic sign is a classical icon of anti-Semitic propaganda that has been widely used by extreme right propaganda throughout modern history. The visual world of anti-Semitic propaganda is crowded with bloodsucking insects, vermin, spiders, rats, and other repelling animals. The motive of the blood-thirsty animals has often been used as illustrations in various editions of the "Protocols of Elders of Zion", and appeared in many other places, such as newspapers, magazines, on stamps, propaganda posters, etc. (Image 3). Jewish world conspiracy is often represented by vampire-like Jewish figures, such as Leon Trotsky's figure in Image 4.

Image 3.

Image 4.

These pictures are liable to evoke strong feelings of anxiety, since mosquitoes and other parasites might be dangerous to our bodies. Furthermore, they could bring to the surface of our minds myths about vampires and other threatening creatures penetrating under the surface of the skin, inflicting pain, intoxicating our blood, causing infectious diseases and, eventually, death. Our biological skin is a natural defence shield against external stimuli and threats. Analogously, our "skin ego" is, as the French psychoanalyst Anzieu (1989) expressed, a psychological defence shield against penetrations that endanger our integrity or self-identity. Social groups also have a "skin", a protective membrane that divides the internal and external world and defends group integrity. As the main function of the biological skin is *abjection*, that is, eliminating impure, toxic, undesirable substances and bodily products, a similar function can be attributed to the psychological and social "skin". The process of getting rid of the parasites and other similar objects might be the source of intensive pleasure, in as much as it can signify a non-traumatic repetition of the original trauma of the separation from the mother's body. The idea goes back to the early works of the Hungarian psychoanalyst, Imre Hermann, who introduced the notion of a contrasting pair of drives "clinging–going-in-search" (by other theorists referred to as "clinging–exploring"), starting out from contemporary observations of the behaviour of apes, small children, and neurotic or psychotic patients (Hermann, 1976).

For Hermann, skin is a surface where the contrasting pair of drives may meet and fight each other.

> In terms of those parts of his epidermis that can be separated from it or are already almost detached from it, the individual is indeed in a state of dual unity, corresponding to the original state. Small cracks in the skin, scabs, nails, hair, are already alien, in a minimal way, to the living ego. In the forced, often bloody detachment of this minimally alien object, a familiar motive is asserting itself: . . . the ego's striving to experience the trauma-in this case, detachment, not traumatically imposed from outside, as was the case with that prototype of all separation, the detachment of the clinging child from the mother, but as a self-intended, self-apportioned action by a free 'adult'. The pain that arises with these beginnings of self-mutilation is an incentive to carry out the final separation; and at the same time, it is a sign of that liberation which may . . . make itself felt in a state that can only be described as narcissistic intoxication. As such, this liberation may enter consciousness as an emotion, in an eerily pleasurable feeling. Thus, in this group of phenomena, pain arises in connection with the separation that is striven for, while its successful accomplishment brings pleasure. (Hermann, 1976, p. 31)

In his book *On the Psychology of Anti-Semitism*, Hermann (1990 [1945]) applied the concepts on clinging, going-in-search and separation to an explanation of the psychic roots of anti-Semitism, drawing an analogy between the urge to eliminate parasites from the skin, the "delousing" practices, and the persecution of Jews.

Chasseguet-Smirgel also connects abjection to the trauma of separation. In her article quoted above she writes,

> I have postulated the existence of a primary wish—immediate and inborn—to strip the mother's body of its contents in order to regain possession of the place one occupied before birth. All obstacles which,

after birth, make access to the mother's body impossible to achieve, have to be removed. These obstacles are identified with reality and are represented by the father and the father's derivatives: his penis, children. In my opinion the difference between my concept and that of Melanie Klein is that this fantasy is a structural one that forms part of the organization of the human mind. Thought is born from the encounter with the obstacle that thwarts the wish to return to the mother's body. Ridding oneself of obstacles is also directed at retrieving a mode of mental functioning governed by the pleasure principle where free-flowing energy circulates unimpeded. Ridding oneself of paternal obstacles by emptying the maternal body, fighting against reality and thought, form a single, identical wish: that of returning to a world without organization, to primeval chaos, to a universe marked by homogeneity and the continuum present before birth. (Chasseguet-Smirgel, 1990, p. 167)

The purity of blood is one of the most salient motives in *purification fantasies*. Preoccupation with the purity of blood was one of the main features of Nazi ideology; it was not, however, a privilege of Nazism, since it is generally present in racist thinking and imagery. Psychoanalysts and psychoanalytically orientated authors have repeatedly pointed out this specific feature of racist imagery. For example, Adorno and his associates in the interview section of *The Authoritarian Personality* quote a number of examples in which the subjects refer to Jews and other "inferior races" as "rats" or "vermin", which must be annihilated in order to defend the purity of blood (Adorno, Frenkel-Brunswik, Levinson, & Sanford, 1950) Reich, in *Mass Psychology of Fascism* argues that fascist race theory is "a mortal fear of natural sexuality and of its orgasm function" (Reich, 1970, p. 84). According to Reich, fascist irrationalism, manifested in the sanctification of the family and the celebration of the women's chastity, is closely related to the myth of purity of blood as a symptom of sexual repression brought about by a patriarchal society.

Sexual repression, the horror and, at the same time, a secret desire for sexual abuse, are implied in the ancient accusations of ritual murders committed by Jews for ritual purposes. Ritual murder scenes appear on a large variety of visual representations, too. In 1882 the corpse of a young peasant girl, Eszter Solymosi, was found drowned in the river Tisza near the East Hungarian village Tiszaeszlár. Based on stories and gossips which had immediately started to spread among the peasants of Tiszaeszlár and the neighbouring villages, the local Jewish community had been accused of murdering the girl for ritual reasons: they sacrificed her to use her blood for preparing the Pesach matzo. After a long investigation procedure in which verbal and physical force as well as blackmailing were equally used against the alleged crown witness, a fifteen-year-old, psychologically rather unstable Jewish boy and his family, a group of the members of the Tiszaeszlár Jewish community, were found guilty and put on trial. However, after a long and controversial process, the defendants were completely acquitted by the higher court. The acquittal of the defendants was celebrated as a major victory of the progressive, liberal, social and political forces over the anti-Semitic movements which had already started to flourish in that period in Hungary. However, the infamous "Tiszaeszlár Affair" set off a wave of hysterical anti-Semitism across the Austro-Hungarian empire—and much of Europe—in the 1880s (Kövér, 2011).

Eszter Solymosi's name became a symbol, and her story became a recurrent topic in the mythology of the Hungarian extreme right movements. A well known Hungarian poet of the 1930s and 1940s, József Erdélyi, published a poem under the title "Eszter Solymosi's blood", which became a kind of "fascist hymn" during the years of Shoah. Image 5 is a picture of a scene of the commemoration of Eszter Solymosi in 2010 in her native village.

Blood libel is often associated with fantasies of rape committed by Jews—not only of concrete persons, but of a whole nation, like Germany. Adolf Hitler suggests, in *Mein Kampf*, that the epidemics of syphilis in Germany were caused by the Jews who "jewificated" the

Image 5.

soul of the German people, committing the crime of racial mixing, also known as "miscegenation". The Jews, according to Hitler, raped mother Germany. "One often says, it is written in 'Mein Kampf,' that the Jews are human, too. But if someone violated your mother, would you then say that he, too, was human?" (Fenichel, 1940, p. 37).

Let us compare Hitler's words with a statement coming from a young Hungarian extreme right activist in 2004 commenting on the peace treaty of Trianon, near Versailles, in 1920. The treaty redefined the borders of Hungary so that the country lost significant parts of its earlier territory and population. The loss of territories, the division and mutilation of the historical Hungary, is still regarded as a major traumatic event in the Hungarian collective memory. The historical trauma of Trianon has been continuously revitalised by ethno-nationalist and chauvinistic rhetoric (see Image 6).

"Greater Hungary looks like a fetus in the womb of a mother. . . . so what happened in 1920 was an abortion, a catastrophe", said the aforementioned activist. What is most striking about these kinds of

Image 6.

statements is that the difference between fantasy and reality disappears. The nation becomes a biological entity. Chasseguet-Smirgel quotes Rudolf Hess, who said that "National Socialism is nothing but applied biology". In this context, Chasseguet-Smirgel speaks about the "loss of symbolism" in Nazi thinking.

> It is a well-known fact that Nazi propaganda, mass demonstrations and enrolment in the different Party organizations are all aimed at creating the same feeling of identity. However, the doctrine of 'Blood and Soil' brings another dimension to this need for homogeneity. It introduces a biological dimension, an expression of concrete thought, without transposition, without substitution, as if the human race had returned to a form of mental functioning without symbols, to a time when no ram had as yet taken the place of Isaac as the promised sacrifice. (Chasseguet-Smirgel, 1990, p. 171)

In another study (Chasseguet-Smirgel, 1989) she argues,

> The aim of every extremist ideology . . . is to attain a union with the mother and to annihilate the paternal dimension of the psyche. Ideology is the promise of returning to paradise, to the mother's womb from which we were expelled at birth. From this moment on, we live in the knowledge that the mother's body is given over to the father's penis, his children that her psyche is taken up with thoughts that do not exclusively center around ourselves. It follows then that whatever does not conform to ideology has to be pitilessly eliminated. In other words, facts and events that endanger ideological thinking are decreed 'non-existent'. (p. 18)

That is the point where, according to Kristeva (1982) "the abject does indeed draw the subject towards the place where language gives up and meaning collapses" (p. 13).

The need for homogeneity, the elimination of differences, is a central part of Imre Hermann's analysis of anti-Semitism, too. In his above-mentioned book, he quotes a Hungarian popular rhyme, which, in rough translation, reads like this:

> Erger, Berger, Schlossberger,
> All the Jews are bastards.
> A Jew bought two geese,
> One white, and one brindle,

The bloody Jew,
Why does he need two geese?
And if he did buy two,
Why didn't he buy two similar ones?
(Hermann, 1990[1945], p. 66)

Psychoanalytical studies might help to understand the underlying assumptions, needs, and motifs of racist imagery expressed in visual representations. This imagery has a self-generating capacity to activate passions and emotions, over and above the hatred against Jews. However, in contemporary Hungary, the main target of the "Jobbik" party posters is not only, and not even primarily, Jews. Although the whole campaign of the party was based on the patterns and symbolism of Nazi-like anti-Semitism, the main target of the present day extreme right propaganda is, in fact, the Roma population (which does not exclude a simultaneous presence of anti-Semitic hatred).

The years 2008–2009 were a fatal period for Hungarian Romas. A wave of extremely violent attacks against them swept over the country. Explosions, arsons, shootings, and other atrocities had been committed in several villages and towns, resulting in many victims. Six people (including children) were killed; several others were seriously injured. After a year-long investigation, the suspected assassins (or at least a few of them) were arrested. However, their real motives and connections with extremist organisations remained unclear, and the process is still going on (the first degree sentence, life-long imprisonment for the perpetrators, was announced recently, in May 2013). In any case, the series of killings and other atrocities must be regarded as extreme manifestations of a growing hatred. One election poster, for example, focuses on the so called "Gypsy criminality". These words, in the vocabulary of the right-wing activists, are a closely related term written in one word: "*gypsycriminality*" (see image 7). However, the question arises: what are the appeals of this kind of propaganda? To what extent is the extreme right able to mobilise larger segments of the population to vote and to provide support for them?

At the national elections in 2010, the conservative party alliance, FIDESZ-KDNP ("young democrats" and Christian democrats), obtained a two-thirds majority (68.13%). In the national parliament at the present there are three opposition parties: Jobbik (12.18%), Socialists (15.28%), and ecologists (LMP = Lehet Más a Politika ["Politics Can Be Different"], 4.15%).[1] The overwhelming majority of

Image 7.

the ruling party alliance allows them to pass any law they wish, and, moreover, to change fundamental laws, including the constitution of the country. Therefore, FIDESZ can govern the country without brakes and counterbalances, that is, practically without an effective opposition, thus introducing a *de facto* one-party system and creating a new, more authoritarian constitution which seriously limits the working of the democratic institutions and fundamental rights. In the past few years, Hungary has become more isolated in the European Union, and several actions of the government have been harshly criticised by different European bodies and committees.[4]

The relative success of Jobbik (which reached its culmination at the European election in 2009, still under the Socialist government) was a story of rapid emergence on the ruins of other small right-wing extremist parties. Their rise from early 2000 and onwards was partly due to the impact of the world economic crisis, to the restrictive budget policy of the Socialist government, and to a legitimacy crisis as a consequence of the then right-wing opposition's ceaseless attacks against the ruling Socialist–Liberal coalition. This situation led to several demonstrations, riots, and even violent street fights during the autumn of 2006.

Jobbik is now one of the strongest extreme right-wing parties in comparison with those of the rest of Europe, and on the basis of

DEREX (Demand for Right-Wing Extremism Index) poll results[3] it seems that Hungary is extremely high on all factors of DEREX scale: "prejudice and welfare chauvinism", "anti-establishment attitudes", "right-wing value orientation (Figures 1 and 2). It should be emphasised, however, that Jobbik is not satisfied with purely "political" methods: it has organised its own paramilitary units, the so-called "Hungarian Guard", equipped with its own uniforms, marches, symbols, and rituals, which evoke in many people a strong association to the Arrow Cross movement (a Fascist movement in Hungary in the 1940s). The Guard—now officially banned—has been involved in several violent conflicts with Roma inhabitants all over the country.

The now ruling government led by Viktor Orbán has made several promises to stop, or at least push back, extreme right activities, its hostile rhetoric, and its violence. However, there are several signs that might lead us to infer that Orbán and his government, at least partly, share "the underlying frame of interpretation" of Jobbik: ethnonationalism, anticommunism, and "Euro-scepticism". In Hungary, according to the recent polls, Jobbik enjoys more than twenty per cent popularity among those citizens who expressed their willingness to vote at the election that will be held in 2014.

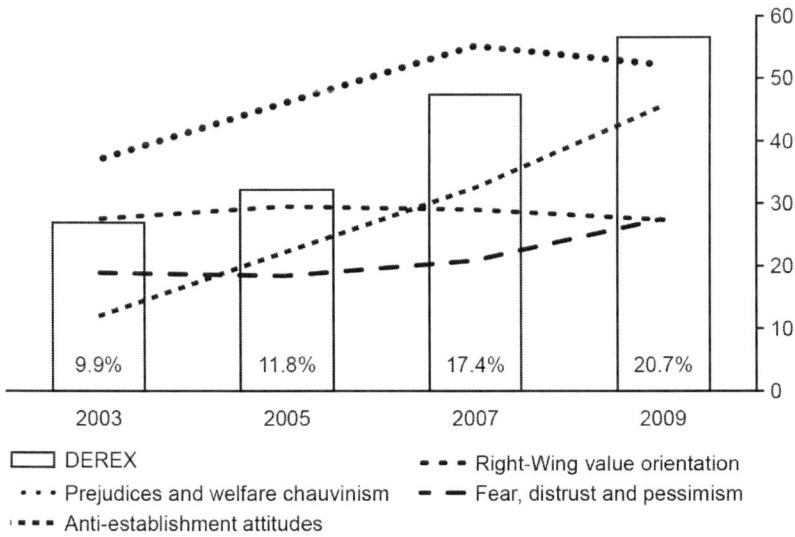

Figure 1. Development of Hungary's DEREX components (percentage of respondents in each category).

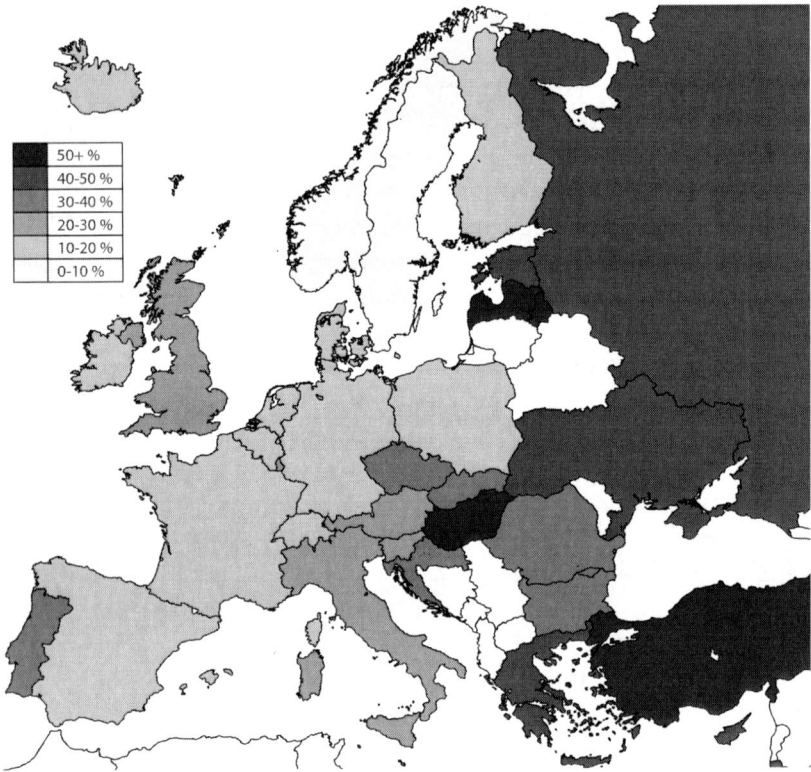

Figure 2.   DEREX Index: Prejudices and welfare chauvinism.

Notes

1. In 2012 LMP split into two fractions: the "old" LMP and a new group called "Dialogue for Hungary".
2. See, for example, the recent report of Rui Tovares, a Portuguese member of the European Parliament to the Committee on Civil Liberties, Justice and Home Affairs "on the situation of fundamental rights: standards and practices in Hungary". www.europarl.europa.eu / sides / getDoc.do?pub Ref=–%2f%2fEP%2f%2fNONSGML%2bCOMPARL%2bPE–508.211%2b0 2%2bDOC%2bPDF%2bV0%2f%2fEN
3. The DEREX index is issued regularly by the Political Capital Risk Forecast Division (PC RFD), an international network of analysts (macroeconomists and econometric experts, political scientists, sociologists, social psychologists, and mathematicians) who analyse various fields of

political risks that can have an impact on political stability or the economic environment of a given country or region. See www.riskandforecast. com/

References

Adorno, T. W., Frenkel-Brunswik, E., Levinson, D. J., & Sanford, R. N. (1950). *The Authoritarian Personality*. New York: Harper & Brothers.

Anzieu, D. (1989). *The Skin Ego*. New Haven, CT: Yale University Press.

Auestad, L. (2012). Subjectivity and absence: prejudice as a psycho-social theme. In: L. Auestad (Ed.), *Psychoanalysis and Politics. Exclusion and the Politics of Representation* (pp. 29–42). London: Karnac.

Chasseguet-Smirgel, J. (1989). Reflexions on some thought disorders in non-psychotic patients. Certain disturbances of thinking in individuals and groups. *Scandinavian Psychoanalytic Review, 12*: 5–21.

Chasseguet-Smirgel, J. (1990). Reflections of a psychoanalyst upon the Nazi biocracy. *International Review of Psycho-Analysis, 17*: 167–176.

Darré, R. W. (1928). *Das Bauerntum als Lebensquell der Nordischen Rasse*. Munich: J. F. Lehmanns.

Fenichel, O. (1940). Psychoanalysis of antisemitism. *American Imago*, 18:24–39,

Hermann, I. (1976). Clinging—going-in-search—a contrasting pair of instincts and their relation to sadism and masochism. *Psychoanalytic Quarterly, 45*: 5–36.

Hermann, I. (1990)[1945]. *Az antiszemitizmus lélektana* [The psychology of Anti-Semitism]. Budapest: Cserépfalvi.

Kövér, G. (2011). A tiszaeszlári drama [The Drama of Tiszeszlár]. Budapest: Osiris.

Kristeva, J. (1982). *The Powers of Horror. An Essay on Abjection*. New York: Columbia University Press.

Reich, W. (1970). *The Mass Psychology of Fascism*. New York: Simon & Schuster.

Editor's introduction to Chapter Three

The chapter examines the anthropologist Marianne Gullestad's (1946–2008) concept of "imagined sameness", describing how the majority of Norwegians "must consider themselves as more or less the same in order to feel of equal value", thus tracing the connections between egalitarian cultural themes and a racially coded majority nationalism. Sameness is created, rather than simply found, via a style of interaction that focuses on what is similar between the parties in the conversation. The imaginary construal of the other as essentially similar to oneself consists both in seeking out harmony and agreement and in avoiding others who are seen as being "too different" to maintain the illusion. "Imagined sameness" and collective narcissism is exemplified using a famous photograph of the late King Olav taking the tram (1973), and the philosopher Gunnar Skirbekk's book on Norwegian national identity (2010). It goes on to examine a more extreme form of narcissism, self-construction, and identity confusion in the case of the Norwegian terrorist and self-appointed crusader Anders Behring Breivik. The author argues that the perpetrator's propaganda material is characterised by a high degree of continuity with earlier anti-Semitic and racist propaganda and by very explicit sexualisation. Sexism and racism are intertwined in the

material, and the hated, feared, and denigrated other is simultaneously of great sexual interest. The final section of the chapter points to
the contiguity between the more extreme statements of xenophobia
and Islamophobia and recent statements made in the mainstream
media. The voices of those who defend a revived nationalism and
xenophobic attacks against "others", Muslims, Roma, refugees, and
immigrants in particular, have become the more dominant ones. Thus,
the chapter ends by emphasising the responsibility of the general
population for undertaking renewed reflection on how "we" see
ourselves, and on whom "we" may include, a willingness to listen to
and sustain such a painful enquiry.

CHAPTER THREE

Idealised sameness and orchestrated hatred: extreme and mainstream nationalism in Norway

Lene Auestad

The first part of this chapter was presented to the "Nationalism and the body politic" winter symposium in Oslo, 25–27 March 2011, four months before the Breivik massacre. It aims to explore how an analysis of narcissism and the logic of idealisation can help us understand neo-nationalist articulations by members of the social mainstream. The later events necessitated a focus on the more extreme varieties; thus, the second part interprets some of the fantasies of the perpetrator. The third part focuses on the reactions of the general population, emphasising the responsibility of the bystander.

Likeness and idealisation

In his *Introductory Lectures*, Freud proposes studying some very common, familiar phenomena which "since they can be observed in any healthy person, have nothing to do with illnesses" (1916–1917, p. 25). These are what we know as parapraxes, slips of the tongue, saying something other than what was intended, or doing the same thing in writing, or hearing something different from what was said to one. His mention of how people speak of a "demon of misprints" (p. 31) indicates how there is a general unwillingness to understand or identify with such errors, which are normal actions, only not the ones one had planned to perform. The ability of psychoanalysis to wonder about, and be struck by, features pertaining to the seemingly trivial and ordinary and Marianne Gullestad's (1946–2008) chosen method of pinpointing and presenting for debate details of a culture with which she was intimately familiar. Her decision to do "anthropology at home", to devote her work to studies of the ordinary, that is, the majority of, Norwegians, was unusual when she started out (Lien & Melhuus, 2008). The portrayal of people in relative positions of power, rather than of marginalised people used to being misunderstood and misrepresented, caused discomfort as well as anger from parts of her audience.

Examining the popular reinforcement of majority nationalism, with a focus on commonality of culture, ancestry, and origin, she identified connections between egalitarian cultural themes and racially coded majority nationalism (Gullestad, 2006, p. 168). The concept of "imagined sameness" emphasises how "equality", in a Norwegian context, is linked with "identity", how, in order to feel equal, people must feel that they are the same. She wrote,

> In previous studies, I formed a set of ideas about egalitarianism in Norway based on how 'ordinary people' relate to differences in ways of life and lifestyle. The central value concept is *likhet*, meaning 'likeness', 'similarity', 'identity' or 'sameness'. *Likhet* is the most common translation of 'equality', implying that social actors must consider themselves as more or less the same in order to feel of equal value. . . . This often leads to an interaction style in which commonalities are emphasized while differences are played down. (Gullestad, 2006, p. 170)

Thus, sameness is created, rather than simply found, via a style of interaction that focuses on what is similar between the parties in the conversation. The imaginary construal of the other as essentially similar to oneself consists both in seeking out harmony and agreement and in avoiding others who are seen as being "too different" to maintain the illusion:

> Open conflicts are seen as a threat to other basic values, such as 'peace and quiet'. [D]iversity is concealed by avoiding those people who, for

one reason or another, are perceived as 'too different', and by playing them down in social interaction with those who are regarded as compatible. The result is that the dividing lines between people in terms of social class have become blurred. At the same time, the differences between 'Norwegians' and 'immigrants' have become discursively salient. (Gullestad, 2006, p. 171)

One may observe that when the confrontation with what appears as "too much difference" in this scenario results in a collapse of the picture of seamless similarity, the other, as the seeming cause of this disruption, is easily given the blame for it. As a result of the previous exaggeration of likeness, the difference that looms too large to be ignored appears in an exaggerated version as well, and the encounter can result in rage towards this disruption of "peace and quiet". Klein's descriptions of the phenomenology and logic of idealisation can serve to clarify this process. Idealisation is bound up with splitting and denial of external as well as psychic reality, thus "not only a situation but an object-relation is denied and annihilated, and therefore a part of the ego, from which the feelings towards the object emanate, is denied and annihilated as well" (1946, p. 7). Furthermore,

> Since the destructive and hated part of the self which is split off and projected is felt as a danger to the loved object and therefore gives rise to guilt, this process of projection in some ways also implies a deflection of guilt from the self on to the other person. (Klein, 1946, p. 12)

We are allowed to see how, in this case, the relationship to the one who is regarded as similar is kept peaceful and harmonious at the cost of the relationship to the seemingly more dissimilar other, whose appearance entails an unwelcome encounter with denied hostility and guilt. So, the aspect of idealisation that is not immediately obvious is the splitting involved. To paraphrase Klein, while parts of the ego attempt to unite with the ideal object, other parts are kept busy striving to deal with internal persecutors (1946, p. 10).

A good illustration of "imagined sameness" and also of the unambiguously positive adjective *folkelig*—being like the people, like ordinary people—is the famous photograph of the late King Olav sitting on the tram on his way to going skiing, on a Sunday in December 1973. As a result of the Yom Kippur war, OPEC had cut off their oil supplies, resulting in a drastic price rise referred to as "the oil crisis".

Driving motorised vehicles was forbidden at weekends. The picture shows the King handing a 10 kr bill to the conductor, but his fare had already been paid for. The identities of some of his fellow passengers were only disclosed much later. Berit Okkenhaug, a first-year student of Christianity, had planned a quick break from looking after her first-born daughter to go skiing, had plumped down on the free seat next to the King unaware of who he was, and looked down in embarrass-ment when the photographers started shooting. She later became a priest, left the priests' association in protest against the attitudes of the Norwegian Church towards female priests, but joined it again, and has written a book about shame (Bjånesøy, 2010). The man sitting behind the king was Mohammad Fayyaz. Having arrived as an immi-grant from Pakistan the year before, he was on his way to work— scrubbing in a restaurant kitchen. One of the pictures shows him having fallen asleep, resting his head in his hands. He later settled in Drammen with his family, where he set up this industrial town's first fast-food restaurant. He died in 2001 at the age of forty-nine (Bjånesøy, 2010).

This photo has been reproduced again and again, and it was even re-staged many years later, with Berit Okkenhaug and the new King, Harald, celebrating a re-opening of the tramline after a restoration. The celebrated image of equality—"Look, he is just like us"—is, of course, thrilling only because it is actually the King sitting there. An earlier picture in the series shows a servant walking next to him carry-ing his skis, and we know that he did not really pay his own fare. When the photographers started shooting, he treated their attention as being appropriate for a public person, while the woman next to him, feeling invaded by the sudden, unwelcome attention, looked down in shame. While King Olav and Berit Okkenhaug were on their way to partake in the leisurely activity of skiing that Sunday in 1973, Moham-mad Fayyaz was on his way to work, to low-paid, unskilled work, possibly falling asleep out of exhaustion. Being among the first work immigrants from Pakistan, he proceeded to set up his own small busi-ness (finding better employment would have been difficult), a not untypical situation before Norway was anything like a multi-cultural society. One can speculate perhaps, that he died prematurely, only hoping that his children would have better opportunities than he had.

What is the excitement about with regard to this image? One could say that "If the King is just like us, then we are just like the King", thus it allows for a vicarious identification with a grander version of oneself, or an ego ideal. But in what sense is it then egalitarian?

To Freud, according to the narcissistic type of object love, a person may love "(a) what he himself is (i.e. himself), (b) what he himself was, (c) what he himself would like to be, [or] (d) someone who was once part of himself" (1914c, p. 90). Thus, we can see that certain hierarchies are allowed for, in so far as I, or we, can be imagined as having been the other in question, striving to become this other, or having once been united with him. This is paradoxical in the case of a king, the royal family being the only remainder of the nobility that was abolished with the constitution in 1814. Since the nobility represented a cultural difference in relation to the majority of people, being more highly educated and, as commentators would say, of foreign origin, "imagined sameness" could not be maintained, whereas a king who affirms some values assumed to be shared by "the people" is capable of this imaginary feast. Thus, a certain meritocracy is allowed for, provided its markers are essentially the same. If someone from a working-class or lower middle-class background has become rich and famous, the reassurance to the public that he or she feels just as before, the small, ordinary person from that particular place, is greeted with enthusiasm, and a demand to share the wealth is generally not raised, but another kind of sharing, that of narcissistic love, is accepted instead. According to this logic, a difference that can be imagined as quantitative is unproblematic; the investor, athlete, or celebrity can be thought to be like me, only with more money, or better looking, or with a better physique, while the artist or the professor would appear to be beyond the reach of this stretch of the imagination, and come across simply as odd. Also, it does not work to say "just like me, only a woman", or "just like me, only black".

In a helping relationship, a suitable object is one that resembles a past self, and the demand is that the person accepts being formed into his current self; the failure to comply with this norm gives rise to the accusation, "I have given you all this support and assistance, and yet you haven't become me": the cause is suspected to be inherent unworthiness and malevolence. The parallel accusation repeated today towards immigrants or descendants of immigrants is that "you have failed to become like us". If we ask, "Who is the welfare state for?", it appears that there is an increasing tendency to tie the political system to an idea of national origin, an ethnification of the state apparatus.

The philosopher Gunnar Skirbekk's book on Norwegian national identity identifies an experience of mutual trust as a basis for what he calls a "national–political solidarity" which founded the welfare state (2010, p. 67). This mutual trust, linked with thinking of others as fair and as rational, is challenged, as he puts it, by

> immigration from countries where the ideas of what it means to live in a welfare state are unclear (for instance with regard to social virtues, such as solidarity beyond one's own family). Thus, there is a danger of a weakening of the mutual trust and the self-restrictive solidarity which is demanded in a generous and universal welfare state. (Skirbekk, 2010, p. 145, translated for this edition)

In making this statement, he refers in a footnote to the issue of tax avoidance by taxi drivers which was given a lot of press attention some years ago, where some of those who were found guilty were of a Pakistani family background (fn, p. 228). He uses the example to imply that their crime was culturally determined; they lacked the necessary preconditions to form a part of a welfare state. Summing up what he sees as necessary requirements for meaningful participation in Norwegian society, he states that everyone should know today's society has developed through an interaction between state officials and ordinary people, the former secular jurists and Christian theologians, the latter law-orientated and literate common people with a puritan work ethic. Together, these people led a pastoral enlightenment to parliamentary democracy with social solidarity and a rule of law (fn, pp. 229–230). Skirbekk's historical account is jointly descriptive and normative; recognition of this narrated background is explicitly demanded in the double sense of realisation and affirmation.

Gullestad's remarks on "symbolic kinship", made in a different context, seem suitable at this point. "Culture" does not figure as something that is continuously being built, but as something completed. Young and middle-aged majority Norwegians are imaginatively construed as having "built the country", even though factually they did not, while people regarded as "immigrants", irrespective of citizenship or length of stay, are excluded from this conceived participation (2006, p. 180). "Imagined sameness" is, thus, operative in that the former are thought to be not just similar to, but the same as past generations who are seen as having built an entity where "the state" and "ethnic nationality" is deliberately blurred.

Rationality is central to Skirbekk's account of Norwegian identity; in his historical narrative, the rural, as opposed to the city, "common people", as opposed to elite representatives, the nation conceived as an "ethnic unit", and Protestant Christianity are tied together and identified with the form he values the most—self-critical rationality. It is an account that favours the traditional; Gro Harlem Bruntland, three times prime minister for the Labour Party and known for her engagement in environmental issues, as a representative of modern-isation, is granted only technical–instrumental rationality in this picture. Descriptions of cultural battles over modernisation from the 1920s and 1930s onwards, where the Church would be found to take a stand against it, are entirely absent.

The conception of "rationality" is further illustrated in an inter-view, where the journalist states, with reference to citizens of Oslo with a background from Pakistan, that "we must find a way to live together". Skirbekk replies,

> Does that mean that we shall no longer trust the Norwegian state? That we shall no longer relate to science as fundamental to society? Or that the Qur'an should be above science? . . . No, when it comes to . . . rationality, there is no compromise. (Dypvik, 2010, translated for this edition)

His response is reminiscent of Freud's statement that "self-love works for the preservation of the individual, and behaves as though the occurrence of any divergence from his own particular lines of devel-opment involved a criticism of them and a demand for their alter-ation" (Freud, 1921c, p. 102). The figure of the citizen with a Pakistani background is identified as someone who presents a demand for a radical change, seemingly conversion to Islam of a fundamentalist variety and disidentification with the state, its laws, and its system of welfare. The premises are those of a zero sum game: either I have to become you, or, more correctly, my image of you, or you have to become me—any idea of mutuality is absent. Perhaps the only modern feature of his statement is the normative appeal to rationality, usually thought of as a universal human characteristic, but in this case rationality serves the function of supporting a claim for superiority, to the effect that "we" are rational and enlightened and "they" are not. The rationality in question is a very culturally specific one, inter-twined with a notion of trust based on, as he says, "deep, shared experiences" (Dypvik, 2010)—shared, the presumption is, even by people who were not around when the historical events in question unfolded. The book is written with both younger generations and what he calls "new countrymen" in mind and with the aim that if they do not share these experiences, then they ought to do so. Those who are granted Norwegian passports, he states, must acquire more than just the language and knowledge of the laws; they must be subject to a re-socialisation (Dypvik, 2010).

Most often, when one hears the phrase "basic Norwegian values", the content is not further specified, so one is left to wonder what they are, but, in this case, we are presented with at least one candidate; trust as a political virtue. Hoggett (2009, p. 97) with reference to "Instincts and their vicissitudes", has argued that an emotion cannot, in itself, have an inherent moral value; its value depends on the aim and object of the feeling. I would like to follow up on that point here by arguing that the claim that a state of feeling is inherently morally good is often paired with a narcissistic way of thinking. Emotions are ways in which we interact with, and respond to, others and our environment; the word "attunement" captures how they may allow one to discern what is going on, what is at stake, or what is relevant in a situation, whereas the word "mood" points in the opposite direction, describing how the world takes on the colour of one's subjective state. The claim that my state of feeling is morally good *per se* entails the demand that the environment fits with my emotional attitude. If I have decided that trust is inherently morally good, the environment's failure to appear as trustworthy, or another's person's failure to approach me with a similar attitude of trust, will be taken to be offensive. As seen above, the journalist's question about different experiences, emotional and intellectual horizons, is answered with a demand for sameness, for re-socialisation. Thus, the other side to the seemingly beautiful description of a state of mutual trust is the threat to "the other" that you had better adapt so as to comply with this given picture. In what follows, we shall examine a more extreme version of narcissism, both in an individual and a collective sense. Young-Bruehl has suggested that narcissistic societies "do not necessarily put the self first. That is, they do not produce the kind of heedless self-promotion that earned the American middle and upper classes the title "narcissistic" in the 1970s (1996, p. 37). Rather, they combine innovative ambitions for power with profoundly conservative self-images. The Norwegian mass killer did not set aside his megalomaniac beliefs in his own individual importance, though at some point, when he acquired a belief in "something larger than himself", it was a sub-culture that fitted this description of a deeply conservative vision of a future society devoid of "others".

A self-made (wo)man

"Layer upon layer of false identities, secret accounts, white and black lies. And underneath all the layers a single, burning wish: to become great, to become famous" (Borchgrevink, 2012, p. 162, translated for this edition). This is a characterisation of Anders Behring Breivik by his biographer, Aage Storm Borchgrevink. It describes the terrorist who took great pleasure in posing in homemade uniforms with self-invented medals as decorations and distributing the pictures, who was absorbed with his looks, and whose most successful business venture was the founding of a company that sold false diplomas (p. 153): narcissistic personality disorder was the only diagnosis the psychiatrists could agree on. He had dropped out before finishing school and was contemptuous towards academics, thus explaining the reason for his business, which he closed down when it came under investigation for tax avoidance. After that, in 2006, aged twenty-seven, he moved back home to his mother, engaging in a project of self-transformation. The computer game *World of Warcraft* took up most of his time for years thereafter: he had three avatars, one male and two female. His biographer expresses uncertainty as to what was a cover up for what; according to Breivik himself, dependence on computer games was a cover story for a project of distancing himself from his old life (2012, p. 160), of de-sensitivisation as a preparation for killing. Extensive usage of steroids was employed to alter his body and mind. Inspired by a range of international, ultra right-wing, "contra-jihadist" and racist bloggers, he put together a compendium out of which he arose as "Andrew Berwick, Justiciary Knight Commander, Knights Templar Europe" (2012, p. 164). After his arrest, it took the police a while to conclude that no such order existed.

At home with his mother, according to her testimony, Anders failed to keep his distance, especially in the last year; he would practically sit on top of her on the sofa (p. 190). The accused stated in court

that the media and the prosecution had claimed that he had an incestuous relation to his mother, although no such claims had been made
(p. 336). The counterpart to this tendency towards merging with his
mother was a paranoid fear of contagion; from time to time, he would
wear a surgical mask at home to avoid catching her germs. The theme
of women as a source of venereal and other disease permeates
Breivik's compendium (p. 227). This double stance of appearing to be
united with his mother and attempts to protect himself from contact
with, or influence by, her, to avoid fusion, is echoed in accounts of his
childhood. Breivik was born in Oslo in 1979; his mother was a nursing auxiliary, his father a diplomat.[1] Both had moved to Oslo from
elsewhere in the country, so they had few local social ties. The parents
divorced when the boy was eighteen months old; she referred to her
ex-husband as "a monster", he called his ex-wife "mad" (p. 43). Six
months later, the mother asked the social services for help, describing
her son as restless, violent, and temperamental. The State Centre for
Child and Youth Psychiatry, SSBU, observed the family together and
separately. The mother alternated between rejecting and being furious
with the boy and showering him with signs of affection. His mother
had told SSBU that she had wanted an abortion when she was pregnant with him, but had been unable to make up her mind about it by
the legal deadline. She had found the toddler very difficult and
demanding, had expressed a wish to "get rid of" him, and stated to
the SSBU that she wanted to "peel him off her" (pp. 334–335)—a peculiar expression indicating that she saw the boy as part of her own
body. She allied with his older half-sister in attacking the boy, whom
she appeared to identify with his hated father (p. 44). The SSBU
described a child who was unable to play, found it difficult to express
his emotions, and lacked joy and spontaneity (p. 46). They judged that
the boy was subject to neglect and recommended that the care should
be taken away from his mother (p. 49). In 1983, the child protection
service agreed that he should be placed in a foster home. In the same
year, the father and his new wife, who now lived in Paris, went to
court to be given custody. In spite of the SSBU's conclusion that the
boy was "in danger of developing more severe psychopathology" due
to his home situation, the court ruled that he should stay with his
mother, and the father and his new wife withdrew their case (p. 53).
The father was, and remained, distant and remote. It was due to his
stepmother that the couple had applied to be given custody, and she

later maintained some degree of contact with the boy, teenager, and adult, while his father neglected both him and his other half-siblings (p. 60). In spite of this fact, the absent father was the only close relative who remained clear of the rage of the later author of the compendium. In 1984, the child protection authorities followed up the case by paying three visits to the home, and described the boy and his sister as safe, relaxed, and well-behaved. The case was closed two months later (pp. 54–55), after which nothing unusual was reported

There are two striking features of the propaganda material Breivik produced, a film and a 1500-page "compendium": one is the degree to which the imagery echoes earlier anti-Semitic and racist propaganda. (See Ferenc Erős's illuminating chapter in this volume.) The fantasies evoked appear as frightening repetitions of similar material, about conspiracies for world domination and control over the media, only now applied to "the Muslim". The second striking feature is the explicitly sexualised nature of these fantasies; it is apparent that sexism and racism are intertwined, and also that the hated, feared, and denigrated other is simultaneously of great sexual interest. The terrorist complained in his compendium that he had been feminised by having been raised by women (Borchgrevink, p. 236), and enthusiastically endorsed another ultra-right wing writer's description of "the Western man" as having been castrated (p. 179). A part of his plan that failed, that of beheading Gro Harlem Bruntland, can be read as an extension of this thought, as Jegerstedt (2013, p. 164) also suggests, an act of symbolic castration.

Gro Harlem Bruntland was Norway's first female prime minister. She served three terms in office for the Labour Party (1981, 1986–1989, 1990–1996) and has served as the Director General of the World Health Organisation. She was often referred to as "the mother of the country". This expression could be seen to refer to her status as a very powerful woman and an advocate for women's rights, as well as a representative of a party that was in continuous government from 1945–1965 and has held a strong position ever since, associated with rebuilding the country after the war and with building the welfare state, so that she could be conceived as a generous, caring mother. The plan had been to cut off Bruntland's head while reading out a text about her "crimes", and to post this as a film on the internet (Borchgrevink, 2012, p. 240). Reflecting on the "narcissism of minor differences", Figlio (2012, p. 11) stated that "the horror of castration opposes a wish to be castrated".

Breivik could serve as an illustration of this claim; he voiced a fantasy about being himself castrated—in the service of Al-Qaeda. He imagines a collaboration between Islamist groups and "Knight templars" as these are both anti-establishment. To enable the Islamists to distinguish between knights and CIA agents, the knights must show their willingness to sacrifice "by surgical removal of penis and testicles and/or by executing a certain number of civilian children" (Borchgrevink 2012, p. 221). This peculiar statement reveals an imagined parallel between violence towards others and self-mutilation; these appear as exchangeable, or the same. It also points to a wish for an erotic union with "the Islamist", a submissive relationship where the other is the dominant party. I shall venture to add that, to Breivik, there is no distinction between being "the Muslim's" passive gay lover and being a woman to him as a man. Thus, we could add to the understanding of two of the most sexualised images from his propaganda film by reading them simultaneously as self-portraits. The first shows a picture of a white woman with long, blonde hair. Her hair is messy, her face covered in blood. A caption below the image reads: "Has your daughter, sister or girlfriend experienced CULTURAL ENRICHMENT by the local Muslim community yet?" From the context, we are meant to understand that she has been raped, and that "the Muslim community" is responsible. We may also note that the text does not say "have *you* experienced . . ." or "has your *son, brother* or *boyfriend* experienced . . ."; it appears to speak to a man, not a woman, and state that the victim is a woman, not a man. Furthermore, the text does not refer to older generations than that of the addressee ("has your *mother/father* experienced . . ."). Thus, the combination of text and image appeals to an experience of victimisation while also implicitly placing the addressee in a superior position to that of the victim; it avoids direct identification with the victim, thus seemingly contradicting the thought expressed in the "manifesto" that it is the white, Christian man who has been raped or castrated by an alliance of "Islamists", "cultural Marxists", and "feminists", though, by extension of the same logic, since Breivik feels he has been raped and castrated, he has become a woman, so in this sense he is the white woman in the picture. The image of rape can serve as a metaphor for a feeling of being exploited more widely understood, a sense that one's boundaries have been breached, of experiencing impingement, or of being invaded. In neo-nationalist rhetoric, it is not uncommon to see an implicit parallel being drawn between the German invasion of Norway during the Second World War and today's immigrants, portrayed as if they were hostile occupying forces on Norwegian soil.

A second image shows a woman dressed in a black niqab. She is pregnant, although her pregnant stomach is drawn as a bomb that is lit and about to go off. Her hands, resting on her tummy, are those of a skeleton. The text in the top left corner reads: "Islamic demographic warfare. Proven strategy for the conquest of infidel nations for 1400 years". This juxtaposition of pregnancy and terrorism might seem surprising and shocking. Fertility or procreation, more commonly associated with creativity, life, and renewal, is likened to an act of war. Giving life is portrayed as equal to killing. In André Green's words,

> The narcissistic organisation attacks difference, between inside and outside, ego and object, masculine and feminine. The narcissistic sense of plenitude comes both from the ego's fusion with the object as well as from the disappearance of the object and the ego into the neuter, ne-uter. (Green, 2001, p. 23)

Accordingly, life and death are equated; life becomes the same as death. Such an idea of "demographic warfare" is shared by other right-wing extremists and forms part of a conspiracy theory known as the Eurabia theory (Fangen, 2012, pp. 182–183). In an autobiographical part of his "manifesto", Breivik considers the alternative of marrying and having many children (Jegerstedt, 2012, p. 170), which, given these premises, could be read as entering into competition with "the fertile Muslim", though he rejects this thought as insufficiently radical; why reproduce in a world where Europeans are engaged in "cultural suicide", deprived of control over their own lives? (p. 170). From the point of view of a logic of narcissism, we might venture the idea that the problem with having children is that a child would have half the genes of another, and, thus, the solution is insufficiently satisfying. We might venture to say that having children was a position that was not available to Breivik, as he was perhaps, to his mind, a woman. The only transformative option that was available was that of phallic, defensive masculinity. Along these lines, the projects of self-brutalisation via playing computer games, combining stereoids with exercise, and dressing up in uniforms can be read as transforming himself from a woman into a man. Or, he could be seen as transforming himself from the white raped woman into the pregnant Muslim terrorist woman, whose only "creative gift" to the world is that of destruction. Or, via "positive thinking", from a "bitter old goat" behind a computer (Borchgrevink, 2012, p. 217) to a knight in shining armour. "Know", he writes to himself, "that you are not alone" (p. 217).

The hangman and the noose: mainstream support for extremism

As already mentioned, the police searched in vain for a terrorist group of which the perpetrator claimed to be a member. In that sense, the "we" that runs through the manifesto is a fiction, the terrorist's multiple transformative projects defending against genuine contact with others, though the "we" is real in a different sense: it reflects some fantasies shared by a sub-culture. Breivik's document was largely made out of lengthy quotations from other writers. Among them are the Norwegian blogger Fjordman, whose real name is Peder Jensen, Bat Ye'or, real name Gisele Littman, and the American Robert Spencer, whose site is called Jihad Watch. He was also inspired by a blog called Gates of Vienna, run by the American Edward "Ned" May (Brown, 2011). Breivik had been a member of the Norwegian Progress Party, but had left it again (Brown, 2011); he greatly admired the English Defence League (Milne, 2011). There is a continuum between the more extreme statements of xenophobia and Islamophobia and statements in the mainstream media. The manifesto included a lengthy quotation from the *Daily Mail* writer Melanie Phillips, who stated that the former Labour government was guilty of "unalloyed treachery" for using mass immigration to "destroy what it means to be culturally British and to put another 'multicultural' identity in its place" (Milne, 2011). The leader of the Progress Party, Siv Jensen, had warned against what she referred to as "the hidden Islamisation" of Norwegian society in January 2010 (Bjurvald, 2011, p. 199). After Breivik's terror attacks, she described what had happened as horrible, while adding that it would be equally horrible to try to link the events to her party. She later attempted to withdraw that statement. In September of the same year, she repeated her statements to the effect that "Islamisation" was a threat to the entire Western world, and also declared that she had never said anything wrong or discriminatory (Bjurvald, 2011, p. 210).

Immediately after the terror, the attack was seen "as an attack on Norway, on our way of life. In the streets of Oslo, young women wearing hijabs and Arab-looking men were harassed as soon as the news broke" (Myhre, 2011). People assumed that the evil came from "the other", and it was already culturally established that "others" were Muslims and dark-skinned people, "immigrants" or descendants of immigrants. When it was discovered that the perpetrator was a blond, white man, as Norwegian as any, the majority was faced with an identity problem. If the terrorist had been "culturally other", explanations of his actions by reference to "cultural factors" would have been expected. Since, instead, he represented the mainstream, examining why he grew out of Norwegian society would have amounted to painful self-examination. It might be too categorical to state that such a process has not yet begun; perhaps it is under way, though there are alarming signs that point in the opposite direction.

More than three million Norwegians participated in public mourning ceremonies after 22 July 2011. There were processions in which people carried roses, sang hymns, and hugged one another. Public spaces were covered in candles and flowers, commemorating the victims. The Prime Minister for the Labour Party, Jens Stoltenberg, declared in a speech that "You shall not be allowed to destroy us. You shall not be allowed to destroy our democracy and our engagement for a better world", and stated that his response to the violence would be "more democracy, more openness, more humanity" (Vettenranta, 2012, p. 275, translated for this edition). The Crown Prince's description appeared to be expressive of the general mood: "The streets are filled with love this evening. We have chosen to answer cruelty with closeness. We have chosen to meet hatred with unity" (Vettenranta, 2012, p. 276, translated for this edition). Despite the officially conveyed sense that everyone was united in mourning and in love for one another, clinging together in despair and incomprehension, a more recent survey has revealed systematic differences with regard to participation in these ceremonies. Women and people in urban areas were overrepresented, as were people whose education and income were lower than the average. Employees in the health sector and social services were more likely to participate, as were people who voted for the socialist party (SV) or the social liberal party (V). Perhaps unsurprisingly, Progress Party (FrP) voters were least likely to do so (Nipen, 2013).

In a twist on the old expression "in the house of the hanged, you should not mention the noose", Adorno described how it was "the victims of Auschwitz who had to take its horrors upon itself, not those who, to their own disgrace and that of their nation, prefer not to admit it", and continued; "But in the house of the hangman one should not mention the noose; otherwise one might be suspected of harbouring resentment" (2010, p. 208). In his 1955 group study of post-war West Germans, he encountered virtuosic deployment of defences against guilt, manifestations of "collective narcissism", among which was that of placing the blame somewhere else, with third parties or with the victims (2010, p. 23). Thus far, in Norway, the result of the call for "more openness" has been a larger space, or stage, for those who more or less sympathise with the perpetrator to voice their opinions. In April 2013, the blogger Fjordman was assigned a major space in the Norwegian newspaper *Aftenposten*. He used it to state that

> those who are critical of Islamisation and mass immigration are both the majority and the voice of reason. We shall no longer let ourselves be bullied by a radical minority which unfortunately commands most of the stream of propaganda through the mass media. (Jensen, 2013, translated for this edition)

The piece is headed with line "By branding certain opinions that the ruling elites dislike the media attempts to frighten people into silence". The irony is easily spotted: through the serious attention they are given in a major newspaper, the claims about being bullied and censored are thoroughly disproved. The attention has been followed up with interviews, and the blogger has recently received funding from the Freedom of Speech Foundation in Norway in order to write a book (Svendsen, 2013). When Eskild Pedersen, the leader of the Labour Party's youth organisation, AUF, and a survivor from Utøya, protested, stating, "The web overflows with racism, harassment towards gay people and women and hatred of the social democracy. Do we need to pay to get it in a book format as well?" (Pedersen, 2013), he was referred to as an "enemy of democracy" (Ravnaas 2013). In a similar vein, Thomas Hylland Eriksen, professor of social anthropology and a public intellectual famous for defending diversity and tolerance, was accused in another newspaper article (Bandehy, 2012) of provoking Breivik's terror attack by expressing his positive views on multi-culturalism.

We might wonder why, after the most serious terror attacks in Norway since the Second World War, which killed seventy-seven people, including many children, extremists' perspectives are thus affirmed and supported by mainstream representatives. The press might, of course, be led by a commercial interest in producing excitement by giving attention to fascists. The official arguments state that "freedom of speech" legitimises their claim to be heard. This stance could be motivated by fear; a fear of even more violence resulting from suppression of their views, expressive of a strategy of "appeasement". It might also be motivated by partial support for their point of view. The result is that expressions of xenophobic hatred have received a large share of uncritical attention, so that after the terror attacks the divide between extreme and mainstream variants of nationalism is even more blurred than it was before. According to the latest polls, support for the Labour Party and other parties on the left is receding, while the support for the right is increasing. The Conservative Party, with 33% of the vote, in coalition with the racist Progress Party, with 18% support (TV 2, 2013), is set to take over the government after the next election (in September 2013). Thus, the terror attacks can be seen to have been remarkably successful; the intended victims lose support, those who sympathise with the aggressor are victorious. "The beautiful words after July 22nd seem to have withered with the roses", wrote Marie Simonsen (2013) in a comment on the virulent expressions of hatred towards visiting Roma in Oslo that followed the expressions of mourning after the terror attacks:

> The TV news broadcasts a film clip of a Roma who defecates under a bridge, accompanied by the comment: He did not even care that we saw him. The question is whether anyone really saw him. Or whether a gradual dehumanisation has taken place, which defends such an unworthy newsreel. . . . Today it is the Roma. Tomorrow it may be another group that challenges with its difference. It does not only affect the others, it influences us all: how we think of weakness, of ethnicity, of people who end up on the outside. It impacts on politics and, finally, the whole of society. (Simonsen, 2013, translated for this edition)

Sadly, this columnist's stance is uncharacteristic. The voices of those who defend a revived nationalism and xenophobic attacks against "others", Muslims, Roma, refugees, and immigrants in particular, are the dominant ones. They meet with no strong opposition. Unless there is renewed reflection on how "we" see ourselves—victims? perpetrators? bystanders?—and whom "we" may include, a willingness to listen to and sustain such painful enquiry, there is reason to fear for the future.

Note

1. A sociological point could be made about the differences in social status between Breivik's parents. When his parents divorced, these differences meant that instead of growing up as the child of a diplomat, he grew up as the child of a single mother and nursing auxiliary in a part of Oslo's west end, where success was considered important and where he was surrounded by classmates with a higher social status than himself.

References

Adorno, T. W. (2010). *Guilt and Defence. On the Legacies of National Socialism in Postwar Germany*, J. K. Olick (Ed. & Trans.), A. J. Perrin (Ed.). London: Harvard University Press.

Bandehy, L. (2012). Våre antirasistiske helter. *Aftenposten*, 23 November.

Bjånesøy, K. B. (2010). Da Kongen tok trikken. *Dagbladet Magasinet*, 8 March.

Bjurvald, L. (2011). *Europas skam. Rasister på frammarsj*. Oslo: Cappelen Damm.

Borchgrevink, A. S. (2012). *En norsk tragedie. Anders Behring Breivik og veiene til Utøya*. Oslo: Gyldendal.

Brown, A. (2011). Anders Breivik's spider web of hate. *Guardian*, 7 September.

Dypvik, A. S. (2010). Her kan det ikkje vera noko gi og ta. Interview with Gunnar Skirbekk. Klassekampen, 26 November 2010.

Fangen, K. (2012). Mellom konspirasjonsteori og galskap. In: S. Østerud (Ed.), *22. juli. Forstå - forklare - forebygge* (pp. 178–198). Oslo: Abstrakt forlag.

Figlio, K. (2012). The dread of sameness: social hatred and Freud's "narcissism of minor differences". In: L. Auestad (Ed.), *Psychoanalysis and Politics. Exclusion and the Politics of Representation*. London: Karnac.

Freud, S. (1914c). On narcissism: an introduction. *S.E., 14*: 67–102. London: Hogarth.

Freud, S. (1916–1917). *Introductory Lectures on Psycho-Analysis. S.E., 15–16.* London: Hogarth.

Freud, S. (1921c). *Group Psychology and the Analysis of the Ego. S.E., 18*: London: Hogarth.

Green, A. (2001). *Life Narcisssim. Death Narcissim.* London: Free Association Books.

Gullestad, M. (2006). *Plausible Prejuaice.* Oslo: Universitetsforlaget.

Hoggett, P. (2009). *Politics, Identity and Emotion.* Boulder, CO: Paradigm Publishers.

Jegerstedt, K. (2012). Frykten for det feminine. In: S. Østerud (Ed.), *22. juli. Forstå - forklare - forebygge* (pp. 150–177) . Oslo: Abstrakt forlag.

Jensen, P. N. (2013). Medienes myter. *Aftenposten*, 25 April.

Klein, M. (1946). Notes on some schizoid mechanisms. In: *Envy and Gratitude* (pp. 1–24). New York: Delacorte Press/Seymour Lawrence.

Lien, M. E., & Melhuus, M. (2008). Overcoming the division between anthropology 'at home' and 'abroad'. Marianne Gullestad in conversation with Marianne Lien and Marit Melhuus. www.easaonline.org/Gullstadeasa.pdf.

Milne, S. (2011). In his rage against Muslims, Norway's killer was no loner. *Guardian*, 28 July.

Myhre, A. S. (2011). Norway attacks: Norway's tragedy must shake Europe into acting on extremism. *Guardian*, 24 July.

Nipen, K. (2013). Sorgen etter 22. juli var ikke for alle. *Aftenposten*, 25 June.

Pedersen, E. (2013). Å kjempe for toleranse. *VG Nett*, 18 June.

Ravnaas, N. R. (2013). Eskild Pedersen er en fiende av demokratiet. *Nettavisen*, 18 June.

Simonsen, M. (2013). Rosetoget har visnet. *Dagbladet*, 27 April.

Skirbekk, G. (2010). *Norsk og Moderne.* Oslo: Res Publica.

Svendsen (2013). "Fjordman" får penger fra Fritt Ord. *VG Nett*, 16 June.

TV 2 (2013). Partibarometeret. *NorStat/Vårt Land*, 27 June.

Vettenranta, S. (2012). Statlige sorgriter og kollektiv smerte. In: S. Østerud (Ed.), *22. juli. Forstå - forklare - forebygge* (pp. 271–288). Oslo: Abstrakt forlag.

Young-Bruehl, E. (1996). *The Anatomy of Prejudices.* Cambridge, MA: Harvard University Press.

PART II
CONSTELLATIONS OF NATIONALISM

Editor's introduction to Chapter Four

The chapter analyses what the author calls "mourning populism" based on Ernesto Laclau's theory of populist reason, Carl Schmitt's idea of the political, and Freud's thoughts on group psychology and mourning. The author follows Laclau in his observation that populism has its own logic, a transcultural approach that can, in principle, be applied to any content. Laclau's concept of populism is strictly formal; its definition relates exclusively to a specific mode of articulation, independent of the actual contents. If we ask to what extent any given movement could be populist, it is argued, we come up with two ideal extremes of the continuum of political practices: (1) an institutionalist discourse dominated by a pure logic of difference, and (2) a populist discourse, in which the logic of equivalence operates unchallenged. Where the former would lead to a society so dominated by administration and by the individualisation of social demands that no politics would be possible, the latter would involve such a dissolution of social links that the notion of "social demand" would lose any meaning, and the image of society would be that of a "crowd" or "mass". The author follows Laclau in his observation that populism has its own logic, a transcultural approach that may, in principle, be applied to any content, while arguing for the need to also analyse the cultural context specific to a given country to understand its specific embodiment of populism. "If the English are preoccupied with the weather", he states, "the Poles are with suffering." Polish populism, it is argued, performs best when exploiting a trauma—the partitions of Poland in the eighteenth century, the uneven war in the twentieth century, the genocide of the Polish intelligentsia in Katyń 1940, the Warsaw Uprising, or the Smoleńsk tragedy of 10 April 2010.

CHAPTER FOUR

Funeral policy: the case of mourning populism in Poland

Szymon Wróbel

Populism in question

The concept of populism has seemingly become an indispensable part of any democratic political culture. The fact that it is so widely acknowledged in the analyses of social, political and institutional phenomena by historians, social scientists, journalists and politicians alike indicates that populism tends to emerge at different times and in various places. It also seems that, today, populist slogans are not only used by radical parties, as is often said in the literature. Populist rhetoric has been exercised by vast political platforms, not only on the right but also on the left of the political scene (Betz, 1994, p. 33; Kazin, 1995, p. 78; Mudde, 2000, p. 67; Taggart, 1996, p. 14; Zakaria, 2003, p. 56). Populism today is not restricted to populist parties as such, but it is increasingly associated with European leaders and social movements.

Mudde defines populism as "an ideology that considers society to be ultimately separated into two homogeneous and antagonistic groups, 'the pure people' versus 'the corrupt elite', and which argues that politics should be an expression of the general will of the people" (Mudde, 2007, p. 41). Leaving aside the question of whether the above definition considers populism an ideology or not, it undoubtedly provides a collection of the features of populism of which the first and foremost is negativism. Populism reacts against elites and institutions and, thus, it is perceived as anti-capitalism, anti-Semitism, anti-urbanism, anti-modernism, anti-etc. Populism derives its expressiveness from negativism. Negativism and expressiveness are presented by a discourse. Here, the discourse plays an important role and is based on the rhetoric that expresses not who the populists are for, but who the populists are against. The second feature of populist thinking is the sense of betrayal and treachery. Populists usually claim that the people have been betrayed by an establishment. Usually, all political elites are accused of abusing their position of power instead of acting in conformity with the interests of the people as a whole (Mény & Surel, 2002. p. 13). To go further, populists argue that there is a conspiracy of elites against the people (Szacki, 2004, p. 33). This is also based on simple rules derived from the common wisdom of the people and is deeply rooted in local tradition and culture.

The weakness in defining populism as an ideology lies in a tacit assumption that populism simply expresses the inner nature of some political subjects (Canovan, 1981, p. 56). Here, in this chapter, I claim that we would be better off assuming that the political practices do not, in fact, express the nature of social agents, but instead constitute it. Such a solution has been proposed by Laclau, who suggests that it is the practices that constitute primary units of analysis, and that the group is the result of an articulation of social practices.

Thus, what makes a movement populist is not its apparent "populist take" on politics or its apparent "populist ideology", but a particular logic of articulation of populist content—whatever this might be. Individuals, in the theoretical context, are not coherent totalities, but merely referential identities that, at best, could be split up into a series of localised subject positions. The articulation between these positions is a social rather than an individual affair. Laclau's concept of populism is, therefore, strictly formal, for all its defining features are exclusively related to a specific mode of articulation which is independent of the actual contents that are articulated. That is the reason why "populism" falls into an ontological and not an ontic category (Laclau, 2005, p. 34). Most of the attempts at defining populism have tried to identify a specific and particular ontic content and, to that end, they have proved unsuccessful. In fact, there have been only two predictable alternative results of such an undertaking: those based on empirical content could by no means provide for numerous excep- tions, and those appealing to an "intuition" could not provide for all given conceptual contents (Laclau, 1996, p. 45).

Approaching the question of populism formally reveals another, otherwise intractable issue. If, instead of a question as to whether or not a movement is populist, we begin with a question as to what extent any given movement could be populist, we come up with two ideal extremes of the continuum of political practices: (1) an institu- tionalist discourse dominated by a pure logic of difference, and (2) a populist discourse, in which the logic of equivalence operates unchal- lenged. The former, if unchallenged, would lead to a society so domi- nated by administration and by the individualisation of social demands that no struggle for internal frontiers, and, consequently, no politics, would be possible. The latter, on the other hand, would involve such a dissolution of social links that the very notion of "social demand" would lose any meaning, and the image of society would be that of a "crowd" or "mass", as depicted by the nineteenth-century theorists of "mass psychology", such as Taine (1878) or Le Bon (1896).

Laclau maintains that the first precondition of that mode of poli- tical articulation we call populism is a social situation in which demands tend to reaggregate themselves on the negative basis and all remain unsatisfied. While the institutional arrangement is grounded in the logic of difference, in the populist situation we have an inverse scenario, which can be described as the logic of equivalence. In such a case where all demands, in spite of their differential character, tend to reaggregate and form what Laclau calls an equivalential chain (Laclau, 2005, p. 178), each individual demand is constitutively split: on the one hand, it is its own particularised self; on the other, it points, through equivalential links, to the totality of other demands.

Laclau's conceptualisation of chains of equivalences that forge links between not necessarily connected demands draws upon Saus- surian linguistics, with its distinction between syntagms and para- digms predicated on a non-referential and non-essentialist conception of language and relations among elements more generally. The crea- tion of equivalences occurs through processes of articulation, which bring together elements that do not necessarily belong together. It is only through the creation of equivalences that a set of relational differ- ences can be drawn together into a totality defined as a unity against something it, in itself, is not. The separate, differential demands that emanate from a variety of different sectors of society are unified through their common opposition to an oppressive regime. In other words, while each of the particular demands is distinctive, what they share is the opposition to a common enemy: the oppressive regime. In this respect, they are rendered equivalent.

The unity of the chain of equivalences is established by one of the elements of the chain representing the chain as a whole and, thus, operating as an *empty signifier*. In this way, the democratic subject emerges in and through the process of making demands, which in turn may come to perform as *empty signifiers*. It is important to note that the *empty signifier* plays a dual role in the constitution of a populace. On the one hand, it is instituting a populace in the very process of representing them and, as such, it does not simply reflect a preordained totality. On the other hand, it represents the people as a not entirely autonomous marker of identification. Given this, the constitution of "the people" causes tension. If the totalising moment—that of equivalence—prevails, representation is destroyed. If, on the other hand, there is a complete autonomisation of demands, where difference prevails, the moment of totalisation necessary for the constitution of some form of unity is blocked. To put it more simply, if the constitutive function of representation prevails without attention to the fact that a particular actor is being represented, the link between the representative and the represented is broken. If, on the other hand, the representative simply reflects the represented, there is no possibility of drawing together a number of distinct demands into a unity that exceeds the specificity of each of the demands. Hence, the *political* function of representation is, of necessity, one of maintaining the tension between the two extreme points of the continuum.

In each case, the subject of the demand is different. In the first case, the subject of the demand is as specific as the demand itself. Laclau describes the subject of a demand conceived as a differential particularity a/the democratic subject. In the other case, the subject is broad, for its subjectivity results from the equivalential aggregation of a plurality of democratic demands. Laclau calls a subject constituted on the basis of this logic a/the popular subject (Laclau, 2005, p. 148). This clearly shows the conditions for either the emergence or disappearance of a popular subjectivity: the more social demands tend to be differentially absorbed within a successful institutional system, the

weaker the equivalential links are and the more unlikely is the constitution of a popular subjectivity. Conversely, a situation in which there
coexists a plurality of unsatisfied demands and an increasing inability
of the institutional system to absorb them differentially constitutes a
prerequisite of a populist rupture.

For Laclau, the very logic of hegemonic articulation also applies to
the conceptual opposition between populism and politics: populism is
the Lacanian "objet a" of politics, the particular figure which stands
for the universal dimension of the political, which is why it is "the
royal road" to understanding the political. Populism is not a specific
political movement, but the political at its purest: the "inflection" of
the social space that can affect any political content. Its elements are
purely formal: populism occurs when a series of particular "democratic" demands (for better social security, health services, lower taxes,
against war, etc.) is enchained in a series of equivalences, and this
enchainment produces "people" as the universal political subject.
What characterises populism is not the ontic content of these
demands, but the mere formal fact that, through their enchainment,
"the populace" emerges as a political subject, and all the different
particular struggles and antagonisms appear as parts of a global
antagonistic struggle between "us" (people) and "them". Again, the
content of "us" and "them" is not prescribed in advance, but is,
precisely, the stake of the struggle for hegemony.

For Laclau, the fact that some particular struggle is elevated into
the "universal equivalent" of all struggles is not a predetermined fact,
but itself the result of the contingent political struggle for hegemony:
in one constellation, this struggle can be the workers' struggle, in
another constellation, the patriotic anti-colonialist struggle, in yet
another constellation, the anti-racists struggle for cultural tolerance.
The struggle for hegemony, thus, not only presupposes an irreducible
gap between the universal form and the multiplicity of particular contents, but also the contingent process by means of which one among
these contents is "transubstantiated" into the immediate embodiment
of the universal dimension. For example, in Poland of the 1980s, the
particular demands of Solidarność were elevated into the embodiment
of the people's global rejection of the Communist regime, so that all
the different versions of the anti-Communist opposition (from the
conservative–nationalist opposition through the liberal–democratic
opposition and cultural dissidence to Leftist workers' opposition)

recognised themselves in the empty signifier *Solidarność* (Žižek, 2006, p. 56).

Populism in Poland

Before we start to elaborate on populism in Poland, one issue needs to be briefly outlined. It concerns the 1989 settlement reached between the opposition leaders of *Solidarność* and the former communist regime in "the round table" talks. It was summed up by the opposition leader Adam Michnik: "your President, our Prime Minister" and the suggestion by the first non-communist PM, Tadeusz Mazowiecki, to draw "a thick line" to mark off the communist past from the democratic future. Although Mazowiecki's intention was to make communists responsible for their era and the new government responsible for the future, in Polish parlance, the "thick line" came to signify that past Communist misdeeds are non-issues. Soon, however, the *Solidarność* camp split over the idea of building a democratic system together without referring back to the past. The vengeful ones claimed the Communists should never be forgiven and conceived that there must have been a silent settlement between the opposition leaders and the Communists. They would later pursue de-communisation and the vetting law, a bone of contention between two political camps emerging form *Solidarność* shaping Polish democracy in general and populist movements specifically (Krasnodębski, 2005; Śpiewak, 2005).

To exemplify Laclau's thesis that "a populism" as such does not exist but there are only different ways of doing politics with the help of populism, and that instead of defining a party or a given movement as populist one should rather ask to what extent is a movement populist, I will try to analyse the different logics of populist reason in Poland. In January 2005, the Law and Justice party (*Prawo i Sprawiedliwość, L&J*) won the parliamentary election and its victory gave the party a mandate to pursue "social justice" by the implementation of the vetting law and combating corruption (Kaczyński, 2006). The latter seems to have provided a capacious "empty signifier" to accommodate various social claims, including that of the nurses and the intelligentsia alike, all mesmerised by the idea that the troublesome social reality is indeed the corrupt fruit of the Roundtable Talks in 1989, resulting in their rights being taken away, their helplessness and poverty, and a distorted political scene. The Law and Justice party championed a populist agenda and, in the course of implementing it, tied up with populism by referring to the nation and claiming to represent the nation, by carrying out policy by acclamation, anointment, and delegation of power.

On the other hand, the victory of Civic Platform (*Platforma Obywatelska, CP*) in the parliamentary elections in September 2007 had much to do with the promise of Poland's economic progress matching that of Ireland's. The fact that it was such a success and a true banner of the victory also allows us to view CP's agenda as populist. In this case the "empty signifier" was to accommodate the claims of the entrepreneurs and the populace for more economic freedom, more support for free initiative, access to better education and better health care. Quite worryingly, contemporary politics looks like a mere mix of various populisms, addressing varied groups of society with the help of varied structural combinations. While L&J managed to seduce a disenfranchised nation, CP did the same with an entrepreneurial nation. Both parties accuse each other of pandering to the electorate and formulating hollow promises.

One of the objectives of this chapter is to establish whether a distinction between "good" and "bad" populism is implicitly assumed in analyses of populism. If so, "good" populism would be the one celebrating democracy as its core value, asking for more power on behalf of the people, and appearing to go along the lines of the customary way of conducting politics. "Bad" populism, on the other hand, would question the delegation of power to a few chosen people, the foundation of today's representative democracy, as well as most of the democratic institutions and long established democratic procedures. "Bad" populism, while shaking the foundations of democracy, its core ideas and procedures, is even more critical towards guarantors of the constitutional order, other than those democratically chosen by the nation: for example, the Chairmen of Central Banks or the Judges of the Constitutional Tribunal.

Based on Laclau's definition, Polish populism regards the society as being ultimately separated into two homogeneous and antagonistic groups. "The pure people" can be represented by different social classes, such as workers, farmers, Catholics, but also by the smaller entrepreneur. All of them are disappointed with the transformation (meaning democratisation, Europeanisation, globalisation, etc.) and blame the establishment for its failures. They are all united in disagreement with "the network", which, for the Polish populists, means everything that has any connections with communism. Interestingly, that includes not only post-communists, but also those who settled the agreements with them and, according to populists, blended the past with the future. Populists stress that such conduct has led to the divisions of society, pathologies, and corruption on different levels (political, economic, or social).

However, the good, or should we rather say, the "blessed", populism of CP is ready to sacrifice some of the beneficiaries of the transformation in new middle classes. This includes doctors who have their own profitable practice, successful academics employed at various institutions, bankers, presidents and directors of big companies, etc. These examples all too hastily believed in their success being the inevitable outcome of positive changes, as well as their own hard work and skills, and, thus, justified liberalism as a free market ideology at the expense of the security of the unfit, unskilled, and unlucky ones. Those beneficiaries used to see liberalism as the religion of a strong and victorious, self-confident man, who takes from God and Nature whatever he justly deserves. The teaching of this religion is a promise of a better future to all and contempt for those who delay the coming of this better world, like the helpless and irrational clerical masses. Polish populism is, thus, trapped between the discourse of desire for success and the success necessitated by the CP, which is essentially a discourse promising heaven and salvation here on earth, and the discourse of frustration triggered by the corruption of the elites who renounced their ties with the people and allowed them to perish in a liberal hell. To exaggerate, one could see Polish populism in a continuum where the extremes are the "rebellion of the elite" alienated from society, and the "revolt of the masses" alienated from the corrupt elite.

Coming back to Laclau's distinction, one could even say that CP's populism and L&J's populism seek to attain what Laclau recognises as inconceivable: (1) the CP's aim is to establish an institutionalist discourse dominated by a pure logic of difference, and (2) the L&J's aim is to establish the rule of a pure logic of equivalence. Let me only recall that pure difference would probably result in the death of politics, and pure equivalence would probably result in a dissolution of social links, making the very notion of the populace obsolete.

Populism after trauma

Before we move on, I would like to make a few general remarks on the dynamics of populism in Poland. In the early 1990s, at the frontier of populism in Poland, there were dissatisfied peasants, remnants of the state economy, still treasuring the memory of a robust past, resenting their assignment to the so called Poland "B". They took the coming of capitalism to be the prescribed St John's apocalypse and, equipped with nothing but a survival instinct, they began invading the cities, thus introducing populism to the political scene. As the side effects of the transformation piled up, other social groups also fell for state controlled economy. Meanwhile, the post-Communists appeared to accept the inevitable shift to a liberal economy and to leave the disenfranchised to their own devices. The disenfranchised, for their part, started to form a unified front of discontent and hastily assigned their problems to the Nation; the vows were renewed and corporations, together with the European Union and the State, were put on watch (Bauman, 2003; Wysocka, 2009).

While the majority of the population and the media continued to be blindly optimistic about the effects of the transformation and cheered the accession of Poland to the EU, new prophets appeared, teaching of a threat to the Nation and the apparent conspiracy to forsake the motherland. Radical populism was soon embodied in a grassroots party called "Self-Defence" (*Samoobrona*) which, in the years preceding the accession, declared a state of emergency. Its vocation was to do justice. The popularity of the fearless peasant leader, Andrzej Lepper, had peaked by the day of elections in 2004, but, as with the accession day, when the borders were opened and no one invaded, it declined together with other nationalist parties. Importantly, however, the left wing was to be marginalised in the years to come and it was the right wing that remained to appeal to the majority of the constituency. The banking crisis instigated by Lehman Brothers' bankruptcy was not that much of a problem to the Polish economy. Thus, it seemed that populism and its late parliamentary formation lost currency for good (Dzwończyk, 2000; Marczewska-Rytko, 2006; Markowski, 2004).

Then, one fatal day in 2010, everything changed. The Polish Air Force Tu-154 crash occurred on 10 April 2010, when a Tupolev 154 aircraft of the Polish Air Force crashed near the city of Smoleńsk, in

Russia, killing all ninety-six people on board: the Polish president Lech Kaczyński and his wife; former president Ryszard Kaczorowski; the chief of the Polish General Staff and other senior Polish military officers; the president of the National Bank of Poland; Poland's deputy foreign minister; Polish government officials; fifteen members of the Polish parliament; senior members of the Polish clergy and relatives of victims of the Katyń massacre. It was an immense loss to the country, taking the lives of the whole board of administrators, members of the state, and above all the late President Lech Kaczyński, who was at the time collaborating with the liberal government and waging wars with it over his competence to represent the nation.

Those underrepresented in the parliament and critical towards the government were in disbelief and their suspicions went beyond measure. This period marks the absorption of politics by two right-wing parties, the liberal CP and social L&J. Mutual accusations were hysterical, the charges all uncorroborated by evidence. Yet, no other political party could possibly steal this show, at best adding fuel to the national tank. By an almost unanimous and, as some now regret, hasty decision, the late President, together with the late First Lady, were buried in Wawel cathedral in Krakow, hitherto a place of burial reserved for Poland's kings and heroes. This moment marks the beginning of a new stage of populism in Poland, which I will, from now on, refer to as "mourning populism". There was no catharsis, since the opposition party L&J leaders parroted each and every insinuation, no matter how nonsensical. The tragedy lingered on and became the key reference point when testing one's own political ascription. The official line was the rejection of the so-called conspiracy theory where one of the parties involved would be the Polish liberal government. The opposition, for its part, charged the CP government with treason, punishable negligence or grave disrespect towards Polish history.

Remembering Smoleńsk remains a key distinction in political life. "Living it" it is a token of patriotism and legacy to the nation, while "living with it" is seen as a disregard of the country and treason. To render it justice, it could be the least exotic form of populism yet encountered. There is a certain level of control over its use in politics, but, since it is an either/or situation, all political stances ultimately reduce to this axis. The division might prove lasting, given the impenetrable mist surrounding the plane crash, but the spin it has today indicates that it must have some footing in culture, and to test this hypothesis we shall now try to trace it back to the classical romantic period, when the framework of today's populism was forged.

Poland's elections in October 2011 produced two significant changes. First, a governing party was re-elected for the first time since the collapse of communism in 1989 and a new anti-clerical party run by an extrovert businessman and a spin-off from CP, Janusz Palikot, was recognized as the third power in the Parliament. While the CP might have been rewarded for its predictability and entrusted with the task of coping with the second wave of the global crisis, Palikot appealed to anti-clerical sentiment and campaigned on legalising abortion, gay marriage, and possession of marijuana—issues considered sexy among younger constituents. Although it might signify some sort of liberal and secular slant, one thing is common to both Palikot and L&J leader, Jarosław Kaczyński. In Palikot's own words: "Being against the system unites us. But while Kaczyński wanted to challenge democracy, I came to strengthen it" (Palikot, 2011, p. 141). This is a superb illustration of populist reasoning: the strengthening of democracy may only be effected by struggle with the system. Using Laclau's concepts, the demands of the Palikot Movement are not democratic, but populist. The distinctiveness of populism is that it gathers together disparate ideological positions or political demands, and stresses their equivalence in terms of a shared antagonism to a given instance of political power or authority. In other words, once again, populism should be defined by its form rather than its content: it tends to divide the social field into two distinct camps, championing the "people" over what Laclau variously terms as "the dominant ideology", "the dominant bloc", "the institutional system", "an institutionalised Other", or even "power" itself.

From a political perspective, romanticising Poland's past is a must (Janion, 1975). What is not so obvious and not so feasible, however, is how to apply romantic imagery to the political agenda and translate it into decision making. The unquestionable legacy of the late president Lech Kaczyński in this respect is his courageous flight to war-stricken Georgia to force Russia to retreat. Needless to say, Russia *is* the enemy in each and every case. From a practical point of view, in order to adopt and later uphold such a political stand one needs to have a strong feeling of a great loss and the ensuing suffering and enormous sacrifice. As for the loss, the most apposite allegory is in the biblical story of Job. In his classical gesture, he is helplessly submerged in his suffering and so devastated by the loss that no explanation and no gratification could suffice. Only by adopting this perspective may we understand that the question "why?" never came to Kaczyński because the answer was already given. Job's loss is so irreparable that no apology or punitive measure can ever soothe his bitter disbelief. We have seen it happen: such is the lesson of Job. Despite his loss. Job never really gets down to the question "why?" Instead, Job persists in his faith in God, despite a prevailing sensation that an injustice has been committed. In other circumstances, we would call it a dignifying loss, that is, loss moral, ultimate, inexplicable. This is exactly how Poles take loss. I should think this is a profoundly Christian trait, making a memory of the departure of the guarantee of salvation, as epitomised by Job.

As for the suffering, it is a position of a new type of a romantic hero: Gustav/Konrad from the Polish romantic poet, Adam Mickiewicz and his masterpiece *Forefathers' Eve*. In its preface we come across an observation that still holds validity. Mickiewicz famously says that the suffering inherent to Poles best complements their understanding of nationality. The drama alone is a voyage into the land of the many irrefutable reasons for his earlier claim. Martyrdom is one of such claims, with the slogan "Poland, Christ of Nations" as a cornerstone of the national myth. In a letter to his fellow-exile, the historian, Joachim Lelewel, on 23 March 1832, Mickiewicz wrote,

> I place great hopes in our nation and in a course of events unforeseen by any diplomacy. . . . I would think only that our aspirations should be given a religious and moral character, distinct from the financial liberalism of the French and firmly grounded in Catholicism. (Mickiewicz, 1899, p. 89)

The third part of *Forefathers' Eve*, which Mickiewicz wrote in Dresden later that spring, develops these ideas in a dramatic form, taking the enigmatic fragments of the earlier parts in quite a different direction. The starting point is Mickiewicz's own biography: its central character, Gustav, who takes the name Konrad, is, like Mickiewicz, a victim of Tsarist oppression in Vilnius in the early 1820s. It is over Konrad's soul, and, by extension, the soul of Poland, that the greater forces of Good and Evil are waging a titanic struggle. As he awaits trial in his cell, Konrad questions the existence of divine justice, given the monumental crime against Poland. His blasphemous conclusion is that God is, in fact, the Devil, identified with the Tsar. However, he is saved from damnation by Father Peter, who leads him to understand the need for expiation and suffering, introducing ideas which Mickiewicz was to expand upon in the *Books of the Polish Pilgrimage and Nation* (Mickiewicz, 1832), specifically that Poland was the "Christ of Nations", whose collapse was a necessary sacrifice in the moral regeneration of Europe. The Vilnius scenes are complemented by a series of realistic, satirical scenes set in Warsaw, showing sections of Polish society collaborating with the Russian oppressor.

If the English are preoccupied with the weather, the Poles are with suffering. An expression of suffering is, in fact, a proper way to begin a conversation. Overall, Polish populism does best when exploiting a trauma: it could be the partitions of Poland in the eighteenth century, uneven war in the twentieth entury, the genocide of Polish intelligentsia in Katyń 1940, then, of course, the Warsaw Uprising. Along the line there comes the last fateful flight of Presidential Topolev 102 approaching Smoleńsk airport near Katyń on the seventieth anniversary of the Katyń genocide, 10 April 2010.

Exposing this non-coincidental link became a big statement in the months following the catastrophe. The dates "1940–2010" soon appeared on T-shirts and in graffiti as a simple yet powerful mission statement. Commemorating the victims became something of an obligation. As of the last count, the late President and his wife have provided names for six roundabouts, five parks, two streets and schools, one bridge, one square, and one City Hall. Undeniably, a roundabout has something of the eternal to it. Reprints of a painting were made available for purchase for whoever wished to ponder the site at Smoleńsk and the dead climbing up to the skies on the rays of the sun with a grin of a deeper understanding of fate and history on their faces. The demand for these symbols serving as pegs of Polish collective memory was unmatched. "1940–2010" marked seven decades of martyrdom and proved that forces of evil defy time—as do perseverance and memory. To add more substance to the argument "Poland Christ of Nations", soon after the crash a large group of protesters marching in front of the official residence of the late President was reported chanting "woe betide those who forbid Jesus to be King of Poland". And in November of that fateful year, a statue of

Jesus was reported standing in Świebodzin, Poland, measuring thirty-three metres, one metre for each year of the Saviour's life. It dwarfed Rio de Janeiro's Christ the Redeemer at only 30.1 metres high, but the record did not prove to be longstanding as, in June 2011, the Peruvians erected a four metres taller Cristo del Pacifico—and so the race continues. Let us now consult Freud.

Freud, in "Mourning and melancholia" (1917e) states that mourning has an affinity for melancholy in that both are affected by the loss of the ability to find a new object of love. The prerequisite of finding a new object of love and thus ending mourning is to distance oneself from the deceased, to refrain from the shared memories, and to avoid places that evoke memories from the past. We have not seen that happen throughout 2011. Instead, the work of mourning was full ahead. We might call this an advanced mourning phase, where the patient has already made a discovery that the beloved object was lost, and has already started questioning the fond memory of those lost in the crash. Also, erecting monuments could be seen as a sign of recovery and a relief to the collective memory. While in progress, attaining the third phase after the trauma and the phase of relieving pain came to a halt as we saw resistance to the idea of finding a new object of adoration. Instead, due to perseverance, the lost were conceived as an empty signifier, and the dead were as if possessed by demons—something which vaguely recalls the living spirit of Hamlet's father.

Freud wrote *explicitly*,

> There is no difficulty in reconstructing this process. An object choice, an attachment of the libido to a particular person, had at one time existed; then, owing to a real slight or disappointment coming from this loved person, the relationship was shattered. . . . The object-cathexis proved to have little power of resistance and was brought to an end. But the free libido was not displaced on to another object; it was withdrawn into the ego. . . . In this way an object-loss was transformed into an ego-loss and the conflict between the ego and the loved person into a cleavage between the critical activity of the ego and the ego as altered by identification. (Freud, 1917e, p. 248)

The above leaves no room for doubt as to why the opposition was messianic and the ruling party had no idea how to react. We may assume that, in the case of Poland, the function of politics is the transformation of an object-loss into an ego-loss.

The opposition party leader, twin brother of late President Kaczyński, shows little resemblance to the romantic hero of Mickiewicz, and, to approximate his image, I could only compare it to a rather peculiar hybrid of Hamlet and King Lear: not only he is mourning over the immense loss, but he is also seeking ways to displace free libido on to another object. In time, the national ego absorbs him and makes him an embodiment of Christ of Nations. This, in turn, would explain why the major party leader and Prime Minister Donald Tusk was, in comparison, a mix of Pontius Pilate and Lady Macbeth, presenting reports on the progress of investigation and defying accusations of lack of diligence before the eyes of the confused public.

From mourning to narcissism

In accordance with the model of political correctness advocated by liberals in the past twenty years, secularisation was the inevitable cost of modernisation. It is now evident that the supporting sociological argumentation was void. Poles were actively participating in the processes of modernisation, but there are no signs of secularisation—how to explain this phenomenon? The only way out of this conundrum is to hypothesise that both Polish modernism and religious beliefs are superficial. Bogus modernists and bogus radicals are equally prone to populism. The modernists have already revealed their affection for populist anti-clerical discourse (Palikot's Movement). The radicals are waiting for the return of the avenger, the Messiah, whose earthly abode is the opposition party and its leader (radical wing L&J Jarosław Kaczyński). Meanwhile, the liberals from the governing party (the one-man show of Donald Tusk, CP) do nothing apart from inciting panic in the populace in the face of roaring extremism and practise what one might call a liberalism of fear. Yet others feel compelled to take action and, equipped with torches and high spirits, once again enter the centre of world events, deny the new president's moral right to represent the nation, and spin tales of how the late President Kaczyński was murdered by the evil forces (Bielik-Robson, 2010, p. 56; Stavrakakis, 2005).

The Smoleńsk 2010 tragedy increased tension between the liberal, enlightened establishment and the unenlightened clerical masses. It makes a comeback of populism plausible, as much as it facilitates return of naïve, profane, quasi-liberal Enlightenment. We tend to forget that science may, in fact, pave the way for a church of atheism in the same way that religion may institutionalise itself as a guardian of the revelation. The unredeemable loss, this evil spell of the land, the unknown malfunction of the plane, the culpable misdoings and irreproachable errors of the government—this was just a beginning of a process that, with time, started posing the question of the very nature of state and politics, from foreign affairs to lower bureaucracy, tracing back to years ago and churning out imputations and pleas to institutions worldwide. On the other hand, the catastrophe brought about the realisation that there was a dimension beyond the state but directly related to the state, where grief poured in and thickened into accusations. This put institutions under surveillance and revealed them as impotent exactly when their might was sought for and their authoritative stand was expected. The state proved not much of an avenger, and neither was it a good shepherd, or a deliverer. What at first seemed a tiny crack or a dent in the body of the state was soon the size of a yawning chasm where, in the deep, only torches flickered. To give only two examples, the state, instead of taking direct control over the plane crash investigation, ceded it to the Interstate Aviation Committee run by the enemies—the Russians. The State Treasury did not initially recognise the immeasurable loss and the families of victims who died in the Smoleńsk air crash were compelled to sue the State for damages, which, only much later, resulted in a rather generous settlement. In both cases the state proved bulky and hollow. And if religion is void, too, one may seriously test the idea of a civil religion, that is, a form of religion reconciled with the state and complementary to its functioning.

My analysis of what I call "mourning populism" is, thus, half-way between the purely formal, structural position of Laclau and the positions analysed by Mudde in reference to the contents of populism. I follow Laclau in his observation that populism has its own logic, a transcultural approach that can, in principle, be applied to any content, be it economic, religious, or racial, etc. However, in attempting to understand the specific embodiment of populism and its syntax, we must also analyse the cultural context specific to a given country. This does not mean that populism is the expression of the very nature of a given population, but it does mean that in a discourse, a given population organises and builds its identity around recurring fixations and themes. It is not nature, however, that provides a pretext for their expression, but discourse, which becomes a prerequisite of apparently natural and irrevocable identity.

To Freud, melancholia borrows some of its features from mourning, with a narcissistic object choice in the regression to self-enclosure. Like mourning, melancholia is a reaction to the real loss of a loved object, but, above all, melancholia is marked by a determinant absent in normal mourning, which, if present, transforms the latter into pathological mourning. It would follow that the politics of mourning is, in fact, the politics of narcissism.

To justify my claim I shall briefly refer to two texts by Freud—the aforementioned essay "Mourning and melancholia" (Freud, 1917e) and "On narcissism: an introduction" (Freud, 1914c). In both texts, Freud enquires into what happens to the libido following the loss of a loved object. In mourning and melancholia, libido regresses to *das Ich*. Such a regression is a complex and indirect process. Freud says that the narcissistic type may love: (a) what he himself is (i.e., himself), (b) what he himself was, (c) what he himself would like to be, (d) someone who was once part of himself. Melancholia is a narcissistic type of love that, upon the loss of a loved object, regresses to a past ego: "what he himself was". Such a regression is indirect, as it is mediated by an *ideal ego*: "what he himself would like to be". This ideal ego is now the target of the self-love that was enjoyed in childhood by the actual ego. The subject's narcissism makes its appearance displaced on to this ideal ego, which, like the infantile ego, finds itself possessed of every perfection that is of value. What he projects before him as his ideal is the substitute for the lost narcissism of his childhood in which he was his own ideal.

To Freud, narcissism was a normal maturational phase of development in all children, a complement to the egoism of the instinct for self-preservation. Development consists in a departure from primary narcissism when people invest their libidinal energy into another person rather than themselves. When people progress from primary narcissism to object love, their own feelings of self-regard are lowered. However, when individuals' love objects are unable or unwilling to return the love, they regress to a state of narcissism, called secondary narcissism, in order to love and gratify themselves as a compensatory mechanism. Freud wrote briefly, "A strong egoism is a protection against falling ill, but in the last resort we must begin to love in order not to fall ill, and we are bound to fall ill if, in consequence of frustration, we are unable to love" (Freud, 1914c, p. 85).

The inability to love again is specific to melancholia. Melancholia, like mourning, is a reaction to the real loss of a loved object, but, above all, it is a regression to narcissism accompanied by the experience of omnipotence. This is probably the reason why funeral policy (mourning populism) is so ambiguous and dangerous. Funeral policy not only reduces and limits the interest of the world, but, above all, it gives an illusion of might.

To sum up: mourning makes the world appear poor and void (the reproach is overwhelming), melancholia makes *das Ich* void (self-incrimination prevails), and only narcissism allows the subject to recover its imaginative power (idealised self-esteem prevails). This is, of course, clinical diagnostics and a clinical vocabulary; in political life, these three strategies are constantly confused, melancholy blends with narcissism and narcissism with mourning. The reason for such confusion is the libido's constant struggle to recover the object, the object that has never been fully abandoned. The struggle involves hate and love; hate aims at the liberation of the libido from cathexis, love aims at securing the position of the libido towards the object.

Perhaps, for us Poles, this bitter time is a revival of national symbols, the moment of identification with one object. If, in the process, we renewed our bonds with community, it was a community of tears. Perhaps the tragedy at Smoleńsk already released a non-modernist, or maybe even anti-modernist, attitude: Smoleńsk was a reunion for "the populace". Today, in retrospect, we already realise how tricky the sense of national unity can be, and how deceptive politics devoid of divisions is, and the vision of a completely reconciled state (society / nation). We, the Poles, already know that this sense of unity can only be temporary, and the work of mourning is to open chasms and test new divisions, as compelled by the libido lacking the object of love. This libido, if it is not bound up with a new object of love after the loss, could only later be absorbed by the national ego. Freud's genius made us painfully aware of the fact that melancholia is akin to narcissism. For as long as we remember, no future loss will ever again set the Polish nation flying so high, as there is no more joy in matters of death. No matter how high melancholia takes us the next time, no matter how divinely detached from the earthly bliss the Polish nation might become, it would always be in the company of an envious radical narcissist.

References

Bauman, Z. (2003). Handlarze strachu [Merchants of fear]. *Krytyka Polityczna*, 4: 15–22.

Betz, H.-G. (1994). *Radical Right-Wing Populism in Western Europe.* Basingstoke. Macmillan.

Bielik-Robson, A. (2010). Polski triumf Tanatosa [Polish triumph of Thanatos]. In: *Żałoba* [Mourning]. Warszawa: Krytyka Polityczna.

Canovan, M. (1981). *Populism.* New York: Harcourt Brace Jovanovich.

Dzwończyk, J. (2000). *Populistyczne koncepcje w społeczeństwie postsocjalistycznym na przykładzie Polski* [Populist Concepts in a Post-Socialist Society as Exemplified by Poland]. Toruń: Wydawnictwo Adam Marszałek.

Freud, S. (1914c). On narcissism. *S.E.*, *14*: 67–102. London: Hogarth.

Freud, S. (1917e). Mourning and melancholia. *S.E.*, *14*: 237–258. London: Hogarth.

Janion, M. (1975). *Gorączka romantyczna* [Romantic Fever]. Warsaw: PIW.

Kaczyński, J. (2006). Interview with Kublik and Olejnik, We mnie jest czyste dobro [There is pure good in me]. *Gazeta Wyborcza*, 3 February.

Kazin, M. (1995). *The Populist Persuasion: An American History.* New York: Basic Books.

Krasnodębski, Z. (2005). *Demokracja peryferii* [The Democracy of the Outskirts]. Gdańsk: słowo/obraz terytoria.

Laclau, E. (1996). *Emancipation(s).* London: Verso.

Laclau, E. (2005). *On Populist Reason.* London: Verso.

Le Bon, G. (1896). *The Crowd: A Study of the Popular Mind.* New York: Macmillan.

Marczewska-Rytko, M. (2006). *Populizm na przełomie XX i XXI wieku. Panaceum czy pułapka dla współczesnych społeczeństw?* [Populism at the Turn of the 20th–21st Centuries: Remedy or Trap for Contemporary Societies?]. Toruń: Wydawnictwo Adam Marszałek.

Markowski, R. (Ed.) (2004). *Populizm a demokracja* [Populism and Democracy]. Warszawa: Instytut Studiów Politycznych PAN.

Mény, Y., & Surel, Y. (Eds.) (2002). *Democracies and the Populist Challenge.* Basingstoke: Palgrave.

Mickiewicz, A. (1832). *Books of the Polish Pilgrimage and Nation*, K. Lach-Szyrma (Trans.). London: James Ridgway.

Mickiewicz, A. (1899). *Wybór listów* [Selected Letters], ułożył Józef Kallenbach, Kraków: Spółka Wydawnicza Polska.

Mudde, C. (2000). *The Ideology of the Extreme Right.* Manchester: Manchester University Press.

Mudde, C. (2007). *Populist Radical Right Parties in Europe.* Cambridge: Cambridge University Press.

Palikot, J. (2011). *Tajemnice Platformy, rządu i parlamentu* [Secrets of the Platform, the Government and Parliament]. Warszawa: Czerwone i czarne.

Śpiewak, P. (2005). *Pamięć po komunizmie* [The Memory of Communism]. Gdańsk: Słowo/obraz terytoria.

Stavrakakis, Y. (2005). Religion and populism in contemporary Greece. In: F. Panizza (Ed.), *Populism and the Mirror of Democracy* (pp. 153–181). London: Verso.

Szacki, J. (2004). Pytania o populism [Questions about populism]. *Krytyka Polityczna*, 4: 28–35.

Taggart, P. (1996). *The New Populism and the New Politics. New Protest Parties in Sweden in a Comparative Perspective.* Basingstoke: Macmillan.

Taine, H. (1878). *The French Revolution*, J. Durand (Trans.). London: Daldy, Isbister.

Wysocka, O. (2009). Populism in Poland: In/visible Exclusion. In: L. Freeman (Ed.), *Junior Visiting Fellows' Conferences: In/visibility: Perspectives on Inclusion and Exclusion*, Vol. XXVI (pp. 78–97). Vienna: IWM.

Zakaria, F. (2003). *The Future of Freedom: Illiberal Democracy at Home and Abroad.* New York: W. W. Norton.

Žižek, S. (2006). Against the populist temptation. *Critical Inquiry*, 32(3): 551–574.

Editor's introduction to Chapter Five

The chapter presents the theory of the fourth basic assumption, which provides a bridge between the Bionian study of group relations and Foulkesian group analysis, and between psycho-analysis and sociology. Bion (1961) conceptualised three basic assumptions associated with specific kinds of anxieties, processes and roles: dependency, fight/flight, and pairing. The author suggests that the unconscious life of traumatised groups is dominated by a fourth basic assumption, which he terms "Incohesion: Aggregation/Massification" or (ba) "I:A/M". When social systems regress following traumatic experiences of failed dependency, they become *like*, or actually become groups. "Aggregation" and "Massification" refer to processes through and by which the group becomes either an aggregate or a mass; two bi-polar forms of incohesion which are equally incohesive. The members of an aggregate hardly relate to one another. They remain silent for long periods of time, and engage in various forms of non-communica-tion such as gaze-avoidance. Where an aggregate is characterised by too much individuality, a mass is characterised by too little. The term may refer to a highly charged political demonstration or a rally in a confined location. People are so physically close that in any other situ-ation they would be experienced as violating one another's sense of personal space, they are mesmerised through staring into one another's eyes or focusing on a common object. The mass' silence differs in quality from that of the aggregate; people feel they do not need words or gestures to communicate, as they are rooted in a shared sense of awe and wonder. These bi-polar intra-psychic constellations are associated with two types of personal organisation:, the "contact shunning" or "crustacean" type as a schizoid reaction against the fear of engulfment; and two, the "merger-hungry" or "amoeboid" as a clinging reaction against the fear of abandonment. The massification of traumatised societies, it is argued, is dominated by processes of fatal purification; massification breeds nationalism and fascism.

CHAPTER FIVE

The theory of Incohesion: Aggregation/Massification as the fourth basic assumption in the unconscious life of groups and group-like social systems*

Earl Hopper

I n this chapter, I will summarise my theory of the basic assumption of Incohesion: Aggregation/ Massification or (ba) I:A/M, which I (Hopper, 2003) have developed at length in *Traumatic Experience in the Unconscious Life of Groups*. Although I have clarified and refined this theory in more recent publications (for example, Hopper, 2005a, 2009, 2010), I believe that this summary is the most lucid statement of it. Of course, it is impossible to discuss here the general theory of both the "work group" and the "basic assumption group". The key text is *Experiences in Groups* (Bion, 1961), and further discussion and applications of Bion's ideas about groups can be found in, for example, "Bion's contribution to thinking about groups" (Menzies-Lyth, 1981) and *Tongued with Fire: Groups in Experience* (Lawrence, 2000), which include extensive bibliography.

The term "group" indicates a social system that is a group, and not some other kind of social system. Although all groups are social systems, not all social systems are groups. A group is not, for example,

---

*This chapter was the basis of my (Hopper, 2012) *Introduction to Trauma and Organizations* (London: Karnac).

a committee, but a committee is a group. Similarly, a group is not a family, but a family is a group, and is sometimes called a "family group". Neither is a group an organisation, a society, or a village, etc. It is sometimes useful to refer to an "actual group" in order to indicate that a particular social system is, in fact, a group and not some other kind of social system.

Actual groups may be understood in terms of their work group dynamics and/or their basic assumption group dynamics, which is a matter of the frame of reference and the gestalt of the observer of them. Although the dynamics of work groups can be studied psychoanalytically (Armstrong, 2005), a more complete understanding of them is best served by the social sciences. However, generalisations about work groups are rare, primarily because there are so many different kinds of work group, and they evince such a vast range of variation in parameters such as size and complexity. None the less, it is widely agreed that the effectiveness and efficiency of work groups are manifest in their social cohesion, which is expressed in the integration (as opposed to the disintegration) of their interaction systems, the solidarity (as opposed to the insolidarity) of their normative systems, and in the coherence (as opposed to the incoherence) of their communication systems, and in many other dimensions of their organisation, such as styles of thinking and feeling, and various aspects of leadership, followership, and bystandership.[1]

Although the work group might use the mentality of basic assumption processes in the service of its work, the basic assumption group is, in essence, both pathological and pathogenic. The pathology and pathogenesis of the basic assumption group are expressed unconsciously in terms of the dynamics of various so-called "basic assumptions". I would remind you that, using a Kleinian model of the mind, Bion (1961) conceptualised three basic assumptions associated with specific kinds of anxieties, processes, and roles: dependency, associated with envy, idealisation, and the roles of omnipotence and grandiosity, on the one hand, and with the roles of passive compliance and low self-esteem, on the other; fight/flight, associated with envy, denigration, and roles of attack, on the one hand, and retreat, on the other; and pairing, associated with the use of sexuality as a manic defence against depressive position anxieties and the roles of romantic coupling, on the one hand, and their messianic progeny, on the other. I would suggest that there are two variants of the basic assumption of pairing: one concerns the conception and birth of the new and desirable; the other, which I (Hopper, 2003) have termed "perverse pairing", concerns the use of pain under the guise of pleasure leading to stasis and an absence of fertility and creativity.

Many Kleinian students of basic assumption theory have argued that it is impossible to conceptualise more than these three basic assumptions, because the Kleinian model of the mind, from which the theory of these three basic assumptions is derived, does not permit the conceptualisation of a fourth. However, using an alternative model of the mind, I have conceptualised a fourth basic assumption in the unconscious life of groups. This model of the mind is associated with the work of many of the founding members of the Group of Independent Psychoanalysts of the British Psychoanalytical Society, such as Fairbairn, Balint, and Winnicott, and is shared by many sociologists and group analysts. Its central tenet is that although it is important to study envy, it is more important to study helplessness, shame, and traumatic experiences within the context of interpersonal relationships, which are at the centre of the human condition. In this model, envy does not arise from the death instinct, but is a defensive or protective development against the fear of annihilation, and is directed towards spoiling the resources of people who are perceived as potentially helpful but who do not, or will not, actually help. In other words, envy might be more of a protective defence than it is a primary impulse.[2]

The basic assumption of Incohesion:
Aggregation/Massification or (ba) I:A/M

Derived from this model of the mind, in which traumatic experience within the context of the relational matrix is privileged over envy and the putative death instinct, my theory of the fourth basic assumption provides a bridge between the Bionian study of "group relations" and Foulkesian "group analysis", and, in a way, between psychoanalysis and sociology. I call this fourth basic assumption "Incohesion: Aggregation/Massification" or, in the tradition of the literature concerning basic assumptions, "(ba) I:A/M". Although each of the three basic assumptions conceptualised by Bion is, in a sense, a source of incohesion in groups, this fourth basic assumption pertains specifically to the dynamics of incohesion. It indicates that the very survival of the group is in question.

The bi-polar forms of Incohesion are Aggregation and Massification. "Aggregation" and "Massification" refer to the processes through which and by which the group becomes either an aggregate or a mass. The terms "aggregate" and "mass" are taken from early sociology and anthropology. The underlying basic assumption is that the group is not really a group, but is either an aggregate or a mass. Although a mass seems to be more cohesive than an aggregate, in fact these two bi-polar forms of incohesion are equally incohesive. They are transitory and incapable of sustaining co-operative work.

An aggregate is neither a group nor merely a collection of people who have absolutely no consciousness of themselves as being members of a particular social system. An aggregate is a very simple social formation that is barely a social system at all. The members of it hardly relate to one another. They are often silent for long periods of time, and engage in various forms of non-communication in general, for example, gaze-avoidance. Among the metaphors for an aggregate are a collection of billiard balls or a handful of gravel. However, these metaphors are not quite right, because they utilise inorganic objects, and it is important to recognise that an aggregate involves a degree of libidinous interpersonal attachment. A better metaphor would be a bowl of whitebait or a flock of ostriches, flamingos, or penguins, the flock having survival value. If sub-grouping does occur, it takes the form of contra-grouping rather than differentiation, specialisation, and co-operation.

A "mass" also refers to a social system that is not quite a group. However, whereas an aggregate is characterised by too much individuality, a mass is characterised by too little. Whereas an aggregate refers, for example, to a collection of people who are window shopping while strolling down a street, or who are walking through a tube station in order to catch many different trains or heading for the exit, a mass refers, for example, to a highly charged political demonstration or rally in a confined location. In the former situations, people rarely touch one another, but in the latter they are so physically close that in any other situation they would be experienced as violating one another's sense of personal space, and might even be accused of frotteurism. Whereas, in an aggregate, people avoid one another's gazes, in a mass they are mesmerised through staring into one another's eyes or focusing on an object that they hold in common. Whereas the silence of an aggregate is one of diffidence, non-recognition, and non-communication, the silence of a mass is rooted in a shared sense of awe and wonder in which people feel that they do not need words or even gestures in order to communicate. In fact, a mass of people prefers slogans and jargon to careful exposition, but, most of all, its members prefer the silence of "true communication". Among the metaphors for a mass are a piece of basalt, a nice piece of chopped fish, or a *quenelle de brochette* (in which the fish from which it has been made can no longer be recognised as a fish, let alone as several fish), a chunk of faeces, or a handful of wet sponges squeezed together. The metaphor of a herd of walruses is also useful.[3] Of course, during states of massification, neither sub-grouping nor contra-grouping is likely to occur, virtually by definition.

It is well known that Turquet (1975, p. 103) referred to the state of aggregation in terms of "dissaroy", which was his neologism for social, cultural, and political chaotic disorder, and that Lawrence and his colleagues (1996, p. 29) referred to it in terms of "me-ness". Similarly, Turquet (1975) referred to the state of massification in terms of "oneness", and Lawrence and his colleagues (1996) in terms of "we-ness". Although these neologisms are appealing, in fact most social scientists would use the terms "aggregate" and "mass", and, therefore, aggregation and massification. However, this is not merely a matter of semantics. In fact, these technical terms cover the confluences of interaction, normation, communication, and styles of thinking and feeling that characterise these polarised states.

Group trauma and the unconscious life of the group

Incohesion is caused by trauma and traumatogenic processes. Before outlining the main steps of these processes, I will stress that personal traumas are different from, but overlapping with, group trauma. Group trauma may occur in several interrelated ways, for example:

- through management failures on the part of the group analyst, or by other events that break the boundaries of holding and containment, causing the members of the group to feel profoundly helpless and unsafe;

- the members of the group regress to an early phase of life in which certain kinds of traumatic experience are virtually universal and ubiquitous;
- the members of the group share a history of specific kinds of trauma;
- processes of equivalence occur through which traumatic events and processes within the contextual foundation matrix of the group are imported and then enacted.

Group trauma provokes social and cultural regression and the collapse of boundaries between people and their groupings. Therefore, it is only in these circumstances that the language and concepts of personal trauma are really apposite for the study of group trauma. This is also why I try not to refer to the life of a group, but to the "life" of a group, conscious or otherwise.[4]

Failed dependency and the vicissitudes of feeling of profound helplessness and the fear of annihilation[5]

The first step in the process through which trauma causes Incohesion is that through various combinations of strain, cumulative and/or catastrophic experience of failed dependency on parental figures is likely to provoke feelings of profound helplessness and the fear of annihilation. The phenomenology of the fear of annihilation involves psychic paralysis and the death of psychic vitality, characterised by fission and fragmentation, and then fusion and confusion of what is left of the self with what can be found in the object. Fusion and confusion are a defence against fission and fragmentation, and vice versa: the fear of falling apart and of petrification is associated with fission and fragmentation; the fear of suffocation and of being swallowed up is associated with fusion and confusion, but the former offers protection against the latter, and vice versa.

Each psychic pole is also associated with both its own characteristic psychotic anxieties and its own characteristic modes of defence against them. Ultimately, disassociation and *especially* encapsulation occur as a defence or protection against the fear of annihilation, which is characterised by psychic motion but not by psychic movement or psychic development.

These bipolar intrapsychic constellations are associated with two types of personal organisation: one, the "contact shunning" or "crustacean"; and two, the "merger-hungry" or "amoeboid". These two types of personal organisation have often been delineated in similar terms, for example, the crustacean type as a schizoid reaction against the fear of engulfment, and the amoeboid type as a clinging reaction against the fear of abandonment (e.g., Rosenfeld, 1965).

Traumatised people tend to oscillate between these bipolar intrapsychic constellations, and crustacean and amoeboid character disorders are very common among people who have been traumatised. Such disorders are apparent among people with gender dysphoria and in more narcissistic homosexuals, whose characteristic "not-me" psychic postures oscillate with fusionary identifications as a way of protecting themselves from psychotic anxieties. Such disorders are also associated with perversions, which are often characterised by early traumatic experience.

The traumatogenic and interpersonal origins
of the basic assumption of Incohesion

Thus, the basic assumption of Incohesion: Aggregation/Massification or (ba) I:A/M derives from the fear of annihilation and its two characteristic forms of personal organisation. The second step in the process through which trauma gives rise to Incohesion is that with respect to those states of mind characterised by fission and fragmentation in oscillation with fusion and confusion, traumatised people tend to use projective and introjective identifications involving the repetition compulsion and traumatophilia (that is, the love and craving for traumatic experience) in the service of the expulsion of their horrific states of mind, and in their attempts to attack and control their most hated objects. These processes are also used in the service of communication of experience that is not available through conscious narrative. In fact, traumatised people feel unconsciously compelled to tell the stories of their traumatic experience.

When they are unable to tell their stories, perhaps because they have no one to listen to them, or when they are unable to tell their stories in a particular way, perhaps according to ritualised procedures, traumatised people attempt unconsciously to communicate through enactments, which may be studied from various points of view in connection with various forms of psychopathology. Enactments are of particular interest to forensic psychotherapists, because they involve a failure of the symbolic process.[6] Within the context of a group, enactments also involve processes of resonance, amplification, and mirroring. Thus, such enactments precipitate the emergence of the basic assumption of Incohesion.

Patterns of enacting the intrapsychic dynamics of traumatic experiences

With respect to the bipolar forms of Incohesion, the group is likely, in the first instance, to become an "aggregate" through a process of "aggregation" in response to the fear of annihilation, as manifest in the psychic processes of fission and fragmentation. However, as a defence against the anxieties associated with aggregation, the group is likely to become a mass through a process of massification. This is partly in response to the fear of annihilation as manifest in the psychic processes of fusion and confusion of what is left of the self with another. The process of massification also involves the "hysterical" idealisation of the situation and the leader, and identification with him and the group itself, as well as with its individual members, leading to feelings of pseudo-morale and illusions of well-being. However, the first group-based defence against the anxieties associated with massification is a shift back towards aggregation, thus precipitating the same anxieties that provoked the first defensive shift from aggregation towards massification.

Thus, a group-like social system in which the fear of annihilation is prevalent is likely to be characterised by oscillation between aggregation and massification. However, such oscillations are rarely total and complete, and, at any one time, vestiges of aggregation can be seen in states of massification, and vestiges of massification in states of aggregation. Moreover, each polar state can become located simultaneously in different parts of a social system, and even in different geographical locations.

Oscillations between aggregation and massification are not only a matter of the externalisation of intrapsychic and interpsychic processes. Such oscillations are also a product of the dynamics of these two socio-cultural states, involving, for example, nomogenic responses to the anomogenic forces of aggregation, and differentiation and specialisation in response to the anomogenisation and homogenisation that are typical of massification.

Sub-grouping characterises the first phases of the shift from aggregation to massification, in the same way that contra-grouping characterises the first phase of a shift from massification back to aggregation. Sub-groups and contra-groups can become more clearly demarcated in the service of attempts to purify the system as a whole; their boundaries become more and more rigid and impermeable, and silence and secrecy prevail.

Intrapsychic encapsulations are the basis of various kinds of subgroups and contra-groups. These groupings are the basis of various kinds of social–psychic retreat.

The emergent roles and their personifications
by crustaceans and amoeboids

During oscillations between aggregation and massification, many typical roles emerge. The role of whistleblower is typical of states of massification, as is the role of jester, or fool. The role of stable-cleaner, characterised by a sense of mistrust, in-fighting, and refusal to co-operate is typical of states of aggregation, as is the role of the endearing but ineffectual peacemaker. More generally, "lone wolf" roles are typical of aggregation and "cheerleader" roles of massification.

Whereas Individual Members (Turquet, 1975) and Citizens (de Maré, 1991; Hopper, 2000) are likely to fill the leadership roles that are properties of the structure of work groups, Singletons and Isolates (Turquet, 1975) are likely to fill aggregation roles, and Membership Individuals (Turquet, 1975) massification roles. In other words, traumatised people with crustacean character structures are likely to become lone wolves, and those with amoeboid character structures are likely to become cheerleaders. As Foulkes would have put it, the former are likely to *personify* aggregation processes, and the latter, massification processes. As Bion would have put it, such people have *valences* for these roles. And as Kernberg, following Redl, would have put it, such people are exceedingly vulnerable to "role" suction, because specific roles offer them skins of identity. However, traumatised people are also likely to create the roles in question. Thus, this process is recursive, and the basis of the relations between personal systems and group systems.

Alford (2001) has provided a profoundly incisive analysis of whistle-blowers, to which I would add moral masochism in the form of altruistic surrender (A. Freud, 1974). I would also suggest that it is only a matter of time before someone is sucked into the role of whistleblower.[7] Whistleblowers are often scapegoated in the search for people to blame for aggregation, involving the splintering of relationships and the state of mind associated with this, and the violation of the sense of perfect conformity and purity and the state of mind associated with this.

The role of jester allows its incumbents to speak to truth, as they see it, sometimes outrageously, often with humour and irony. The incumbents of this role often have an attractive, adolescent quality, which carries a degree of self-protection for them, which tends to blunt the acuity of their message.

The myth of Hercules is entirely apposite to a description of the role of stable cleaner: there is so much to do in order to ensure the survival of the organisation! The female incumbents of the role of stable cleaner often become the housekeepers and cleaning ladies of the organisation, roles that they have rejected within the realms of their own domesticity. The male incumbents are more like worka-holics who sacrifice themselves to the "firm" and to an older male mentor. Stable cleaners are not always reliable, and might suddenly take revenge on their mentors and the organisations as a whole.

The role of peacemaker tends to suck in those who become the voice of platitude and homilies. The peacemaker idealises the need for compromise, but denigrates the recognition of the importance of taking tough decisions that are necessary for survival.

These roles and their incumbents have been described by Shake-speare with brilliance and acuity. Briefly, *Julius Caesar* is an examina-tion of a traumatised society and its traumatised governmental organ-isations. I suppose that Brutus is the main personifier of the whistle-blowing role, although others in the group of assassins and saviours should be considered. With respect to the "fool", any of the plays in which Falstaff appears is relevant, but the fool aspect of the role of Caliban is also important. With respect to the peacemaker, consider Gonzalo in *The Tempest*, and Menenius in *Coriolanus*. So much horror follows the refusal to face reality (Hopper, 2003a).

Aggressive feelings and aggression

Aggressive feelings and aggression are especially important in the dynamics of Incohesion. Both crustacean, contact-shunning characters and amoeboid, merger-hungry characters are likely to personify the processes of aggression associated with Incohesion. They have great difficulty in acknowledging and experiencing aggressive feelings, not only in themselves but also in others. However, when crustaceans become angry, they become cold and over-contained; when amoeboids become angry, they become intrusive and engulfing, based on their tendencies towards vacuole incorporation.

The crustacean personification of the group's rampant aggressive feelings in states of aggregation is fairly easy to understand. It reflects a sense of one against all, and all against one, each and every one.

In contrast, the amoeboid personification of the group's aggressive feelings in states of massification is much more difficult to understand. It is important to recognise the forms of aggression that are typical of massification processes. One form of aggression involves the actual maintenance of massification processes: the manipulation of moral norms and moral judgements in such a way as to control the processes through which certain people and their sub-groups and contra-groups are labelled as deviant, immoral, and corrupt, which leads to their marginalisation and peripheralisation. Also important are anonymisation, rumour mongering, and character assassination, if not actual assassination. Of course, processes of scapegoating and more general attacks on all those who are defined as "Others" or as "Not Me's" support massification processes. In fact, the fatal purification of the system of all that is different, strange, and foreign is central to the study of traumatised social systems. Terrorism involves the use of violence in the service of purification.

Threats to personal and group identity

(ba) I:A/M is an acronym for the first three letters of the words Incohesion: Aggregation/Massification. However, I:A/M can also be read as 'I am!'[8], which is an assertion of personal identity when identity is felt to be threatened. As in the dynamics of exhibitionism, an assertion of identity is not as convincing as an expression of identity based on authentic feeling and belief. An assertion of identity is based on grandiosity and fantasies of omnipotence and omniscience, which come into being when dependency fails, that is, when our parents and our leaders fail us and disappoint us. Such affects and ideas are associated with traumatic experience.

The dynamics of the assertion "I am!" are closely related to the assertion "I am not!", as Winnicott (1955) realised in his discussion of the development of identity as a function of what he called "unit status", in terms of becoming aware of what is "not me", that is, of what one is not within a particular group context. It is in this sense that one develops a sense of being both a subject and an object simultaneously, a self and another, both from the point of view of oneself as a subject and from the point of view of another person as an "other". None the less, regression to this phase of development involves the experience that one's identity is threatened and, thus, is associated with either too much me-ness and too much not-me-ness, on the one hand, or with too much we-ness and us-ness, on the other.

Under conditions of optimal cohesion, the willingness and ability of the members of a group to refer to their sense of "we-ness" and "us-ness" indicate that a social system exists, as do notions of collective identity and of membership. We-ness and us-ness also develop in tandem with a sense of you-ness and other-ness. In this, there is a shared recognition of a boundary concerning who is inside and who is outside, or who should be included and who excluded from a particular social system (Stacey, 2005).

In contrast, the assertions "We are!" and "We are not!" suggest that the existence of the group is under threat, because otherwise there would be no need for the members of the group to assert their identity as members of it. "We are!" and "We are not!" might be statements by the members of a group during states of massification, but such statements are not possible during states of aggregation, because people lack a sense of we-ness and us-ness. The reason why these processes can be conceptualised in terms of a so-called "basic assumption" is that people who have regressed because their groups are under threat enact their fantasy that they are not a group but an aggregate, or a mass, both of which are states of collective being that offer protection from extreme anxieties.

Applications

The basic assumption of Incohesion occurs in traumatised societies.[9] Social traumas range from strain trauma, such as stagflation, to catastrophic trauma, such as economic and natural disasters. Massification breeds nationalism and fascism, which are always associated with racialism of various kinds. Fascism can be understood as a set of properties of interaction and normation systems. Despite their inequalities of economic and status power, all members of massified systems become equal with respect to their commitment to shared core values and norms. Fundamentalism can be understood as a set of properties of the communication system. Fundamentalism involves the transformation of words into objects based on the ritualisation of language (Klimova, 2011).

Although the protection of socio-cultural diversity is essential for the long-term survival of the society as a whole, encapsulated contra-formations are, in essence, enclaves and ghettos, which might be sanctuaries for those within them, but might also be sources of suffocation (Mojovic, 2011). Although life within enclaves and ghettos may be culturally rich and nourishing, these social–psychic retreats might also be rubbish dumps which reflect processes of splitting and projection that lead to the depletion and distortion of the "cultural capital" of the society as a whole.

The basic assumptions of traumatised societies are likely to be perpetuated across the generations, recapitulated by macro-social systems and by their component micro-social systems, and vice versa. Based on projective and introjective identifications and other forms of interaction and communication between parents and children, teachers and students, etc., these processes occur within the foundation matrices of contextual social systems. In order for people to break these vicious circles and cycles of equivalence, adequate and authentic mourning and reparation are necessary. Yet, people rarely have or take opportunities for such work. Actually, unauthentic, ritualised mourning can make matters worse. Circles of perversion, in the sense of turning away from the truth, involve chosen traumatic events and the perpetuation of sadomasochistic experience (Long, 2008, and in Chapter Three of this volume). After all, if the golden rule of civilised societies and mature people is to do unto others as you wish them to do unto you, then the leaden rule of traumatised and regressed societies is to do unto others as you have been done by.

Of special interest are those spontaneous communities that emerge after disasters of various kinds, such as floods and earthquakes. Although they are highly transitory, tending to become structured and institutionalised very quickly, they evince the defining parameters of large groups. Under certain circumstances, the members of these groups are extremely altruistic (Solnit, 2009), but I wonder whether this is an expression of massification as a defence against aggregation, and, thus, an example of how people make use of the basic assumption of Incohesion in the service of survival. Knowledge of (ba) I:A/M should inform the work of government agencies and local and community authorities in their interventions in the aftermath of natural disasters.

The fourth basic assumption of Incohesion is typical of traumatised organisations, and perhaps especially of organisations within traumatised societies. It is especially typical of prisons, mental hospitals, and perhaps even our professional societies and training institutes in which the capacity to suffer mental anguish is virtually a criterion for admission. Large, complex organisations are especially vulnerable to aggregation and massification, because, in essence, they comprise units of various kinds, both with respect to their membership populations and with respect to sets of roles. This involves the paradox of complexity in which aggregation is characterised by excessive differentiation and specialisation of work combined with the greater need for co-ordination of it. Knowledge of (ba) I:A/M should inform the work of consultants to traumatised organisations.

The basic assumption of Incohesion is also typical of large groups, in which the trauma of regression is ubiquitous and often overwhelming. Large groups are especially vulnerable to aggregation, and, therefore, massification is also typical of them. However, although we work in and with large groups in conferences, large groups rarely occur in "social situ", with certain exceptions, such as certain kinds of audience, meeting, and rally.

With respect to small groups in the context of traumatised organisations and organisations associated with trauma, the unconscious life of committees tends to be characterised by constant oscillations between aggregation and massification, which is why it is so difficult to accomplish their work agendas over a reasonable period of time. The members of such committees have difficulty in co-operating with one another, and in holding a sense of common purpose. Similarly, committees can become massified, as seen in the tendency of their members to agree with one another all the time, and to intrude into one another's work. Although patience in the chairmanship of such committees is certainly a virtue, it is often necessary to acknowledge the anxieties that threaten to overwhelm the members of them, and offer the space for discussion of the personal dimensions of the work.

The basic assumption of Incohesion also occurs in small groups who meet in order to study themselves or for the purpose of providing psychotherapy for their members, especially for the treatment of traumatised patients. In these treatment groups, all attempts by patients to express their individualities must be treated with care, because "individuality" might actually indicate schizoid isolation and an inability and refusal to co-operate with others, or be a step towards volunteering for becoming a scapegoat. The emotional life of treatment groups characterised by Incohesion is likely to be either very cold or laden with affect. Intense demands are made on the group analyst and his use of countertransference processes (Hopper, 2005b). It is especially difficult to help clinical groups of forensic patients who are often caught in the throes of enacting and perpetuating traumatic experience (Welldon, 2009). None the less, the personification of this basic assumption must not be met with containment and holding forever, but subjected to understanding and interpretation.

Yet, the basic assumption of Incohesion: Aggregation/Massification or (ba) I:A/M does not constitute a closed system. Incessant and eternal oscillations between aggregation and massification are not inevitable. People and their groupings can be resilient and can manifest mature hope. This depends on the development of citizenship and the recognition of the rights of others. It also depends on our making identifications with people who will be alive after we have died. These are the key elements of the transcendent imagination. I believe that pure and applied psychoanalysis and group analysis may be of help in the realisation of this "project" in the existentialist sense of the term.

Notes

1. The nature of social cohesion depends on the type of social system in question. For example, the main source of the cohesion of a societal social system is the integration of the patterns of interaction of its work group,

whereas the main source of the cohesion of an actual group is the coherence of the patterns of communication of its work group. The reason that the cohesion of an actual group depends primarily on the coherence of its communication system is that so many of an actual group's essential functions are fulfilled by people and organisations within its social context. For example, an actual group does not have to provide for the economic needs of its members, because these needs are met through activities in its wider social context.

2. This is not merely a piece of esoteric meta-psychology. In his Introduction to *Traumatic Experience in the Unconscious Life of Groups*, Kreeger suggested that in essence I had re-punctuated Turquet's work, and in so doing changed its meaning. In so far as it was Kreeger (1975) who extensively shaped Turquet's notes into the now famous "Threats to identity in the large group" in *The Large Group: Dynamics and Therapy*, Kreeger's comment was really a suggestion that I had re-punctuated his version of Turquet's argument. I think that, apart from using the sociological concepts "aggregate" and "mass" rather than Turquet's neologisms of "dissaroy" and "oneness", and apart from making several clarifications of his argument, my main departure from Turquet's theory was to emphasise the importance of trauma and the relational matrix. This slight turn of the kaleidoscope of psychoanalytical theory permitted the conceptualisation of the fourth basic assumption of Incohesion, which really should be regarded as the first of the four, because it is prior to dependency. In other words, unless trauma is privileged over envy, it is impossible to conceptualise a basic assumption that is prior to dependency, which is based on envy and idealisation, which, in the Kleinian model, are assumed to be primary.

3. It is hardly surprising that when I lectured on this topic in Dublin, several women in the audience suggested that whereas a bowl of boiled potatoes is the perfect icon for aggregation, a bowl of mashed potatoes is perfect for massification. Potatoes are a potent symbol of traumatic experience in Ireland (and in some other countries, too), involving starvation, on the one hand, and emigration and loss, on the other. During the discussion, an argument ensued about the best way to make mashed potatoes. I remember thinking that in much the same way that a shift towards aggregation provides transitory relief from the pain of massification, a simple bowl of boiled potatoes would have settled the argument.

4. It is important to remember that although in the study of social systems it is sometimes useful to think in terms of organismic and "personistic" *analogies*, it is rarely useful to think in terms of organismic and

personistic *homologies*. Social systems are *like* organisms and persons, but they are *not* organisms and persons. This distinction is especially relevant to the study of social systems that are changing, and when they are characterised by political conflict. (Incidentally, the same points can be made with respect to the use of "mechanistic" analogies and homologies, although they have the opposite implications.) Although it is not entirely apposite to this outline of my theory of Incohesion, Weinberg and I (2011) have discussed this issue in greater depth in the Introduction to *The Social Unconscious in Persons, Groups and Societies: Volume I: Mainly Theory*. Also, since writing this particular outline, I have read Weinberg's (2006) discussion of regression in groups, which provides a useful review of the literature on regression in social systems and some clinical illustrations of this.

5.   I have learnt from Gordon Lawrence that at more or less the same time that I began to use the notion of failed dependency, Eric Miller (1993) also began to use this term, although we were working independently of each other. Gordon preferred to use his own notion, "thwarted dependency". This is typical of innovation in the community of intellectuals of London. Of course, we were all influenced by Winnicott's ideas about development from dependency to independent unit-status.

6.   Consider the masturbatory movements of traumatised patients in hospital settings, such as in the films that we have seen of Romanian orphans painfully and incessantly banging their heads against their cots. Or the rhythm, cadence, and repetitions of "trauma poetry", for example, in Kipling's narratives of war, influenced by life in English boarding schools, or in Coleridge's *The Rime of the Ancient Mariner*, the hero of which was compelled to find a wedding guest to whom he could tell his story. It was hardly accidental that Coleridge knew something about addiction to opium: the use of addictive substances is ritualised, involving unconscious masturbation, often with other people, involving a tense balance between isolation and merger.

7.   Actually, the perceived threat that the role of whistleblower will soon be filled leads to the process of hiring a consultant from outside the organisation. In this context, the first task of the consultant is to be wary of processes of manipulation and seduction through which the existing management attempt to protect themselves from the shrill voices of those who are at the margins of power.

8.   It is ironic and of more than passing interest that, as Buber (1923) noted in *I and Thou*, when, as reported in the Old Testament, Moses asked God his name and what he wished to be called, God replied "I am." This

highly condensed dialogue occurred during a period of massive social trauma, at the beginning of the attempts by Moses to lead the Jewish people out of slavery. However, "I am" was also used in the New Testament when Jesus referred to himself in terms of his personifying a number of essential qualities, for example, "I am the light". This, too, was a time of trauma. As discussed in *The Times* (20 March 2010) by the Right Reverend Geoffrey Rowell, Bishop of Gibraltar in Europe, the poet Samuel Taylor Coleridge argued that

> If you begin with 'it is' – that everything is reducible to the material – if you have no place for the experience of being a human person. If you begin with 'I am', with the experience of being a person, then that reality is as fundamental as the nature investigated and explored by the science of material things. So, too, if God is no more than nature then there is no source of transforming grace, of forgiveness.

Rowell continues, "The tension of explanation between 'It is' and 'I am' continues to challenge us in our own world, and in our own lives . . . The language of 'I am' cannot be reduced to the language of 'It is'". I do not wish here to open up my argument to a consideration of the spiritual aspects of identity, but note that when personal and group identities are severely threatened, the boundaries between the realms of the sociocultural, the psychic and the somatic, tend to be dissolved, and there is a very strong tendency to both doubt and explore one's relationship with both our neighbours and with God.

9.   The Panel Report by Ira Brenner (2006) provides a useful but limited discussion of societal regression from a psychoanalytical point of view, most of which involves the implicit assumption that traumatised societies begin to regress, taking on the structure and functions of large groups. Some of these ideas can also be found in the work of Hannah Arendt (2007).

References

Alford, C. F. (2001). *Whistleblowers: Broken Lives and Organizational Power.* Ithaca, NY: Cornell University Press.

Arendt, H. (2007). *The Jewish Writings,* J. Kohn & R. Feldman (Eds.). New York: Schocken Books.

Armstrong, D. (2005). *Organization in the Mind: Psychoanalysis, Group Relations and Organizational Consultancy.* London: Karnac.

Bion, W. R. (1961). *Experiences in Groups and other Papers*. London: Tavistock.

Brenner, I. (2006). Terror and societal regression: a panel report. *Journal of the American Psychoanalytical Association*, 54(3): 977–988.

Buber, M. (1923). *I and Thou*, R. Gregor Smith (Trans.). New York: Charles Scribner's Sons, 1958, p. 26.

De Maré, P. (1991). *Koinonia*. London: Karnac.

Freud, A. (1974). Beating fantasies and daydreams. In: *The Writings of Anna Freud: Volume I* (pp. 137–157). New York: International Universities Press, 1974.

Hopper, E. (2000). From objects and subjects to citizens: group analysis and the study of maturity. *Group Analysis*, 33(1): 29–34.

Hopper, E. (2003). *Traumatic Experience in the Unconscious Life of Groups*. London: Jessica Kingsley.

Hopper, E. (2005a). Response to Vamik Volkan's Plenary Lecture "Large group identity, large group regression and massive violence". *Group Analytic Contexts*, 30: 27–40.

Hopper, E. (2005b). Countertransference in the context of the fourth basic assumption in the unconscious life of groups. *International Journal of Group Psychotherapy*, 55(1): 87–114.

Hopper, E. (2009). The theory of the basic assumption of Incohesion: Aggregation/Massification of (ba) I:A/M. *British Journal of Psychotherapy*, 25(2): 214–229.

Hopper, E. (2010). Ein Abriss meiner Theorie der Grundannahme der Incohesion: Aggregation/Massification oder (ba) I:A/M. *Die analytische GroBgruppe. Festschrift zu Ehren von Josef Shaked*, 4: 55–76.

Hopper, E., & Weinberg, H. (Eds.) (2011). *The Social Unconscious in Persons, Groups and Societies: Volume I: Mainly Theory*. London: Karnac.

Klimova, H. (2011). The false collective self. In: E. Hopper & H. Weinberg (Eds.), *The Social Unconscious in Persons, Groups and Societies, Vol 1: Mainly Theory* (pp. 187–208). London: Karnac.

Kreeger, L. (Ed.) (1975). *The Large Group Dynamics and Therapy*. London: Constable [reprinted London: Karnac, 1994].

Lawrence, W. G. (2000). *Tongued with Fire: Groups in Experience*. London: Karnac.

Lawrence, W. G., Bain, A., & Gould, L. J. (1996). The fifth basic assumption. *Free Associations*, 6(37): 28–55, reprinted in 2000 in *Tongued with Fire: Groups in Experience*. London: Karnac.

Long, S. (2008). *The Perverse Organisation and its Deadly Sins*. London: Karnac.

Menzies-Lyth, I. E. P. (1981). Bion's contribution to thinking about groups. In: J. Grotstein (Ed.), *Do I Dare Disturb the Universe?* (pp. 661–666). Beverley Hills, CA: Caesura Press.

Miller, E. (1993). *From Dependency to Autonomy*. London: Free Association Books.

Mojovic, M. (2011). Manifestations of psychic retreats in social systems. In: E. Hopper & H. Weinberg (Eds.), *The Social Unconscious in Persons, Groups and Societies, Volume 1: Mainly Theory*. London: Karnac.

Rosenfeld, H. A. (1965). *Psychotic States: A Psychoanalytical Approach*. London: Maresfield Reprints.

Solnit, R. (2009). *A Paradise Built in Hell: The Extraordinary Communities That Arise in Disaster*. London: Viking.

Stacey, R. (2005). Organizational identity: The paradox of continuity and potential transformation at the same time. *Group Analysis, 3*(4): 477–494.

Turquet, P. (1975). Threats to identity in the large group. In: L. Kreeger (Ed.), *The Large Group: Dynamics and Therapy* (pp. 87–144). London: Constable [reprinted London: Karnac, 1994].

Weinberg, H. (2006). Regression in the group revisited. *Group, 30*(1): 1–17.

Welldon, E. V. (2009). Transference and countertransference in group analysis with gender dysphoric patients. In: G. Ambrosio (Ed.), *Transvestism, Transsexualism in the Psychoanalytical Dimension* (pp. 81–106). London: Karnac.

Winnicott, D. W. (1955). Group influences and the maladjusted child: the school aspect. In: C. Winnicott, R. Shepherd, & M. Davis (Eds.), *Deprivation and Delinquency* (pp. 189–199). London: Tavistock, 1974.

Editor's introduction to Chapter Six

The author interprets Gilles Deleuze and Felix Guattari's concepts of the schizophrenic and paranoid poles using the example of the Lithuanian political scene, where the revolutionary drives of 1990 were quickly replaced by reactionary nationalist forces. *Anti-Oedipus: Capitalism and Schizophrenia* provides an analysis of the processes of desire production. Deleuze and Guattari do not differentiate between libidinal economy and political economy: libidinal and political flows form the processes of desire produce what we call the real. In this sense, schizophrenia designates not the clinical state of mental illness, but the deepest tendency of capitalism. It is associated with the creative tendency of capitalism, its potential for change and permanent revolution. The counter-tendency of capitalism is seen as paranoia. In this context, paranoia does not mean the clinical state, but the libidinal tendency to stick to stable and fixed meanings, beliefs, and authorities. A good example, it is argued, is the comparison between the two events related to the Lithuanian parliament: in 1991 the unarmed population defended the parliament from external forces, while in 2009 the same population attacked its own parliament as a reaction against the first shock of the financial crisis and social cuts. The author argues that the unconscious paranoiac investments manifested themselves shortly after the Re-establishment of Independence in 1991. The independent state started functioning as an apparatus of repression, defending in a paranoiac way a pre-war system of codes and beliefs and excluding ethnic and sexual minorities. The increasing outbursts against minorities, it is argued, reveal the deep connections between the paranoid form of the psyche and the nation state.

CHAPTER SIX

The schizoanalysis of Gilles Deleuze and Félix Guattari, or the political between schizophrenia and paranoia

Audronė Žukauskaitė

G illes Deleuze and Félix Guattari's *Anti-Oedipus: Capitalism and Schizophrenia* provides an inspiring analysis of the processes of desire production. Deleuze and Guattari do not differentiate between libidinal economy and political economy: libidinal and political flows form the processes of desire which, in their turn, produce that which we call the real. In this sense, schizophrenia designates not the clinical state of mental illness, but the deepest tendency of capitalism, its potential for change and permanent revolution. The counter-tendency of the same capitalism is seen as paranoia. Paranoia here means the libidinal tendency to stick to stable and fixed meanings, beliefs, and authorities. Thus, schizophrenia and paranoia designate two poles of social libidinal investment which are analysed in terms of deterritorialization and reterritorialization, the molecular and the molar, and the revolutionary and fascist drives in the political. In this chapter, the schizophrenic and paranoid poles are examined using the concrete example of the Lithuanian political scene: the revolutionary drives of 1990 were quickly replaced after twenty years of independence by reactionary nationalist forces which reveal the deep connections between the paranoid form of the psyche and the nation-state.

Psychoanalysis vs. schizoanalysis

In *Anti-Oedipus: Capitalism and Schizophrenia*, Gilles Deleuze and Félix Guattari provide a systematic critique of Freudian and Lacanian psychoanalysis. Their main reproach to psychoanalysis is that it always remains—positively or negatively—dependent on the notion of subjective identity. Arguably, though Lacanian psychoanalysis postulates the notion of a "barred" or "split" subject, it presupposes a virtual identity which was lost and allegedly could be gained through the process of analysis. By contrast, Deleuze and Guattari argue for the project of schizoanalysis where the schizophrenic is free from any forms of identity and is open to follow new flows of desire. Deleuze and Guattari claim that "A schizophrenic out for a walk is a better model than a neurotic lying on the analyst's couch. A breath of fresh air, a relationship with the outside world" (Deleuze & Guattari, 2004, p. 2). They compare the schizophrenic with the characters of Samuel Beckett's novels who decide to venture outdoors and who, after all their trips, trajectories, and methods of locomotion, become a "finely tuned machine" (Deleuze & Guattari, 2004, p. 2).

In *Negotiations*, Deleuze defines schizoanalysis as a project which has two sides: it is both a criticism of the Oedipus complex and psychoanalysis, and a criticism of capitalism and capitalist production.

> We attack psychoanalysis on the following points, which relate to its practice as well as its theory: its cult of Oedipus, the way it reduces everything to the libido and domestic investments, even when these are transposed and generalized into structuralist or symbolic forms. We're saying the libido becomes unconsciously invested in ways that are distinct from the ways interests are preconsciously invested but that impinge on the social field no less than invested interests. (Deleuze, 1995, p. 20)

Psychoanalysis gets stuck on domestic investments and never gets to the social investments of the libido; that is why psychoanalysis should be replaced by schizoanalysis, which examines libidinal investments as a form of social, political and economic investment. To achieve this, Deleuze and Guattari replace the notion of the unconscious with the notion of the machine, and a linguistic paradigm of psychoanalysis with the functionalist model of desire production.

Deleuze and Guattari compare the unconscious with the factory which produces different affects. In this sense, they define themselves as strict functionalists:

> what we're interested in is how something works, functions – finding the machine. But the signifier's still stuck in the question 'What does it mean?' – indeed it's this very question in a blocked form. But for us, the unconscious doesn't *mean* anything, nor does language. . . . The only question is how anything works, with its intensities, flows, processes, partial objects – none of which *mean* anything. (Deleuze, 1995, pp. 21–22)

The unconscious is machinic rather than structural or linguistic; that is why it should be analysed not in terms of signification and meaning, but in terms of desire production. The unconscious works as a factory producing different intensities and flows, but sometimes it breaks down. This was the case of Antonin Artaud, one day "finding himself with no shape or form whatsoever, right there where he was at that moment" (Deleuze & Guattari, 2004, p. 9). At that moment, Artaud interrupts the proper functioning of desire production and invents his "body without organs"—a term for antiproduction.

> Desiring-machines make us an organism; but at the very heart of this production, within the very production of this production, the body suffers from being organized in this way, from not having some other sort of organization, or no organization at all. (Deleuze & Guattari, 2004, p. 8)

An "absolutely rigid stasis" can appear in the midst of the production and produce the body without organs as an element of antiproduction.

By stressing the processes of functioning instead of the processes of meaning, Deleuze and Guattari suggest a parallel between desire production in schizoanalysis and the production of the goods in the capitalist political economy. In this respect, desire does not have any particular form of existence which could be called "psychic reality". If desire exists, it exists only when assembled or machined (Deleuze & Parnet, 2006, p. 71). In other words, desire is not a spontaneous reality, but something constructed. Another important aspect is that desire is not an individual affair, but the expression of a collective.

"Since every assemblage is collective, is itself a collective, it is indeed true that every desire is the affair of the people, or an affair of the masses, a molecular affair" (Deleuze & Parnet, 2006, p. 71). Desire impregnates every field of social and political reality in such a way that the libidinal economy is assembled together with the political economy. From this, it follows that desire production has the power to organise social production: in other words, desire produces what we call social reality. As Deleuze and Guattari point out, "If desire produces, its product is real. If desire is productive, it can be productive only in the real world and can produce only reality. . . . The objective being of desire is the Real in and of itself" (Deleuze & Guattari, 2004, p. 28). In this respect, Deleuze and Guattari oppose the Lacanian idea that the unconscious is structured like a language, and interpret the unconscious in terms of the machinic. By contrast to Lacanian "idealism", Deleuze and Guattari define their project of schizoanalysis, or materialist psychiatry, as a method which investigates the unconscious materialist processes immanent to the social fabric:

> There is no such thing as the social production of reality on the one hand, and a desiring-production that is mere fantasy on the other. . . . The truth of the matter is that *social production is purely and simply desiring-production itself under determinate conditions*. We maintain that the social field is immediately invested by desire, that it is the historically determined product of desire, and that libido has no need of any mediation or sublimation, any psychic operation, any transformation, in order to invade and invest the productive forces and the relations of production. *There is only desire and the social, and nothing else.* (Deleuze & Guattari, 2004, pp. 30–31)

Desire production does not exist in any other way than as embodied in social, political, and economical assemblages. In this respect, Deleuze and Guattari neglect such psychoanalytic notions as dream or fantasy:

> It is not possible to attribute a special form of existence to desire, a mental or psychic reality that is presumably different from the material reality of social production. Desiring-machines are not fantasy-machines or dream-machines, which supposedly can be distinguished from technical and social machines. Rather, fantasies are secondary expressions, deriving from the identical nature of the two sorts of

machines in any given set of circumstances. (Deleuze & Guattari, 2004, p. 32)

In fact, Deleuze and Guattari deny the very opposition between psychic reality and material reality and assert that all psychic phenomena are immanent to the material reality of production. In this respect, the unconscious is also described as a material, rather than a linguistic, phenomenon:

> For the unconscious itself is no more structural than personal, it does not symbolize any more than it imagines or represents; it engineers, it is machinic. Neither imaginary nor symbolic, it is the Real in itself, the 'impossible real' and its production. (Deleuze & Guattari, 2004, p. 60)

The materialist notions of desire and the unconscious explain the specific role that schizophrenia takes in Deleuze and Guattari's project. Desire functions as a machinic desire production and, likewise, capitalist production consists in following the paths of desire and, in this sense, opens an unlimited space for libidinal investment. Deleuze and Guattari argue that capitalist production follows a schizophrenic model of desire production because both capitalism and the schizo are trying to overcome defined codes and territories. Thus, capitalist flows and schizophrenic flows have a great affinity, but it would be an error to consider them as being identical. Schizophrenic flows involve both decoding and deterritorialization; capitalist flows also involve decoding and deterritorialization but later decoding is replaced by axiomatization which transforms goods or qualities of any kind into quantitative monetary flows. This means that both capitalism and schizophrenia follow decoded flows, but not in the same way: "they are not at all the same thing, depending on whether the decodings are caught up in an axiomatic or not" (Deleuze & Guattari, 2004, p. 268). In other words, capitalism arrests the decoded flows and transforms them into axiomatics, whereas schizophrenia makes the flows proceed in a free state and produce the desocialised body without organs. "Hence schizophrenia is not the identity of capitalism, but on the contrary its difference, its divergence, and its death" (Deleuze & Guattari, 2004, p. 267). Capitalism inhibits this schizophrenic tendency by making it its basic principle of functioning. Thus, capitalism is more schizophrenic than schizophrenia itself, because it permanently transforms external limits into internal ones and, in this way, ensures its permanent overproduction.

> Hence one can say that schizophrenia is the *exterior* limit of capitalism itself or the conclusion of its deepest tendency, but that capitalism only functions on condition that it inhibit this tendency, or that it push back or displace this limit, by substituting for it its own *immanent* relative limits, which it continually reproduces on a widened scale. It axiomatizes with one hand what it decodes with the other. (Deleuze & Guattari, 2004, p. 267)

Capitalism arrests the schizophrenic flows by transforming the decoded flows into the network of axiomatic relationships. In this way, capitalism opposes the revolutionary potential of schizo-flows by posing a new interior limit.

Hence, there is an affinity between a revolutionary and the figure of the schizophrenic, though it is important to stress that not every schizophrenic is, by definition, a revolutionary and *vice versa*. As Deleuze and Guattari point out,

> there is a whole world of difference between the schizo and the revolutionary ... The schizo is not revolutionary, but the schizophrenic process – in terms of which the schizo is merely the interruption, or the continuation in the void – is the potential for revolution. (Deleuze & Guattari, 2004, p. 374)

The same is true for the revolutionaries:

> We're not saying revolutionaries are schizophrenics. We're saying there's a schizoid process, of decoding and deterritorialization, which only revolutionary activity can stop turning into the production of schizophrenia. We're considering a problem to do with the close link between capitalism and psychoanalysis on the one hand, and between revolutionary movements and schizoanalysis on the other. We can talk in terms of capitalist paranoia and revolutionary schizophrenia ... (Deleuze, 1995, pp. 23–24)

If codes and territories represent molar structures and aggregates of power, then the process of decoding and deterritorialization seeks to escape these structures and engender new molecular forms of social organisation. Schizophrenic flows create what Deleuze and Guattari call "the lines of flight or escape":

We set against this fascism of power active, positive lines of flight, because these lines open up desire, desire's machines, and the organization of a social field of desire: it's not a matter of escaping 'personally', from oneself, but of allowing something to escape, like bursting a pipe or a boil. (Deleuze, 1995, p. 19)

Schizophrenic escape creates the potential for a revolutionary investment and, in this sense, breaks free from conformist, reactionary, and fascistic investments.

Schizophrenia and paranoia as two forms of libidinal investment

As far as every libidinal investment is simultaneously a social investment, schizoanalysis can be seen as a "militant libidino–economic, libidino–political analysis". As a result of this analysis, Deleuze and Guattari define two major modes of social investment, which are similar to two poles of delirium: these are schizo and paranoid poles.

> At times we contrasted the molar and the molecular as the paranoiac, signifying, and structured lines of integration, and the schizophrenic, machinic, and dispersed lines of escape; or again as the staking out of the perverse reterritorializations, and as the movement of the schizophrenic deterritorializations. At other times, on the contrary, we contrasted them as the two major types of equally social investments: the one sedentary and biunivocalizing, and of a reactionary or fascist tendency; the other nomadic and polyvocal, and of a revolutionary tendency. (Deleuze & Guattari, 2004, p. 373)

If the paranoiac formula is: "I am one of your kind", "I am a pure Aryan, of a superior race for all time", then the formula of the schizo would be: "I am of a race inferior for all eternity", "I am a beast, a black". As Deleuze and Guattari explain, these two poles, paranoia and schizophrenia, coexist with each other in the unconscious, and all the oscillations from one formula to the other are possible. This is why one of the major tasks of materialist psychiatry or schizoanalysis is to investigate these oscillations of the unconscious from one type of libidinal investment to the other.

It is important to stress that both schizophrenia and paranoia designate not the clinical state of mental illness, but the deepest tendency of capitalism and capitalist desire production. As far as desire production determines social production, schizophrenia and paranoia express the two tendencies of libidinal–social investment: the first tendency is to set free desire production, to open the potential for new social and political formations; the second tendency is to stop and bind desire production, to stratify social and political territories, and, in this way, subjugate individuals. Schizophrenia is associated with the creative tendency of capitalism, its potential for change and permanent revolution. Paranoia is associated with the counter-tendency to fix meanings, beliefs, and authorities, to stick to defined territories. As Holland (2003) points out, "despite their psychological origins, the terms 'paranoia' and 'schizophrenia' for Deleuze and Guattari designate effects of the fundamental organizing principles and dynamics of capitalist society" (p. 3). Paranoia represents capitalism's archaic or traditional tendencies, whereas schizophrenia refers to capitalism's revolutionary potential. As Holland points out,

> if we understand schizophrenia (in this first approximation) to designate unlimited semiosis, a radically fluid and extemporaneous form of meaning, paranoia by contrast would designate an absolute system of belief where all meaning was permanently fixed and exhaustively defined by a supreme authority, figure-head, or god. (Holland, 2003, p. 3)

In the last chapter of *Anti-Oedipus*, titled "Introduction to schizo-analysis", Deleuze and Guattari define the negative task of schizoanalysis and the two positive tasks of schizoanalysis. The term schizo-analysis itself suggests that Deleuze and Guattari see the schizophrenic processes as having the potential for liberating the individual from psychic, social, or political constraints. In this respect, the negative task of schizoanalysis is to destroy everything that Deleuze and Guattari define as the molar, that is, stratified, fixed to specific codes or territories: "schizoanalysis must devote itself with all its strength to the necessary destructions. Destroying beliefs and representations, theatrical scenes" (Deleuze & Guattari, 2004, p. 345).

> In its destructive task, schizoanalysis must proceed as quickly as possible, but it can also proceed only with great patience, great care, by successively undoing the representative territorialities and reterritorializations through which a subject passes in his individual history. (Deleuze & Guattari, 2004, p. 349)

The destructive phase is necessary because schizophrenia as a process of deterritorialization is necessarily involved in the counter-reactive processes like neurosis, perversion, and psychosis. All the counter-productive elements should be destroyed and all the recodings and reterritorializations should be undone to liberate the schizoid movement of decodings and deterritorializations.

After this stage, the first positive task of schizoanalysis can be enacted: to discover in the subject the nature, the formation, or the functioning of his or her desiring machines. As Deleuze and Guattari point out, the task of schizoanalysis is that of learning what a subject's desiring machines are, how they work or stop working. As I mentioned before, Deleuze and Guattari point out that desire production or, as they call it, libidinal–social investments, oscillate between two poles:

> The two poles are defined, *the one* by the enslavement of production and the desiring-machines to the gregarious aggregates that they constitute on a large scale under a given form of power or selective sovereignty; *the other* by the inverse subordination and the overthrow of power. *The one* by these molar structured aggregates that crush singularities, select them, and regularize those that they retain in codes or axiomatics; *the other* by the molecular multiplicities of singularities that on the contrary treat the large aggregates as so many useful materials for their own elaborations. *The one* by the lines of integration and territorialization that arrest the flows, constrict them, turn them back, break them again according to the limits interior to the system, in such a way as to produce the images that come to fill the field of immanence peculiar to this system or this aggregate, *the other* by lines of escape that follow the decoded and deterritorialized flows, inventing their own nonfigurative breaks or schizzes that produce new flows . . . And to summarize all the preceding determinations: *the one* is defined by subjugated groups, *the other* by subject-groups. (Deleuze & Guattari, 2004, p. 401)

The first distinction between the schizophrenic revolutionary flows and the paranoiac reactionary breaks of antiproduction seems quite persuasive. If we agree with Deleuze and Guattari that desire is the most important principle in organising the socius, it follows that desire can be both active and reactive, or productive and counter-productive. As far as the capitalist economy always oscillates between schizophrenic production and antiproduction (or the body without organs), the libidinal economy also oscillates between the schizophrenic flows of flight or escape and the reactive paranoiac attempt to bind those flows. Whereas paranoiac investments are always at the service of molar structures and aggregates of power, trying to define territories and codes, schizophrenic investments break these structures and aggregates apart and liberate molecular movements of multiple singularities. Multiple singularities retain the revolutionary potential to the extent that they are not convertible into the axiomatic logic of capitalism.

Although schizophrenic impulses seem for Deleuze and Guattari quite "natural" (everyone wants to change the status quo, to jump from or escape from his or her stratified territory), the opposite paranoiac impulse is more difficult to explain:

> why do many of those who have or should have an objective revolutionary interest maintain a preconscious investment of a reactionary type? And more rarely, how do certain people whose interest is objectively reactionary come to effect a preconscious revolutionary investment? (Deleuze & Guattari, 2004, p. 378)

In fact this is the well-known Reichian question: "Why did the masses desire fascism?" Or, as Guattari has formulated it, "everyone wants to be a fascist". Why does someone who is repressed desire his or her repression? Why does desire desire its own repression? This is the reactionary force of desire which Deleuze and Guattari call the anti-production: "antiproduction is loved for itself, as is the way in which desire represses itself in the great capitalist aggregate. Repressing desire, not only for others but in oneself, being the cop for others and for oneself – that is what arouses, and it is not ideology, it is economy. (Deleuze & Guattari, 2004, p. 380)

Besides the interplay of production and antiproduction, the capitalist dynamics is defined by the opposition between decoding and recoding, deterritorialization and reterritorialization. Decoding can be seen as a positive aspect of capitalist axiomatization: the flows of capital, labour power, or libidinal energy are unleashed from the restrictions of code; on the other hand, this positive aspect is counterattacked by an opposite tendency to recuperate the free flows of capital or libidinal energy (private ownership, family institution). These two aspects of decoding and recoding can be associated with deterritorialization and reterritorialization. As Holland points out, on the one hand, capitalism devotes itself to production as an end in itself, to developing the productivity of socialized labor to the utmost: this is the moment of deterritorialization. Yet, on the other hand, due to private investment in the means of production, social labor and life are restricted to production and consumption that valorize only the already-existing capital-stock: this is the moment of reterritorialization. (Holland, 2003, p. 80)

In other words, the moment of deterritorialization frees both the forces of production and consumption, and at the same time revolutionises the labour power; the moment of reterritorialization, by contrast, stops this free movement by recouping the results of production.

Another distinction, which is important in defining the opposition between the schizophrenic and paranoid poles, is the distinction between the subjugated groups (*groupe assujetti*) and subject groups (*groupe-sujet*). The subject group has the ability to formulate its ideological statement, whereas the subjugated group simply adopts a certain ideology without verifying it. As Genosko (2008) points out,

> the subject group's alienation has an internal source arising from its efforts to connect with other groups . . . whereas the subjugated group's alienation is thought to have an external source, from which it protects itself by withdrawing into itself and constructing richly paranoid protective formations, providing a kind of refuge and a distorted sense of security for its members. (p. 57)

The subjugated groups are based on traditional roles, hierarchies, modes of inclusion and exclusion; such a group usually identifies with a particular institution, which grounds its permanent existence (church, army, party, nation). The subject group, by contrast, questions every institution and acquires a transitional identity which can be easily overcome (Bogue, 1989, p. 86). Although this definition is quite relative because every subject group can easily assume the form of a subjugated group and *vice versa*, a subjugated group can act as a subject group under certain determinate conditions. This oscillation between a subject group and a subjugated group demonstrates the oscillation between the schizophrenic and paranoid poles in the unconscious: the subjugated group, which protects its own identity by inventing an external enemy, can be seen as representing a paranoid pole, and a subject group, which is permanently inventing new identities, can be seen as representing a schizophrenic pole.

The political between schizophrenia and paranoia

Although the distinction between schizophrenic and paranoid poles is quite clear, Deleuze and Guattari complicate this distinction with the division between what they call the preconscious libidinal investments of class or interest, and the unconscious libidinal investments of group or desire. As Deleuze and Guattari point out, "what is reactionary or revolutionary in the preconscious investment of interest does not necessarily coincide with what is reactionary or revolutionary in the unconscious libidinal investment" (Deleuze & Guattari, 2004, p. 380). According to Deleuze and Guattari, power always speaks in terms of interests, aims, and causality. This is what Marxist theory used to call an ideology (or preconscious investments, according to Deleuze and Guattari). Besides these sets of interests and aims, Deleuze and Guattari introduce the unconscious investments of desire. From this, it follows that the preconscious revolutionary investments (which declare a new socius, new aims, etc.) can have the unconscious reactionary investments (which continue to invest the former social body, the old forms of power and its codes and territories). This means that

> even when the libido embraces the new body – the new force that corresponds to the effectively revolutionary goals and syntheses from the viewpoint of the preconscious – it is not certain that the unconscious libidinal investment is itself revolutionary. (Deleuze & Guattari, 2004, p. 381)

Another important distinction is that a preconscious revolution always refers to a new regime of social production, whereas an unconscious revolution operates within the body of the socius, creating the body without organs: for example, some kind of antiproduction which overthrows power. As Deleuze and Guattari point out, in the case of preconscious revolution "the break is between two forms of socius", but in the case of unconscious revolution "the break is within the socius itself" (2004, p. 381).

These oscillations between the preconscious and the unconscious, the reactionary (paranoiac) and the revolutionary (schizophrenic) investments could be analysed using the concrete example of the Lithuanian political scene. I would like to introduce two examples, which are both connected to some specific "territory". The first example refers to two events which took place in connction with the Lithuanian parliament. The first event took place on 13 January in 1991, shortly after Lithuania re-established its independence in 1990. On the night of 13 January, almost all of the population went out on to the streets to defend the Lithuanian parliament from the Soviet troops. The second event took place on 16 January 2009, when the same population attacked the parliament, protesting against severe social cuts and demanding proper living conditions. Following Deleuze and Guattari, we can describe these two events in terms of preconscious and unconscious revolutionary investments. From a historical perspective, we are used to thinking about the liberation movements and investments which took place in the Baltic countries in 1990 as being revolutionary; they aimed to destroy the old Soviet empire (the despotic State-machine, as Deleuze and Guattari would call it) and establish new independent states. But, together with these preconscious revolutionary drives, which were formulated in terms of interests and aims, we can also discern the unconscious paranoiac desire to revive the old nation-state from the inter-war period (Lithuania was an independent state from 1918 to 1940) with all its codes, beliefs, and territories. The unconscious paranoiac investments became manifest shortly after the re-establishment of independence in 1991. The independent state immediately started functioning as an apparatus of repression, in a paranoiac way defending a pre-war system of codes and beliefs and excluding those members who do not represent the "Lithuanian kind": ethnic and sexual minorities.

By contrast, the events in 2009 never aimed to become preconsciously revolutionary: it was a spontaneous reaction by very diverse social groups to the pressure of power structures. Following Deleuze and Guattari, we can call these reactions the unconscious revolutionary investments. The unconscious investments are not so easy to describe, because, as Deleuze and Guattari point out, "the unconscious revolutionary break implies for its part the body without organs as the limit of the socius". Thus, the unconscious revolutionary drives break with the social order, and arrest its organisation and functioning—this is why the unconscious revolutionary investments lack any organisation or shape. It is interesting to notice that after the events on 16 January in 2009, no political group took responsibility for these events; on the other hand, political analysts seemed to lack political terms to describe these events. This lack of terminology could be a symptom that on 16 January 2009 a new social group had appeared—Hardt and Negri (2004) call it the multitude. Hardt and Negri point out that "the multitude is composed of innumerable internal differences that can never be reduced to a unity or a single identity. . . . The multitude is a multiplicity of all these singular differences" (Hardt & Negri, 2004, p. xiv). Virno, following Thomas Hobbes, defines the multitude in opposition to the concept of the people: the people presuppose a particular identity and always correlate to the existence of the state; the multitude, by contrast, never assumes any form of identity and always acts against the state. As Virno points out, "if there are people, there is no multitude; if there is a multitude, there are no people" (Virno, 2004, p. 23). The main feature of the multitude is that it lacks any positive characteristics and can be described as a multiplicity of singularities which emerges as a reaction to global capitalism. The multitude arises spontaneously from nowhere, expressing its schizo-phrenic desires, but anyone trying to analyse the multitude will encounter the problem that these schizophrenic revolutionary drives act on the border of the social and create a kind of body without organs which means the death of the social.

Trying to explain how this transformation (from people to the multitude) is possible, it is important to stress that the preconscious revolutionary investments (declaring a new independent state, a new socius), contain unconscious reactionary investments, which continue to be constructed on the old forms of power, old state apparatuses, and the reactionary notion of the nation (in this case, based on the historical idea of the nation-state). So, even if the revolutionary discourse is formulated in terms of freedom, liberation, and the creation of a new socius (a new subject group), actually it still retains some paranoiac investments, which are easily masked by the rational discourse of aims and interests. As Deleuze and Guattari point out,

> it covers over the irrational character of the paranoiac investment under an existing order of interests, of causes and means, of aims and reasons; or else the investment of interest itself gives rise to and creates those interests that rationalize the paranoiac investment . . . (Deleuze & Guattari, 2004, p. 411)

The discourse of interests and aims disguises the paranoiac investments in order to create a new socius which could act as a subject group. But, very quickly, this newly established socius becomes subjugated to its own interests and aims and, in this way, starts functioning as a subjugated group, forming its new hierarchies, apparatuses of power, and creating its new codes. At this moment, the unconscious paranoiac investments become preconscious and take the shape of aggressive nationalism. For example, on 11 March 2011, the day of the re-establisment of independence in Lithuania was celebrated by an officially sanctioned, neo-fascist demonstration, whose activists carried the slogans "Lithuania for Lithuanians", and "Lithuania nation, homeland, race". I think it is not a coincidence that a neo-fascist demonstration appears on Independence Day, because it expresses the paranoiac investments of the nation-state. It is important to stress that the neo-fascist demonstration was sanctioned by the state authorities. At the same time, the same authorities were trying to ban the Baltic Pride demonstration on May 2010. The permission to organise the demonstration was given only a few hours before the demonstration actually had to take place (and only after numerous warnings from the EU). In the end, the Baltic Pride demonstration took place, and even if there were more policemen than gay and lesbian activists, the activists were still attacked by members of parliament! Here we can speak not only about the unconscious, but also about preconscious paranoia: in this case, the nation-state itself starts functioning as an archaic despotic machine. As Deleuze and Guatari point out, paranoiac investments try to re-establish what they call the molar: if the schizophrenic investments correspond to molecular flows which transversally cross defined territories and subvert established norms, then molar or paranoid investments correspond to traditional, conservative social norms, trying to protect defined territories such as the nation, family, or race. In this case, the nationalist interests and aims, which carried a revolutionary character in 1990, now are converted into fascist slogans, celebrating the nation, homeland, and race. By contrast, the revolutionary events in 2009 did not formulate any revolutionary rhetoric. It signalled the break within the socius itself and the emergence of the multitude. The multitude's revolution aimed to undo the unitary notion of the nation, and the rhetoric of patriotism and ethnic fanaticism, which actually means the eternal debt to capital and a total subjection to the logic of axiomatization.

A second example, which is also linked to a specific territory, again shows the differences between 1990 and the recent moment. In

2010, Lithuania was celebrating the twentieth anniversary of the re-establishment of independence. For this occasion, an artist, Tadas Gutauskas, suggested that he create a special monument to commemorate the twenty years of Lithuanian independence. This monument, called "The way of freedom", consists of a brick wall coloured like the national flag. Everyone who wanted to support the building of the monument could buy a brick with his or her name written on it. This desire to build the wall seems like the ironic reversal of the events in 1990, which started with the fall of the Berlin wall in 1989. By contrast, the recent monument represents not only the paranoiac drive to reterritorialize and redefine a territory, but also is the perfect realisation of capitalist logic: you can celebrate freedom by buying a brick and taking your place in a nationalist columbarium. More surprising is the fact that this "columbarium of freedom" was initiated by a generation who used to sing (together with *Pink Floyd*) about being just another brick in the wall.

This last example reveals the ambivalent nature of any revolutionary movement as well as the functioning of the capitalist machine. As Holland points out, capitalism

> is ambivalent: it borrows paranoia from despotism . . . in conjunction with its drive to reterritorialize and recode; yet at the same time it promotes schizophrenia in its inevitable propensity to deterritorialize and decode. And it earns its inaugural position in universal history on the side of decoding and schizophrenia . . . (Holland 2003, p. 94)

The revolution is needed to create a new socius, a new territory, a new code, but as soon as new territories are taken over, the capitalist machine starts functioning as an apparatus of power, trying to subjugate revolutionaries to its control. As Holland points out,

> whereas capitalist ambivalence combines the freedom of economics with the tyranny of power, permanent revolution eliminates power and paranoia in order to give free play to schizophrenia and enable molecular investments of desire to prevail over molar ones. (Holland, 2003, p. 95)

Although Deleuze and Guattari believe in the revolutionary potential of capitalism, in a paradoxical way, revolution does not eliminate capitalism as an economic formation, but gives a "second breath" to capitalism itself. The permanent oscillation between the paranoid and schizophrenic poles assures the living potential of a capitalist machine.

References

Bogue, R. (1989). *Deleuze and Guattari*. London, New York: Routledge

Deleuze, G. (1995). *Negotiations 1972–1990*, M. Joughin (Trans.). New York: Columbia University Press.

Deleuze, G., & Guattari, F. (2004). *Anti-Oedipus. Capitalism and Schizophrenia*, R. Hurley, M. Seem, & H. R. Lane (Trans.). London: Continuum.

Deleuze, G., & Parnet, C. (2006). *Dialogues II*, H. Tomlinson & B. Habberjam (Trans). London: Continuum.

Genosko, G. (2008). The life and work of Félix Guattari: from transversality to ecosophy. In: F. Guattari, *The Three Ecologies*, I. Pindar & P. Sutton (Trans.) (pp. 46–78). London: Continuum.

Hardt, M., & Negri, A. (2004). *Multitude: War and Democracy in the Age of Empire*. New York: Penguin Press.

Holland, E. W. (2003). *Deleuze and Guattari's Anti-Oedipus: Introduction to Schizoanalysis*. London: Routledge.

Virno, P. (2004). *A Grammar of the Multitude: For an Analysis of Contemporary Forms of Life*, I. Bertoletti, J. Cascaito, & A. Casson (Trans.). Los Angeles, CA: Semiotext(e).

Editor's introduction to
Chapter Seven

The chapter recounts how fundamentalism as a term was born in America in the early twentieth century, derived from a series of pamphlets on "The fundamentals" of the Christian faith, published in the 1910s. These publications formulated a strict commitment to the belief that the Bible was infallible and historically accurate. When the debates sparked by fundamentalism reached Norway, the psychologist and philosopher Ingjald Nissen responded by providing an account of fundamentalism, both Christian and scientific, as characterised by the tendency to render concepts absolute and an unusual confidence in logical inference. In the early 1930s, he came to believe that National Socialism, which was on the rise, was related to a similar mentality. Nissen resorted to Adler's theory of the inferiority complex; feelings of inferiority, he argued, would drive the individual to accept compensatory ideas, logical and conclusive reasoning being the most compelling. The compensatory superstructure protects the individual against feelings of inferiority, and its construction and flaws are more or less hidden from consciousness. This was also a psycho-social mechanism; the creation of feelings of inferiority in the masses that were fed with compensatory ideology could explain the large scale growth of National Socialism. This view guided Nissen's analysis not only of Nazism, but also of dogmatic, scientifically inspired movements, such as the "orthodox" psychoanalytic movement. The author argues that Ingjald Nissen's work exposes an important kinship between Alfred Adler and Hans Vaihinger's ideas, and points to a possible reading of Nissen's books as a warning against contempt for weakness and against holding strength and superiority as ideals. An obsession with masculine strength and a fear of weakness and the feminine can be observed in today's fundamentalists and fascists, which could be seen as a frustrated and exaggerated version of tendencies found deep in mainstream culture.

Fundamentalism, Nazism, and inferiority

Haakon Flemmen

Introduction

What is fundamentalism? In which different forms does it appear? What are the forces behind it? Such questions have been asked frequently, especially during the past decade or so, usually with Islamists in mind. We often forget, though, that the concept is far from a new one: fundamentalism as a term was born in the early twentieth century, originally referring to the Christian faith and, interestingly, even in the first part of the last century, there were scholars who aimed to explore the *psychology* of the fundamentalist.

In this chapter, I intend to show how an Adlerian analysis of fundamentalism and National Socialism took form in the writings of the Norwegian philosopher and psychologist Ingjald Nissen, an important inspiration being the debate on Christian fundamentalism in the 1920s and the work of Norwegian psychiatrist Ragnar Vogt.

In other words, I do not intend to carve out any supra-historical definition of fundamentalism—this is a historical account, an exploration of how the concept was treated in Nissen's own context; the natural starting point, therefore, is the mid-1920s and the religious groups that first were named "fundamentalists".

Fundamentalism: the first debate

The story begins in America and the state of Tennessee in the summer of 1925. During a hot July, the small town of Dayton was the scene of a massive international media event: The State of Tennessee *vs.* Scopes trial, also known as the Monkey Trials; the issue was the charge that John T. Scopes, a science teacher in the town's public high school, had violated state law by teaching evolution. It turned into a dispute over the *literal* truth of the Bible: was Jonah really swallowed by an actual whale? Is the earth really only 6,000 years old? And just where did Cain find his wife?

It was a fierce debate between the defenders of traditional religion, emphasising the literal truth of the Bible, and those who saw themselves as a force of modernism, relying on science and interpretation. However, the state law was quite clear: teaching evolution was prohibited, and Scopes was found guilty. (The judgement was later reversed because of a technicality, but the trial none the less led to evolution being de-emphasised in American textbooks for years to come.) The trial generated enormous interest even in Europe, and not purely because of the case itself; in many European countries this was the first time the public had been confronted with a group labelled "fundamentalists", and a phenomenon called "fundamentalism".

It is easy to forget, in our time, that fundamentalism was originally a Christian movement in America. The term derives from a series of pamphlets on "The fundamentals" of the Christian faith published in the 1910s. These essays formulated a strict commitment to biblical inerrancy, which became the prime characteristic of fundamentalism: a belief that the Bible was infallible and historically accurate. The term "fundamental*ist*" was first used in 1920 to describe the advocates of these fundamentals. By the first years of that decade, it had taken shape as a recognisable religious movement, and, by the middle of the decade, with the victory in the Criminal Court of Tennessee, it was at the pinnacle of its power.

Ragnar Vogt on fundamentalism

The story also reached Norway, making headlines and generating debate. One important question was, of course, to what extent the

Bible could and should be read literally. Some writers chose to take a step back and approached the issue more analytically. One such person was Ragnar Vogt, who had become Norway's first professor of psychiatry in 1915. In an article in 1926, Vogt approached the question of fundamentalism, as it then had become known from the Monkey Trials, attempting to give a *psychological* account of the phenomenon.

Vogt's (1926) starting point was the word "fundamentalism" itself. This is, of course, a metaphorical concept; it has to do with a fundament, the underlying part of something else, a structure, for example, with a fundamentalist being a person who is convinced that he stands on solid ground, an unshakable foundation.

"It goes without saying," Vogt writes, that an objectively true "fundamentalism cannot be based on experience" (Vogt, 1926, p. 280, translated for this edition). Experience will always expand and correct our knowledge, and a world view based on this will never be stable, as empirical science is always incomplete and temporary. The challenge for the fundamentalist is that empirical science is expanding to an increasing number of fields of knowledge, relativising old truths. No philosopher of today would dare to claim that he could ultimately explain existence. Even Kant's categorical imperative is relativised, in sociology. So, the piece of knowledge, the patch of solid ground the fundamentalist is standing on, is eroding; it is becoming smaller and smaller. "That is why," Vogt writes, "the most dogmatic fundamentalists preach with such pathos, that science will plunge us into the abyss" (Vogt, 1926, p. 280, translated for this edition).

In themselves, Christian ideas about faith and grace are not necessarily harmful. What makes fundamentalism dangerous, according to Vogt (1926, p. 281, translated for this edition), is that such "ideas of the highest order are brought to an absolute conclusion". The fundamentalist is turning a small field of knowledge into the ultimate foundation of the world. In that way, fundamentalism represents an intellectual closure; free and enquiring thought is rejected in favour of a safe fundament.

A central point for Vogt is that the fundamentalists were not irrational (as they were portrayed in the media). The structure that the fundamentalist builds on top of his religious fundament is not illogical or inconsistent at all: the problem is the contrary—the fundamentalist has an extreme confidence in logical coherence and a strong feeling of certainty when making his logical inferences. Vogt even suggests calling the phenomenon "hyper-logicism".

So, what is Vogt suggesting? Psychologically, he argues, this has to do with a kind of emotional displacement; the fundamentalist, as mentioned, shows a very strong feeling of certainty when making logical *inferences*. This feeling apparently radiates to the *premises* of the logical argument. The feeling of security and coping associated with a steady and logical conclusion overshadows the presumptions the conclusion is based on, and, in that way, the fundamentalist mind neglects the fact that logic always rests on premises that, in principle, could be different. (Even what some claim to be the highest form of logic, mathematics, depends on its unproven axioms.) Apparently, we are dealing with people who have an extraordinary need for coherence, which, of course, does not guarantee that their conclusions are sound. "Often, those who express the strongest conviction are the last people one should trust" (Vogt, 1926, p. 284, translated for this edition).

Vogt elaborates further on the fundamentalist's type of personality: that the fundamentalist needs a sensation of certainty and coherence to keep his personality together (not unlike how the delusion, according to Freud, acts as a patch covering the breach between the ego and the external world). We all have a tendency to draw conclusions that support our own basic beliefs—it gives us a feeling of security and peace of mind—but, in addition, Vogt suggests, some people also have a *particular* need for self-assertion and self-esteem: "There is a connection between a strong need for self-esteem and an overstressed mechanism of logical inference" (Vogt, 1926, p. 285, translated for this edition). (Even though he was highly aware of Freud's concept of the unconscious, Vogt does not discuss the unconscious factors that appear to underlie such a "strong need for self-esteem".) So, there is a backward thrust in the arguments of the fundamentalist, where his need for a consistent outlook on life cements the fundament it is based upon. In that sense, the letter of the scripture does not really dictate the fundamentalist's thinking; it is the other way round: his need for security rules the letter of the scripture.

In the courtroom in Tennessee, the cocksure main witness of the prosecutor, Mr William Jennings Bryan, rejected the idea that the Bible should be interpreted at all. Even in his own articles on the Christian faith, there were supposedly no interpretations of the Bible, only, as he said, "comments to the lesson" (Moran, 2002, p. 144).

So, according to Vogt, the fundamentalist is a hyper-logicist. That, he says, does not mean that straight thinking and logical integrity is wrong; not as long as we always make a reservation in our conclusions to operate with an "as if" or an "as far as we know". With a ring of pragmatism, Vogt sums up, "Where the fundamentalist speaks of rational necessity, the anti-fundamentalist confines himself to speak of what is appropriate or useful" (Vogt, 1926, p. 286, translated for this edition). That is not to say that values and morals should be kept out of the argument. Rather, Vogt seems to support a less deductive and more flexible way of thinking: instead of believing moral guidelines can be mechanically deduced from basic values, one should openly consider which guidelines and actions would contribute the most to realising one's values.

Scientific fundamentalism?

It is interesting that Vogt starts with the American fundamentalists and ends up by describing fundamentalism as a way of thinking in general, yet he does not really elaborate greatly on this. The person to pick up this notion was the young philosopher, Ingjald Nissen. Nissen would later become a psychotherapist, elaborating such ideas in his books on popular psychology, but at this time he had recently finished his studies in philosophy and was inspired by Vogt's analysis, seeing the potential in applying it to something very different from conservative Protestantism: *science*.

At this time, Nissen was a part of a conservative, Neo-Kantian circle in Oslo, deeply critical of the scientism of the day. They were especially concerned about the notion that natural science comprises the most authoritative world view or form of human knowledge, an idea often accompanied by the belief that the natural sciences are, at least potentially, value-free (Flemmen, 2012).

In 1929, he published a work on the philosophy of science, titled *Die methodische Einstellung* (The Methodical Attitude), a book partly inspired by Vogt's ideas. In the book, he defends a radically open and cautious attitude towards the ideas of science (both natural and social), warning against *scientific* fundamentalism.

Scientific theories, Nissen points out, often appear as value-free and coherent systems of logical relations, easily giving the impression that they represent unchangeable facts. However, under the guise of logic and empiricism, there are always implicit assertions—ideas and patterns of thought that are taken for granted. (So, there is a parallel with Vogt here.) Drawing on the philosophy of Hans Vaihinger, Nissen (1929) thinks of these as *fictions*: they are concepts not based on simple facts, but, rather, on useful assumptions; we think and act "as if" this or that. It could be anything, ranging from the atom to the economic individual or the causal relations in the psyche: we act "as if" they exist or are real because it is useful to do so. This makes our theories add up and it produces the desired results. However, there is a constant danger that we mix up what is empirically founded, what is logic, and what is fiction; we easily treat fictions as external reality. In other words, scientific concepts and theories are objectified. The problem is that our fictions are not neutral; they disguise normative judgements and values that we might not be aware of. In this way, fictions, permeated by ideology—or as Nissen calls it, *immanent valuations*—are transformed into truths. (This was also a mistake made by orthodox Freudians, he thought: they confuse their heuristic point of view with reality.)

We tend to create logical structures that become so dominant and important to us, that we stop questioning the fictions that make them possible. Believing that the knowledge available to us is necessarily correct is the core of fundamentalism, Nissen continues, "One could say that Fundamentalism . . . consists of immanent valuations being absolutised, thereby paving the way for a logical quasi-objectivism that is so dangerous because it appears behind the sincere face of science" (Nissen, 1929, p. 136, translated for this edition).

Alfred Adler

Interestingly, after writing this book, Nissen turned to the study of psychology. He soon joined a group intellectually related to Vaihinger, that is, the school of individual psychology, founded by Freud's collaborator Alfred Adler. Adler had been a central figure in the psychoanalytic movement but broke with Freud in 1911, primarily because he could not accept Freud's concepts of libido and repression.

The central concept for Adler, such as his theory had developed by this time, was the striving of the individual to overcome feelings of inferiority (these would be feelings emerging from bodily defects or experiences of helplessness). Individuals under the sway of such feelings develop compensatory ideas and behaviour. An individual's "social interest" is also central to Adler; in cases of psychopathology, the aptitude for social interest is not adequately developed, such persons are uselessly striving for personal power over others, instead of nurturing a healthy, socially useful desire to achieve constructive goals (Weiner & Craighead, 2010).

Another of Adler's notions is adopted from Hans Vaihinger: that of the concept of fiction. He believes that the individual develops what he calls a "guiding fiction". This is a compensatory structure, originally designed to protect a child from feelings of inferiority, and later amplified by successful behavioural patterns. This "leading fiction" then shapes the cognition of the individual, including apperceptions and memory; it becomes a schema to organise reality. Its final purpose, Adler writes, "aims at freedom from the feeling of inferiority in order to ascend to the full height of ego feeling, to complete manliness, to attain the ideal of being above" (Adler, cited in Stepansky, 1983, p. 155). (When this compensation takes form as an attempt to cover up one's inferiority with a sense of dominance over others, this would be a neurotic tendency.)

If we return to Vogt's thoughts on fundamentalism, one question remains unanswered. If the fundamentalist has such an extraordinary need for coherence, where does it come from? What are the motivational forces behind it? For Nissen, that could now be answered using Adler's theory. A person prone to fundamentalism is likely to be someone with very strong feelings of inferiority who builds certain compensatory cognitive and behavioural patterns; he will cling to a fiction that gives him a feeling of coping and a psychological defence.

That is, of course, not to say that the individual is consciously aware of this process. The compensatory superstructure protects against feelings of inferiority, and its construction and flaws are more or less hidden from consciousness. (Adler, however, did not adhere to Freud's model of the unconscious, where instinctual drives are repressed by socialised consciousness. "What Freud saw as the products of repressed libido, Adler saw as consequences of the guiding fiction, designed to protect the individual from inferiority feelings" (Edwards & Jacobs, 2003).)

Suggestion

The question is, then: could these mechanisms be exploited? According to Nissen, yes; if you create feelings of inferiority in people, it makes them prone to fundamentalist ways of thinking. If you then offer them certain ideas, well suited for compensation, they might adopt them as their own. This is known as the phenomenon of *suggestion*, which becomes a central concern in Nissen's writings in the early 1930s, (the problem of suggestion actually seems to have been a burning question of the day). It appears that several commentators during this period were concerned about the danger of suggestion, both in personal and social life, especially in political propaganda and advertising.

A crucial point for Nissen is that suggestion is not manipulation through unconscious processes; rather, he claims that suggestion exploits the conscious, rational, and logical parts of the mind. (Picking up a point from William Stern, Nissen describes suggestion as "the adoption of an alien opinion that appears to be arrived at freely and independently" (Nissen, 1930).) This means that the most suggestive ideas are not those arousing the strongest emotions, instead they are rational ideas that *fit easily* into the logical defence framework of the individual. Coherent networks of ideas, ideologies that offer a unified system of thought, are the most compelling, but the idea that there is a fixed system can be dangerous, because, as Nissen puts it, it "seems to be making demands on our thinking coming from outside ourselves" (Nissen, 1930). Such systems often appear to be merely descriptive or logical, concealing their normativity. Nissen, therefore, claims that suggestion is fundamentally value judgements being accepted as mere instances of regularity or laws in line with the logical apparatus of the individual. It is valuation disguised as necessity.

The "energy" that makes suggestion work is still found in the individual's striving. As Nissen writes, "It is around their feelings of inferiority that human beings are the most suggestible. The deeper and more extensive the feelings of inferiority, the more suggestible one is" (Nissen, 1966, p. 43, translated for this edition). That is why suggestion so often involves sexuality—in a wide sense. Even though they rejected Freud's theory of the drives, the Adlerians saw sexuality as a domain where the individual was especially vulnerable. Nissen thought that the man's vulnerability, his dependence on the woman and the fear of sexual incapability, could contribute to a particular pattern of compensation. In an effort to overcome fear, men worship strength and independence, sometimes frenetically.

Nissen on National Socialism

Nissen picked up these intellectual impulses in the early 1930s, corresponding with Adler and staying at the movement's institutions in Vienna and Berlin. But there was something else happening in the Weimar republic and Austria at the time, as he writes in a newspaper article in 1932:

> When one has seen the trains of motorcycles with swastika youth rushing through the streets of Berlin and Vienna, when one has seen some of the fanaticism in these people, one starts to realise that here lies a power to be reckoned with in the future. (Nissen, 1932, translated for this edition)

It must have made an impression on him, seeing the hunger for power, the worship of strength and aggression in the growing Nazi movement, while, at the same time, studying Adler's ideas on inferiority feelings, compensatory masculine protest, and the striving for superiority. It is perhaps no surprise that Nissen's next book, in 1934, dealt with the topic of discipline. Space does not allow me to go into detail here, but suffice it to say that he considers all forms of discipline being based on people's deepening feelings of inferiority, while offering collective compensatory strategies. This was typical for the advancing ideologies of the time. He observed, "Strength, superiority, power, ruthlessness and aggressive attitudes are perceived as the most valuable of traits" (Nissen, 1934, p. 10, translated for this edition). There is a fear of weakness, where men live in "an anxiety for not being manly enough, not being the superior, the impregnable, the secure and strong" (Nissen, 1934, p. 10). He continues, "The problem is particularly acute these days as the masculinity complex has become a central phenomenon in politics. The Fascist and the National Socialist movements are building their discipline on the worship of masculinity" (Nissen, 1934, p. 21).

This theory, linking National Socialism to inferiority feelings and vulnerable masculinity, was not very popular among Nazi sympathisers. Nissen was fiercely attacked by the right-wing press, suggesting that his "monomaniac rage against the masculine ideal [arose from] his own physical frailty and weakness" ("Ingjald Nissen," 1935): an interesting analysis.

Five years later, war was upon Europe. Nissen was soon brought in for questioning by the police in a now occupied Norway and eventually imprisoned. However, by that time, he had been able to write a new book, a fiery critique of Nazism, entitled *The Dictatorship of the Psychopaths*, which was published in 1945.

The Dictatorship of the Psychopaths

The manuscript was hidden and published only weeks after German troops left Norway: it sold out in four days. His central claim in the book is that throughout German history certain social groups have cultivated particular manipulative strategies and that these strategies resemble those used by the psychopath. The hallmark of the psychopath, according to Nissen, is the use of what he calls "ruling technique" or "suppression technique[HF1]". As he writes, "In particular this concerns methods for exploiting other people's weaknesses in order to dominate them" (Nissen, 1945, p. 14, translated for this edition). These are behavioural patterns creating a confusing atmosphere of conflict, exhausting people and depriving them of moral initiative. One example of this is the use of *secrecy* or control of information (Nissen, 1945, p. 15). Among other examples are bringing people's weaknesses, shame, and sexual insecurity to the surface. (Later, this became an important concept for Norwegian and Scandinavian feminists, trying to identify the patriarchal "master suppression techniques" (Flemmen, 2009).)

The other part of the book is historical, attempting to show how cults of masculinity and strength have existed throughout German history, culminating with National Socialism (Nissen, 1945, pp. 33, 41–42), and that these groups, for a long period of time, have virtuously cultivated suppression techniques, suggestion, censorship, and the politics of intrigue. Just as the psychopath paralyses others, depriving them of initiative, Nissen believes, these groups have pacified the people of Germany; the Germans have not been able to counteract these tendencies in culture, jurisprudence, or politics. The psychopath has a superb insight into human interaction and rules, but he lacks an emotional kernel and an understanding of what is humanly good. This, Nissen considers, is reflected in the ethical formalism in Germany, consisting, as it does, of abstract laws creating a framework for morals with no clear idea of what is substantially good. As an alternative to this, he points to the intuitionalist ethics of British philosopher G. E. Moore; according to Moore, the moral good is analytically irreducible, only graspable through an act of intuition. Rules and technical reason alone cannot be the basis of social ethics, Nissen concludes, as they can always serve as a pretext for harmful ideologies.

These ideas are an expression of the distrust in rationality that runs through much of post-war thought. It also connects to Vogt and Nissen's ideas about fundamentalism: logic and coherence individually do not ensure the ethically right outcome.

Concluding remarks

If we step out of the strictly historical perspective, we might find relevance in Nissen's thoughts even today. For instance, there is the implication that the root of fundamentalism is not the fundamentalists' ideas in themselves, but the underlying feelings of inferiority. If this is correct, confronting fundamentalist ideas aggressively and disdainfully might harden rather than soften the fundamentalist conviction. Creating a social and psychological climate of trust and safety on the other hand, might curb its growth.

Nissen's books can also be read as a clear warning against contempt for weakness and against holding strength and superiority as ideals. It is not hard to spot both an obsession with masculine strength and a fear of weakness and the feminine among today's fundamentalists and fascists. We should not neglect the idea that this is a frustrated and exaggerated version of tendencies found deep in mainstream culture.

Finally, Nissen warns against personal and structural manipulation based on our feelings of inferiority. He himself reacted strongly against new forms of propaganda to which, today, we are almost blind. In our time, the advertising industry has expanded its reach and impact tremendously, but according to Nissen's line of thinking, its mechanisms are closely related to the techniques of fascist propaganda: they both exploit people's feelings of inferiority, and they offer compensatory strategies to make up for our flaws and weaknesses, of which they themselves so virtuously make us aware.

References

Edwards, D., & Jacobs, M. (2003). *Conscious and Unconscious*. Maidenhead: Open University Press.

Flemmen, H. (2009). Hersketeknikk: en begrepshistorie, *Arr - idéhistorisk tidsskrift*, 1: 97–108.

Flemmen, H. (2012). Drømmen om verdiene - brytningene i den nykantianske Skillelinjen-kretsen, *Norsk filosofisk tidsskrift*(1): 30–41.

Moran, J. P. (2002). *The Scopes Trial. A Brief History with Documents*. New York: Palgrave.

Nissen, I. (1929). *Die methodische Einstellung: Ein Versuch ausgehend von der Fiktionstheorie*. Oslo: Kommisjon hos Dybwad.

Nissen, I. (1930). *Sjelelig forsvar: Mindreverdighetsfølelse, seksualhemning og maktstreben*. Oslo: Aschehoug.

Nissen, I. (1932). Den tyske nasjonal-sosialisme: et forsøk på en tydning I, *Arbeiderbladet*, 1 August.

Nissen, I. (1934). *Seksualitet og disiplin*. Oslo: Aschehoug.

Nissen, I. (1935). *ABC*, 18 juli.

Nissen, I. (1945). *Psykopatenes diktatur*. Oslo: Aschehoug.

Nissen, I. (1966). *Menneskelige oppgaver og utveier: Ledende idéer i mitt forfatterskap*. Oslo: Aschehoug.

Stepansky, P. E. (1983). *In Freud's Shadow: Adler in Context*. Hillsdale, NJ: Analytic Press.

Vogt, R. (1926). Om fundamentalisme (hyperlogisme) i religion og videnskap. *Kirke og kultur, 33*: 279–289.

Weiner, I. B., & Craighead, W. E. (2010). *The Corsini Encyclopedia of Psychology* (4th edn.) Vol. 1. Hoboken, NJ: Wiley.

PART III

HISTORY, LONGING, IDENTIFICATION

Editor's introduction to Chapter Eight

The chapter provides a psychoanalytic account of Mexican national identity. It explores the Mexican essayist and Nobel Prize winner for literature, Octavio Paz's *The Labyrinth of Solitude* (1960), where Paz describes "the Mexican" and gives an account of this character's customs, passions, angst, fantasies, and history. Moscovici's concept of "social representation" is used to clarify what Paz means by "the Mexican": systems of representations conceived as the body of a nation, an agreement about what the "real" of the social group is about. Paz asserts that Mexican solitude is expressed in a feeling of orphanhood that results from the loss of that which contained his reality after the Spanish conquest of Mexico. The author argues that the phantasy of the primal scene is at the basis of the repetition compulsion of Mexican history and the destructive cycle in which Mexican historicity is caught up. This phantasy is both pleasurable and over-exciting and horrific and destructive. Perhaps, it is argued, this phantasy is also at the heart of the Mexican's notoriously pleasurable readiness to contemplate horror and death, that of the self and of the other. To identify with the male object means to become a *Macho*, and, thus, acquire the status of social powerfulness. However, it also means identifying with the Spanish conquistador, he who damages when he rapes, a highly hated image. Thus, the social representations of "what it means to be a Mexican man" are full of contradiction and ambivalence. The author ends by discussing whether a real loss took place in the Conquest, or whether the image of a rape on which Mexican history-telling is centred is a subjective invention, and chooses to leave open the question of whether, or to what extent, historical events are the causes of the Mexican's psychic conflicts and phantasies.

CHAPTER EIGHT

The Mexican: phantasy, trauma, and history

Jonathan Davidoff

This chapter is motivated by a desire to reflect upon Mexican national identity, as depicted by Mexican essayist and Nobel Prize winner for literature, Octavio Paz, in his prominent work *The Labyrinth of Solitude* (1960). In this set of essays, Paz outlines "the Mexican" and gives an account of this character's customs, passions, angst, fantasies, and history. Moscovici's concept of "social representation" (2008) is helpful to describe the type of knowledge that Paz pins down when using the notion of "the Mexican": a set of images, information, and attitudes about Mexican national identity socially constructed and perpetuated. Paz's work proves to be quite psychoanalytically informed, and I will outline my interpretation of his claims and contribute some of my own. The psychoanalytic reading of the national identity of Mexicans, however, presents problematic paradoxes when it comes to attributing history with the causes of the Mexican's psychic conflicts and phantasies. I shall explore some of these problems and, with a paradoxical note, will set forth the conclusions.

What does Paz mean when he writes "the Mexican"? The answer to that is unfolded throughout the whole text of *The Labyrinth of Solitude*. Needless to say, there is no simple answer to that question, but, regardless of the elements that might make up "the Mexican", we can ask *a priori* whether what Paz describes might or might not have a clear and distinct embodiment. Paz acknowledges that his thoughts are "not concerned with the total population of Mexico, but rather with a specific group made up of those who are conscious of themselves, for one reason or another, as Mexicans" (Paz, 1961, p. 11). It is my belief, however, that "the Mexican" is not embodied in any particular group of Mexicans as such, regardless of their consciousness or unconsciousness about their Mexican-ness.

To wit, I believe that "the Mexican" Paz writes about is a figure of thought containing that which, in Paz's view, composes Mexican identity. As I shall explain, Mexican identity would be the sediment of consciousness and unconsciousness that would result from the complex interaction of Mexican history, tradition, customs, folklore, and myth. In other words, Mexico's ancient and modern history shapes the traditions, attitudes, and even the destiny of Mexico by shaping the psychic features of "the Mexican". There is a strong intuition among Mexican intellectuals, historians, and readers—sometimes expressed as a frank certainty—that Paz has a good grip on Mexican identity. In Carrion's words,

> One day, Octavio Paz drew from the boiling pot of images with which he lives due to his poet's soul, the image that shows the actual Mexican as being like Narcissus, who attentively observes his own reflection in the quiet waters of himself. (Carrion, 2002, p. 186, translated for this edition)

Further on, he adds, "Octavio, ultimately a good poet, is disgusted by any means of knowledge and expression other than his accurate, transcendent, intuitive, and poetic procedures" (Carrion, 2002, p. 186, translated for this edition). The general agreement on this seems to be reason enough to take it seriously. More precisely, the particular and shared sense of identification with Paz's "Mexican" that Mexicans experience, while being contestable, seems to prove its thesis: it is a description of the Mexican that many Mexicans accept and identify with, and, on that account, it is considered valuable and valid.

In Mexico, explains Paz, "a variety of epochs live side by side in the same areas or a very few miles apart, ignoring or devouring one another" (Paz, 1961, p. 11). Thus, Mexico is depicted as a tremendously heterogeneous country, a large part of which seems to agree, however, on a certain shared identity. Is that not the case of most nations, but, more importantly, is that not contradictory? In a sense, yes, as the unifying and homogenising idea of national identity does not correspond to the infinite differences that seem to divide nations. However, we would say that this is perfectly possible if national identity is thought of as a tacit agreement between the members of a certain community called "nation". This agreement about what makes up national identity unites and constitutes the nation, and those who accept this agreement, in turn, form the nation. This is by no means the only way to conceive of national identity. Nevertheless, I claim that this agreement, or social knowledge, is made up of a set of shared social representations that might or might not comply with the self-representation of each individual. Social representations would have their own logic and would pertain to that which is shared with other individuals. This amounts to saying that national identity is a complex set of systems of social representations that have particular dynamics, and that, indeed, while they interweave with representations of the individual self, are not simply their collective equivalent.

The French sociologist and social psychologist, Serge Moscovici, considers social representations to be "*sui generis* 'theories' or 'collective sciences' to be used for the interpretation and shaping of the real" (Moscovici, 2008, p. 10). These systems of representations are what might be conceived as the body of a nation: the agreement, in this case between Mexicans, about what the "real" of the social group is about. Therefore, we believe that Paz's account of the Mexican produces that sense of identification in Mexicans not because it describes what each individual might be, but because it describes the agreement between Mexicans, or at least between a great number of them, regarding what the Mexican is. Herein lie, as well, the limits of Paz's thought, for ethnic minorities that might not be represented in this social knowledge, or those who disagree with such ideas, are, *de facto*, excluded from the idea of "the Mexican".

Moscovici discusses the problem of the *function* of such representations. He concludes that social representations are social not because they are socially or individually constructed, but because their function is to shape social behaviour and orientate social communication (Moscovici, 2008). Further on, Moscovici asserts that "the interweaving between social representations and concrete reality is 'total'"

(Moscovici, 2008, p. 32). Thus, it becomes clear that the social representation of national identity is a collective knowledge about what the Mexican *is*. More importantly, it is a type of knowledge that precipitates behaviour and social communication. In other words, it is possible to say that social representations shape—and are immediately shaped by—traditions, attitudes, modalities of interaction, ways to communicate, history, and so on. In my opinion, Paz's image of the Mexican contemplating the waters of himself, as described by Carrion, is the discursive elaboration of these social representations.

Paz takes a step further, for he not only describes, but also interprets, that is, not only aims to answer, "what", but also "why". He offers non-univocal and complex causal explanations of traits, traditions, and customs of the Mexican. In so doing, he reveals his psychoanalytic inclination and opens a new dimension of understanding of Mexican identity. Thus, Mexican identity would not only be made up of the social knowledge to which Mexicans agree more or less "consciously", but also of complex sets of unconscious motivations, phantasies, and conflicts. These unconscious elements, following Paz, are the result of Mexican history and would, thus, underpin the more conscious social representations that constitute Mexican identity.

Paz asserts that Mexican solitude is expressed in a feeling of orphanhood that results from manifold loss:

> The Mexican feels himself to have been torn from the womb of his reality, which is both creative and destructive, both Mother and Tomb. He has forgotten the word that ties him to all those forces through which life manifests itself. Therefore he shouts or keeps silent, stabs or prays, or falls asleep for a hundred years. (Paz, 1961, p. 20)

Thus, Paz establishes that "the Mexican's" feeling of orphanhood is the effect of the loss of that which contained his reality. The conquest of Mexico at the hands of Spain, says Paz, "would be inexplicable without the treachery of the gods, who denied their own people" (Paz, 1961, p. 56). The Aztecs interpreted the conquest as abandonment, for the gods fled the world after being defeated; they let Spaniards take over the land and bring other gods in their stead. According to Paz, Cuauhtémo—the last Aztec emperor—and his people died like orphans, abandoned by everything they knew. Henceforth, Mexico's history seems to be presided over by "the drama of a consciousness that sees everything around it destroyed—even the gods" (Paz, 1961, p. 96).

In addition to this seemingly torn world, Paz argues that the Mexican has a certain relation to "a maternal figure" and a "paternal figure". In this sense, we can think of these descriptions almost like the nation's object (or imago) relations, understood psychoanalytically. Each of these objects consists of a set of social representations, which constitute their texture and contents.

In his outline of the female object, Paz begins by exploring Mexican language. He carries out a serious analysis of the word *chinga*, especially its feminine past participle, *chingada*—a rude word that literally means *raped woman*. The importance and multitude of uses of this term in Mexican Spanish cannot be here elucidated in any great detail or stressed enough. I may point out, however, that to call someone *hijo de la chingada* (son of the raped woman) is perhaps the strongest insult in Mexico. In contrast to the English insult, "bastard", which emphasises the non-recognition of the son by the father, to be the *son of the raped woman* emphasises the abjectness of such a female figure and the wickedness of the raping male. Paz also explores the historical figure of *La Malinche*, or *Malintzin*, in Nahuatl, the Aztec language. *La Malinche* is the woman who became the mistress of Spanish conquistador Hernan Cortes, and identifies her with the *raped woman* figure. In Paz's words, "The *Chingada* is the mother who has suffered—metaphorically or actually—the corrosive and defaming action implicit in the verb that gives her her name" (Paz, 1961, p. 75).

While this might not be exclusive to Mexican idiosyncrasy, the female is regarded as inferior due to her anatomic sex. Women, explains Paz, are thought to be inferior beings because, "in submitting, they open themselves up. Their inferiority is constitutional and resides in their sex and their submissiveness, which is a wound that never heals" (Paz, 1961, p. 30). The dichotomy between *closedness and openness* is regarded by the Mexican as an analogue of the dichotomy between *powerfulness and powerlessness*. Hence, the intrinsic powerlessness that the Mexican attributes to women, moreover, the constant damage to which women must be exposed, is thought to be necessary.

Paz describes another side to the female object, embodied mainly in the Virgin of Guadalupe, the Indian Virgin. Mexico is a profoundly "Guadalupan" country, and Paz explains this as a superimposition of the Virgin Mary on the Aztec goddess Tonantzin. This goddess became central in Aztec cosmology after the masculine deities were defeated by the Spaniards. The Virgin of Guadalupe, above all a non-raped Mother, is regarded, indeed, as the Mother of the poor and the orphans. She brings comfort to all her children, whom she has conceived without being torn open and damaged. Another side of this loving aspect of the object is the image of *La Llorona,* a famous folklore character of an ever-crying woman who laments endlessly the loss of her dead children.

Summing up, I would say that what I have described as the female object is indeed a number of social representations that set a particular place for women in society. They also regulate the interaction between men and women, children and mothers, and also between the Mexican and some female avatars, such as the motherland or a historical event. For example, explains Paz, "if the *Chingada* is the representation of the violated Mother, it is appropriate to associate her with the Conquest, which was also a violation, not only in the historical sense but also in the very flesh of Indian women" (Paz, 1961, p. 86).

Thus, it is a type of knowledge about the woman, or the Mother, that, according to Paz, is determined by historical circumstances. The feminine object is devalued, constantly damaged by the sexual relation, intrinsically inferior due to the openness of her sex, but preserved and idealised on account of her comforting, non-sexual features. Nevertheless, this loving aspect of the object has also a masochistic quality to it, for it is an object that suffers endlessly for her children's suffering. It is in this particular feature, according to Paz, where Mexican feminine narcissism resides: in being able to bear all of life's suffering. I would say, then, that the Mexican's relation to this object is split and sadomasochistic. Nevertheless, it is also tinged with a tremendous sense of guilt, for the object is constantly damaged and still it endures all the suffering that is inflicted upon it.

The masculine object, on the other hand, is thought to be a *Macho.* Paz explains that

> the Mexican *macho*—the male—is a hermetic being, closed up in himself, capable of guarding both himself and whatever has been confided to him. Manliness is judged according to one's invulnerability to enemy arms or the impacts of the outside world. (Paz, 1961, p. 31)

The contrast between the male's closedness with the feminine openness thus becomes quite clear. The *Macho* is a closed entity that penetrates and tears open. Paz resorts to language again and explains this with other usages of the word *chinga*, such as *chingadera* and *chingon*. *Chingadera* is a derivation of the word that literally means "mean or vicious deed", presumably "a rape", and *chignon* literally means "the champion who rapes". In this sense, the *Macho* is he who commits *chingaderas*, mean deeds or rapes, and he is the *chingon*, the one who is exalted because he rapes. It is the *Macho* who damages and tears open the female by raping her. In Paz's words,

> The *macho* commits *chingaderas*, that is, unforeseen acts that produce confusion, horror and destruction. He opens the world, and in doing so, he rips and tears it, and this violence provokes a great, sinister laugh. And in its own way, it is just: it re-establishes the equilibrium and puts things in their places, by reducing them to dust, to misery, to nothingness. (Paz, 1961, p. 81)

In this sense, there is an ambivalent identificatory relationship between the Mexican and the male object. The identification with such an object implies becoming a powerful and damaging object, but also accepting the damage that the object might cause in the female object and in the self of the Mexican. Paz explains that

> it is impossible not to notice the resemblance between the figure of the *macho* and that of the Spanish conquistador. This is the model—more mythical than real—that determines the images that Mexican people form of men in power: caciques, feudal lords, hacienda owners, generals, politicians, captains of industry. They are all *machos, chingones*. (Paz, 1961, p. 82)

In this sense, to identify with the male object means to become a *Macho*, and, thus, acquire the status of social powerfulness. However, it also means to identify with the Spanish conquistador, he who damages when he rapes, an image that is deeply hated by the Mexican. This is the drama of the relation between the Mexican and the male object, and, thus, the social representations of "what it means to be a Mexican man" are full of contradiction and ambivalence. The regulation of behaviour that these social representations exert is remarkable: the relation between the Mexican and his governors, who are typically male; his relation to the figure of the deeply hated, feared, loved, and admired paternal figure, the relation between male colleagues, etc.

Furthermore, another example of the social representation of the *Macho* regulating masculine behaviour is emphasised by Paz. As in the other cases, he resorts to language usage to envisage it. Explains Paz,

> It is likewise significant that masculine homosexuality is regarded with a certain indulgence insofar as the active agent is concerned. The passive agent is an abject, degraded being. This ambiguous conception is made very clear in the word game battles—full of obscene allusions and double meanings—that are so popular in Mexico City. Each of the speakers tries to humiliate his adversary with verbal traps and ingenious linguistic combinations, and the loser is the person who cannot think of a comeback, who has to swallow his opponent's jibes. These jibes are full of aggressive sexual allusions; the loser is possessed, violated, by the winner and the spectators laugh and sneer at him. Masculine homosexuality is tolerated, then, on condition that it consists in violating a passive agent. (Paz, 1961, p. 39)

Thus, the rivalry between men is manifested in the ingenious linguistic fights that inevitably assign one opponent the status of powerful penetrator, and the other that of a powerless, passive, and torn open subject. This homosexual aspect of the relation between men is thus regulated by the social representation of the *Macho*: the winner being the male who tears open, and the loser the shamefully raped female who submits passively to the winner.

We have intimated that the Mexican's social representations of the male and the female, as well as his feeling of orphanhood, can be thought of as a collective version of object relations. In this sense, object relations are a set of phantasies—that is, representations, images, thoughts, feelings, impulses, and affects—that are predominantly unconscious and linked to an object. They regulate the subject's behaviour and view of the world and have an impact on those of the external object as well. In this sense, splitting, projection, identification, and projective identification are the most prominent mechanisms with which the subject relates to external and internal objects. Through the operation of these mechanisms, phantasies about the object are constituted (Hinshelwood, 1989). Thus, the female and male objects have different aspects to them: loving, aggressive, damaging, sadomasochistic, and so on. The relation to those objects is tinged by the phantasies around them, for instance, a raping male object or a raped female object.

To account for the relation between a male and a female object is, I believe, on the right track. In this sense, I agree with Paz in that these imagos shape the Mexican's social behaviour. However, I believe there is more to it, and herein lies my personal interpretation of Paz's account. The raping relation between them, therefore, amounts to a primal scene phantasy where, in Paz's view, the Father enjoys while the Mother suffers. However, Freud explains in his 1918 case study, "The Wolf Man", that the suffering of the Mother is interpreted as pleasurable and the enjoyment of the father implies castration as well. Therefore, what the primal scene conceals is precisely the blurring of pleasure and pain and their coalescence into a sticky, undifferentiated, exciting mass. This is, I believe, a step forward that implies reversing what is visible and commonsensical into its opposite with the idea that truly unconscious representations do not abide by the laws of logic (i.e., of non-contradiction, negation, and the principle of identity). In other words, what is true for one object might be false simultaneously and, furthermore, might be true and false of another object as well, which, in turn, might not be fully "an other" object, but a displacement of the first one, and so forth. This form of relation to the unconscious, fluid and in the spirit of Walter Benjamin's notion of *bricolage*, in my view, is lacking in Paz's account.

What is the contribution of interpreting thus the relation between the male and female objects in the Mexican's phantasy? What is the precise contribution of understanding it as a primal scene? I believe that this phantasy, still not largely understood thus, lies on the basis of the repetition compulsion of Mexican history and the destructive cycle in which Mexican historicity is caught up. This primal scene phantasy, I believe, is at the heart of this, as it has the double property of being horrific, fearful, and destructive, as well as pleasurable and over-exciting, hence its stickiness. Furthermore, perhaps this phantasy is at the heart of the Mexican's notoriously pleasurable readiness to contemplate horror and death, that of the other and of the self. In Paz's words,

> . . . he is even complacent and familiar in his dealings with it (suffering). The bloody Christs in our village churches, the macabre humor in some of our newspaper headlines, our wakes, the custom of eating skull-shaped cakes and candies on the Day of the Dead . . . Our cult of death is also a cult of life, in the same way that love is a hunger for life and a longing for death. (Paz, 1961, p. 23)

While this might be one of the invaluable sources of Mexican cultural richness and singularity, and, thus, a source of potential creativity, as Meltzer (1973) points out, it also has destructive implications for the Mexican psychic economy, Mexican apprehension of reality, and, therefore, the writing of Mexican history. In other words, the question would be "why do all these phantasies (that of the raped Mother, the raping father, or of being an orphan) persist?" Why do Mexicans happily and willingly construct and share the idea of Mexico establishing a relation with the USA, for example, in which Mexico is a victim of rape and the USA the perpetrator? Why do these phantasies still seem to shape Mexico's development? I claim that this is due to the pleasurable pain, painful pleasure, or the state in which these opposites—pleasure and pain—coalesce into an undifferentiated mass of horrid, pleasurable, and viscous over-excitement caused by this primal scene phantasy. I believe this is at the heart of the Mexican's inability to write a different version of history to the one that seems doomed to fail over and over again. To sustain this, it would be easy to find the prolific public rhetoric of "Mexico never changing", "repeating the same all over again", and so forth, everywhere in public discourse.

Psychoanalytic interpretations of history such as this one, where the very writing of history is underpinned by phantasy, have proved to be helpful by expanding the possible understanding of the meaningfulness of historical events. The account I have just advanced, however, leans towards a *subjective or internal* account of Mexican identity, and presents problematic issues for historical practice.

To some extent, this subjective aspect of historicising leans towards an understanding of *the Mexican as a subject that writes history*. This amounts to saying, for instance, that the Conquest, being understood, historicised, and remembered as a rape does not necessarily imply that, in fact, it was a rape. It is only a rape in so far as it is felt, interpreted, remembered, and acted out as a rape. On the other hand, to assert categorically that *it was a rape* (regardless of how many concrete rapes took place) is problematic as well; why call it a rape and not a lost war and a subsequent colonisation? Or perhaps it could be remembered mostly as a robbery? Why a rape?

This is the problem of history taken from a post-structuralist point of view, especially from the point of view of Roland Barthes. We cannot explore Barthes' viewpoint in detail, but only stress his view of the non-referentiality of the historical text. In this context, non-referentiality means the impossibility of the historical text, and of language in general, representing the real. This is due to the closed nature of the Saussurean linguistic sign, and, therefore, of the symbolic on which Barthesian theory relies. The symbolic sign makes no reference to the real, only to other signs. The sign is a closed entity composed of signifiers and the sliding of meaning produced by the linkage of signifiers, that is, the signified. Thus, according to Barthes, the historical narration dies because the sign of history, from then onwards, is not the real, but the intelligible (Barthes, 1964).

Thus, it would be possible to account for the history of the conquest of Mexico as a rape, regardless of the *real* nature of the conquest, which would be inaccessible to the historian anyway. In this sense, *The Labyrinth of Solitude* could be considered as a history book in its own right. This structuralist view would affirm that the *real dimension of the event* would only restrict free play of *difference*, or *dissemination*; it would be an impediment to the infinite possibilities of interpretation available in language. In historical terms, it would restrict the possible infinite versions of history from being written, like that of the Conquest of Mexico as a rape.

Notwithstanding, this point of view brings about the problem of distinguishing fiction from reality within the historic text. Ricoeur (2010) explains, "to the extent that the fictional tale and the historical tale participate of the same narrative structures, the rejection of the referential dimension by the structuralist orthodoxy spans the whole of the literary textuality" (Ricoeur, 2010, p. 322, translated for this edition). Thus, if the referential dimension is rejected, then, indeed, so is the difference between fiction and reality. This, on the one hand, can liberate history and the task of the historian from the constraint against writing more *subjective* accounts of history, such as the one Paz writes. But, on the other hand, it also undermines the possibility of asserting the factual occurrence of the events of the past, *a will to truth* that is central to history and its main, if not only, difference with fiction.

When writing about the Conquest, the recognition of the reality of the events is invaluable for the victims, or heirs, of the historical trauma. Barthes, for his part, suggests that history should be written using the middle voice (Barthes, 1964), an oblique linguistic form that resists dichotomisation and leans on undecidability. This way, the aboutness of a history that writes about trauma is left as an undecidable. While this might be of use when writing history that should not be cornered into any form of narrowness, this form of writing can be felt by the victim of trauma as an alliance with the perpetrator. In this sense, a weakness in the historical denunciation or recognition of the reality of the traumatic experience can be as traumatic as the event itself. Moreover, according to LaCapra, undecidability and unregulated difference, threatening to disarticulate relations, confuse self and other, and collapse all distinctions, including that of present and past and of fiction and history, are related to transference. These prevail in trauma and in post-trauma acting out, in which one is haunted and possessed by the past and performatively caught up in the repetition of traumatic scenes, therefore confused and not being able to tell the difference, in this case, between fiction and history (LaCapra, 2001).

Thus, we encounter the tension between a subjective account of history where language and writing would be the only means and operations at hand, and an objective account of history where the real would be necessary and whose presence would be unquestionable. Paz's account resists a definitive categorisation in this sense. He moves somewhat freely between poetry, history, and interpretation. We do find in Paz's writing, however, evidence of what LaCapra described as features of the traumatised, that is, a disarticulation of relations, which would explain his inclination to ignore the distinction between fiction and history:

> Is it not extraordinary that the effects persist after the causes have disappeared? And that the effects hide the causes? In this sphere, it is impossible to distinguish between causes and effects. Actually, there are no causes and effects, merely a complex of interpenetrating reactions and tendencies. (Paz, 1961, p. 73)

If there are signs of traumatic writing in Paz's account, something real must have occurred and something real must have been lost—something caused the trauma. In this sense, LaCapra asserts that in historic traumatic situations, loss, lack, and absence are confounded. LaCapra understands loss as the sorrowful deprivation of an object in the past and lack would be its analogue in the present. Absence, on the other hand, would point to metaphysics, full unity or ultimate foundations in general: that which has never been had, nothingness

(LaCapra, 2001). When loss is confounded with absence, then the process of mourning the specific loss is arrested and might lead to a melancholic state: an impossible never-ending mourning and possibly to acting out that which is not mourned (LaCapra, 2001). In this sense, we may assert that the repetition compulsion in the case of the Mexican is motivated not only by the primal scene phantasy we described before, but by the fact that there is indeed an unmourned trauma, which has not been worked through due to the misrecogni tion of lack and absence. In Paz's words,

> . . . and (the Mexican) crosses history like a jade comet, now and then giving off flashes of lightning. What is he pursuing in his eccentric course? He wants to go back beyond the catastrophe he suffered: he wants to be a sun again, to return to the centre of that life from which he was separated one day. (Was that day the Conquest? The Independence?) Our solitude has the same roots as religious feelings. It is a form of orphanhood, an obscure awareness that we have been torn from the All, and an ardent search: a flight and return, an effort to re-establish the bonds that unite us with the universe. (Paz, 1961, p. 20)

It is my opinion that this testifies that indeed, the questions of uncertainty of origins—intrinsically related to absence—and the trauma of the Conquest as a deadly war and its consequences—linked rather to loss—are confounded in this passage and in the Mexcian psyche. This suggests that indeed, trauma in Mexican history remains unmourned and unworked through. The Conquest remains being seen and felt as a rape and as a sign of a "lost paradise", and not simply as a part of Mexico's history, albeit a bloody and painful one. This quality in the historisation of the Conquest impedes Mexico from having a present and a non-circular future.

If the interpretation of the rape as a primal scene is taken further, then we find that there is a condition of exclusion from the parental couple: the Mexican becomes a child that observes his father raping his mother and suspects that both parents enjoy it and suffer it. This might arouse in the "little Mexican" a deep impression, excitation, feelings of rage against each parental figure, but also feelings of rage and jealousy about being excluded from the parental coitus. This would be, perhaps, an analogous condition to LaCapra's notion of absence, for the anger about being excluded from the parental couple conceals the longing for the pre-oedipal stage of mother–child symbiosis. This is, as in the case of absence, a longing for something that occurred at the dawn of time, the longing of the metaphysical foundational paradise. The Mexican seems to long for this, and, thus, he conflates the Conquest-rape, a traumatic loss, with his grievance of never having been actually included in the parental sexuality: in this sense, an absence. To recognise this, for the Mexican, would imply coming to terms with feelings of anger, envy, and exclusion. Also, it would imply the insight of the Mexican clinging to a phantasy that prevents his development. In other words, that the putative pre-Hispanic paradise is a chimera and that to cling on to it implies a refusal to develop in the present. This must not obliterate, of course, the trauma and the loss that needs to be mourned as well.

I recognise that in my analysis so far there are two poles: on the one hand, the traumatic, implying that a real loss took place in the Conquest, on the other, that which pertains to the realm of phantasy: a primal scene that precedes the trauma and that accentuates the subjective, rather than the objective, aspect of history. In this problem, posed by history, we bring our investigations to a close. It is pertinent to ask ourselves a few questions to clarify the dilemmas that the historical point of view introduces. Are the social representations of national identity the sedimentation of objective history, or are they the product of writing, that is, of subjective creation? Was the Conquest a rape and, therefore, traumatic, or does the phantasy of the raping male object lead the Mexican to interpret it in that way? In other words, can we conclude that the phantasies that we described are the ones that drive the Mexican to interpret events and history in such a way, or are these phantasies the effect of such history? Have these phantasies shaped Mexico's history, or has Mexico's traumatic history driven the Mexican to amass these fantasies?

In my view, the most pertinent way to understand the relation of these dichotomies is with Winnicott's view of culture and history as a transitional space and, therefore, as necessarily concealing a paradox. According to Winnicott, the transitional space—where history would be produced and thought—is the intermediary space between the subjective and the objective (Winnicott, 1953). However, the subjective is unthinkable without the objective, and *vice versa*. The transitional is a space that freezes the moment of the constitution of the antinomy, when one pole necessitates the other pole to constitute itself. In this sense, I believe that the linguistic sign, the operation of writing, or the

subjective account of history are unthinkable without what is heterogeneous to them: the real, the objective, and the events that occurred
in the past. These two groups hold, indeed, a necessarily paradoxical
relation; hence the impossibility for me to conclude this investigation
other than with a paradox. This paradox, in my view, is a metaphysical question that is concealed in psychoanalytic thought and theory,
about which different authors have different theoretical stands. I
believe Winnicott's transitional space and its inherent paradox of the
objective and the subjective is the most honest one, for it does not
assert the truth or falsity of either of the poles of the antinomy, but
holds fast to their necessary paradoxical relation. I believe this is also
the most honest way in which history, subjective and national, can be
written. Of course, the losing of certainties, historical and subjective,
is what we are left with to face, but is not that a possible outcome of
a successful process of analysis? The bearing of the uncertainty of
ultimate causes and the balance and necessity of subjective and
objective dimensions that inextricably, and paradoxically, penetrate
each other: the bearing, the incarnating, of a question.

References

Barthes, R. (1964). *Le discours de l'histoire*. In: *Le Bruissement de la langue*
(pp. 153–166). Paris: Seuil, 1984.

Carrion, J. (2002). *La raiz y la flor del mexicano*. In: R. Bartra (Ed.), *Anatomia
del Mexicano* (pp. 185–203). Mexico: Plaza y Janes.

Freud, S. (1918b). *From the History of an Infantile Neurosis. S.E.*, 17: 7–122.
London: Hogarth.

Hinshelwood, R. D. (1989). *A Dictionary of Kleinian Thought*. London: Free
Association Books.

LaCapra, D. (2001). *Writing History, Writing Trauma*. London: Johns
Hopkins University Press.

Meltzer, D. (1973). *Sexual States of Mind*. Strathtay, Perthshire: Clunie
Press.

Moscovici, S. (2008). *Psychoanalysis: Its Image and Its Public*, D. Macey
(Trans.). Cambridge: Polity Press.

Paz, O. (1961). *The Labyrinth of Solitude*, M. Kempt & B. Phillips (Trans.).
New York: Grove Press.

Ricoeur, P. (2010). *La memoria, la historia, el olvido*. Buenos Aires: FCE.

Winnicott, D. W. (1953). Transitional objects and transitional phenomena: a study of the first not-me possession. *International Journal of Psychoanalysis, 34*(2): 89–97.

Editor's introduction to Chapter Nine

The chapter discusses Eric Fromm's ideas on politics and the nation. His works relate to Freud and Marx as part of the European humanist tradition. Although he valued Freud's appreciation of the unconscious, Fromm doubted that a destructive instinct is intrinsic to Man, and argued that Freudian analysis over-emphasised the importance of the family while paying too little attention to the person's wider social ties. He valued Marx's thoughts on "positive freedom" and applauded Marx's recognition that, in each historical period, people shaped themselves through the act of living, particularly through economic engagement. Fromm believed he could fill a gap in Marx by explaining how society's economic "base" influenced its political and ideological "superstructure". There were two keys: social character and social unconscious. *Escape from Freedom* provided a path-breaking examination of the socially widespread foundations of National Socialism, while *Anatomy of Human Destructiveness* applied clinical insights to the Third Reich's leadership. In relation to nationalism, Fromm identified a complex of necrophilia, narcissism, and incestuous ties that formed a "syndrome of decay" related to poor mental health and national hatred. He believed modern society was institutionalising elements supportive of the "syndrome of decay"; an environment restricting individuality and spontaneity shapes a new kind of being: organisation man or *homo mechanicus*—a person who has been reduced to a mere item. Although there are some problems associated with Fromm's analysis, the author argues, his body of work provides many sensitive insights into the human condition and society's impact upon it.

CHAPTER NINE

Psychoanalysis and peace: Erich Fromm on history, politics, and the nation

Martyn Housden

Introduction

In the 1950s and 1960s, Erich Fromm supported the American Socialist Party and criticised the nuclear threat to peace; yet, despite his contemporary interests, Fromm's work was permeated by history. This reflected a life spanning a remarkable period. Born to an orthodox Jewish family in Frankfurt in 1900, his life took in the *Kaiserreich* as well as the First World War. He experienced the German revolution followed by Weimar's democracy. He remained in Germany to witness the origins of the Third Reich, but observed the Second World War from a distance. There followed the occupation and division of Germany, the rise of the Cold War, and, more optimistically, the founding of the United Nations. From his vantage point in the Americas (first the USA, later Mexico), Fromm saw McCarthyism, the Korean War, the Cuban Missile Crisis, the assassination of John F. Kennedy, Vietnam, and the civil rights movement (see Internationale-Eric-Fromm-Gesellschaft, e.g., Fromm, 1996a).

Fromm became a cosmopolitan who lived at a time that was a "social laboratory" for the possibilities open to mankind (Fromm, 1980, p. 10). He became convinced that mental health was never unaffected by the impact of social, economic, political, and cultural influences—that psychoanalysis could not abstract the individual from his context (Fromm, 1963a, p. 78). Moreover, he grasped that few human situations were static for long, that the passage of time brought the forming and re-forming of psychologically important social phenomena. The awareness that a person changes both his context and himself as the two interact helps us understand why Fromm discussed history so frequently.

History: autobiography, ideas, and mechanisms of change

Autobiography

Erich Fromm appreciated his autobiography. He knew he had been born into a Europe marked by late nineteenth century optimism (Fromm, 1980, p. 5). Later, he remembered the descent of this out-wardly successful world into conflict, a cataclysm which taught him to doubt that the existence of armaments could ever prevent disaster, and that phrases such as "if you want peace, prepare for war" were weasel words masking less honest desires. As the First World War progressed, he became perplexed that all sides believed they were fighting for justice, freedom, and peace. Understandably, by 1918, Fromm was a troubled young man (Fromm, 1980, pp. 5–10).

If Fromm was right that puzzlement marks the start of wisdom, then his path to knowledge began at this point (Fromm, 1951, p. 3). Subsequent conversations with workers in his father's firm provoked an interest in the idea of peace based on Marxist internationalism; yet personal themes moved him, too. Fromm knew a young woman who broke off an engagement to be married. Thereafter, she spent time with her father, committing suicide after he died and choosing to be buried with him (Fromm, 1980, p. 4). As a youngster, Fromm could not understand her choices, and the case laid the basis for his interest in Freud.

History of ideas: Marx and Freud

Fromm's work related his autobiographical concerns to Europe's history of ideas. He argued that notions of both a common human potential and an unconscious can be traced back to Spinoza, and his writings are full of references to Goethe, Herder, and Nietzsche, less usually Master Eckhardt (Fromm, 1980, p. 96, 2009, pp. 49–54), but it is to Freud and Marx that Fromm returned repeatedly—both of whom he saw as part of the European humanist tradition (Fromm, 1980, p. 24). Although he valued Freud's appreciation of the unconscious, Fromm disputed many features of his work. Fromm doubted that a destructive instinct is intrinsic to man, also that the civilising process necessarily conflicts with the human essence. Freudian analysis was said to overemphasise the importance of the family while ignoring that institution's relationship to wider society and, relatedly, to pay too little attention to the person's wider social ties (Fromm, 1980, pp. 57–58). In the end, Fromm saw Freud's model of the human being as limited: "It is actually the concept of a well-functioning member of the middle-class at the beginning of the twentieth century, who is sexually and economically potent" (Fromm, 1980, p. 62).

Marx's thinking, although chronologically earlier, was considered more perceptive. Marx had a better understanding of the active, productive person. His idea of freedom was richer. It was not just "freedom from" but "freedom to"; that is to say, Marx understood more fully the "positive realization of individuality" attainable by people (Fromm, 1980, p. 64). So, while Freud's individual sought emancipation from his mother, Marx's person laboured for liberation from nature—a quest which opened up many more possibilities in life (Fromm, 1980, p. 64). Admittedly, not everything in Marx was correct. Fromm felt he focused on the economy to the detriment of understanding man's inner life. He neglected morality, assuming that innate goodness would emerge naturally. Likewise, he underestimated the difficulty of achieving socialism, failing to see that social ownership of the means of production could alienate workers; yet there remained a tremendous amount to praise in Marx's work (Fromm, 1963a, pp. 264–265).

Fromm applauded Marx's recognition that, in each historical period, people shaped themselves through the act of living, particularly through economic engagement (Fromm, 1980, p. 39). This was exactly the sort of dynamic undertaking that Fromm required to explain human nature, since society not only shaped people, but they made and re-made society too—hence altering the social and economic constellations acting on them in the first place. So, while

Fromm commended as critical Marx's concept of alienation (the person's failure to have intimate and productive experiences stimulating personal growth), he felt mankind could overcome it, given the right choices. If Marx believed that people could liberate themselves from capitalism's repression and injustice, then they could also liberate the unconscious by overcoming social patterns injurious to mental health.

Social character and social unconscious

Fromm attempted to unite the strengths of Freud and Marx, while rectifying their flaws. Adopting a model of man capable of free will, none the less he maintained that our exercise of reason is more than offset by our socially determined psychological characteristics, only some of which breach our consciousness, despite having decisive importance. As he put it,

> Our conscious motivations, ideas and beliefs are a blend of false information, biases, irrational passions, rationalizations, prejudices, in which morsels of truth swim around and give the reassurance, albeit false, that the whole mixture is real and true. The thinking process attempts to organize this whole cesspool of illusions according to the laws of logic and plausibility. (Fromm, 2009, p. 80)

Meanwhile, the unconscious is

> . . .[a]side from irrational passions, almost the whole knowledge of reality. The unconscious is basically determined by society, which produces irrational passions and provides its members with various kinds of fiction and thus forces the truth to become the prisoner of the alleged rationality. (Fromm, 2009, p. 80)

Pursuing this line further, Fromm believed he could fill a gap in Marx: by explaining how society's economic "base" influenced its political and ideological "superstructure". There were two keys: social character and social unconscious. The former Fromm defined as "the nucleus of character structure . . . shared by most members of the same culture" (Fromm, 1980, p. 74, 1963a, p. 78). It defined those socially transferred characteristics which enabled members of given social groups to behave as required, and was important because conscious choices were deemed inadequate to ensure adaptation to a social system sufficient to sustain its smooth functioning. Social character channelled an individual's energies, ensuring that a person *wanted* to do what the social system *required*. Fromm continued to maintain that ideas gained popularity at any given moment because of the given social character. In turn, he accepted that these ideas could motivate action to reform the economic base that subsequently would have an impact on the social character being produced. To Fromm's mind, then, history involved a constant, reciprocal flow between the economic conditions of a society, its dominant character, and the ideas produced (Fromm, 1980, p. 83).

This was not all. Fromm felt the person can adapt to all manner of circumstances, existing with various social characters and unconsciousnesses. Yet, the individual is not a "blank sheet of paper on which culture writes its text" (Fromm, 1963a, p. 81). Historically, the person has emerged from unity with nature, from primeval ties to clan, blood, and soil. Rational ways to address the loss of oneness with nature revolve around the human being's basic programming to search for "happiness, harmony, love and freedom", the thwarting of which causes psychic revolt (Fromm, 1963a, p. 81). Since the frustration of our basic needs could also be provoked by prevailing social conditions, it followed that groups not only shared a social character, but a social unconscious. By this, Fromm meant

> . . . those areas of repression which are common to most members of a society; these commonly repressed elements are those contents which a given society cannot permit its members to be aware of if the society with its specific contradictions is to operate successfully. (Fromm, 1980, p. 84)

Naturally, the social unconscious helped explain the attraction of given ideas in society and provided a motive force for social change.

Fromm offered an interpretation of social and characterological change over time. For him, the history of the individual and of society had a parallel. The former struggled for independence from the mother, while the latter sought independence from nature, both processes involving loss of an unthinking oneness with something "larger" than ourselves. He defined the human vulnerabilities requiring satisfaction in both processes:

The human desire to experience union with others is rooted in the specific conditions of existence that characterize the human species and is one of the strongest motivators of human behaviour. By the combination of minimal instinctive determination and maximal development of the capacity of reason, we human beings have lost our original oneness with nature. In order not to feel utterly isolated—which would, in fact, condemn us to insanity—we need to find a new unity: with our fellow beings and with nature. (Fromm, 2009, p. 86)

Our capacities to reason and to feel isolated are critical to understanding the trends of human life—individual and collective alike.

Theory of history

Fromm believed that, in the Middle Ages, many of the existential problems troubling us today were absent. Then, the individual experienced "belonging" and "meaning" simply: as defined by his social and economic role enmeshed in feudal ties (Fromm, 1960, Chapter Three). Even if medieval life lacked much of the freedom taken for granted today, in some important psychological respects, society offered greater levels of security. The gradual emergence of capitalism—bringing with it a middle class—challenged traditional social restrictions and, in association with the Renaissance and Enlightenment, prepared the way for modern life. Although the developing person had more options available, ultimately this would have a price. Capitalism and new ways of thinking destroyed the old economic and social orders, such that the "individual was left alone; everything depended on his own effort, not on the security of his traditional status" (Fromm, 1960, p. 60).

Fromm characterised the transformation as from a phase of seeking "freedom from" (from convention, control, and the power of nature) to one of "freedom to" (to develop yourself as you see best) (Fromm, 1963a, p. 60). Initially, the new freedoms yielded positive results. The Renaissance fostered a spirit in which "ideas of human dignity, of the unity of the human race, of universal political and religious unity found . . . an unencumbered expression" (Fromm, 2009, p. 118). Traces of hope were still present in the nineteenth century, when most thinkers still believed production processes should help mankind unfold its powers and acquire justice and truth (Fromm, 1963a, p. 233). Capitalism still operated within limits and there was no boundless quest for expenditure on constantly new satisfactions—as would come later.

Sadly, the First World War shattered the humanism that had been emerging since the Middle Ages. It introduced a period marked by the creation of new national communities in which Fascism, Nazism, and Stalinism provided sanctuary to worried individuals at a terrible cost.

> Man—freed from the traditional bonds of the medieval community, afraid of the new freedom which transformed him into an isolated atom—escaped into a new idolatry of blood and soil, of which nationalism and racism are the two most evident expressions. (Fromm, 1963a, p. 58)

Self-subjugation to state and leader was a kind of "clan worship" which could amount to insanity.

> Nationalism, originally a progressive movement, replaced the bonds of feudalism and absolutism. The average man today obtains his sense of identity from his belonging to a nation, rather than from his being a "son of man". His objectivity, that is, his reason, is warped by this fixation. He judges the "stranger" with different criteria than the members of his own clan. His feelings towards the stranger are equally warped. Those who are not "familiar" by bonds of blood and soil (expressed by common language, customs, food, songs, etc.) are looked upon with suspicion, and paranoid delusions about them can spring up at the slightest provocation. This incestuous fixation not only poisons the relationship of the individual to the stranger, but to the members of his own clan and to himself. The person who has not freed himself from the ties to blood and soil is not yet fully born as a human being; his capacity for love and reason are crippled; he does not experience himself nor his fellow man in their – and his own – human reality. (Fromm, 1963a, p. 58)

Destructiveness, however, reached a new apogee at the end of the Second World War, when nuclear weapons underlined that murder had become "a legitimate means for attaining political goals" (Fromm, 1980, pp. 155–58).

> Against this background, the promise of unlimited progress that seemed possible in the nineteenth century was subverted as, despite increased affluence and freedom, by the middle of the twentieth

century people became 'mentally sicker' than a century before. (Fromm, 2009, p. 2)

They became cogs in bureaucratic machines, their happiness never satisfied by the ceaseless stimulation of passing fancies; economic progress resulted in divisions between rich and poor states; and technological advances only brought environmental disaster and nuclear threat. As a result, in societies supposed to be dedicated to pleasure, there was substantial pain. (Fromm, 2009, pp. 3–5)

Without question, Fromm implied that the discipline of history was impossible without psychoanalytical understanding, but, in the process, he also raised the reverse question: can you have psychoanalysis without historical awareness? Fromm saw intimate links between what we are now, what we have been, and what we are likely to become—all based on individuals and society interacting through constant processes of change, and both Fromm's critique of modernity and his analysis of nationalism had still more to say.

Syndrome of decay

Taking nationalism first, Fromm identified a complex of necrophilia, narcissism, and incestuous ties that formed a "syndrome of decay" related to poor mental health and national hatred.

Necrophilia

Fromm thought a cleavage can exist in people: the love of life (biophilia) *vs.* the love of death (necrophilia). While the former is associated with growth, progress, and mental health, the latter is associated with violence, evil, and mental illness (Fromm, 1964, pp. 37–38). In addition, necrophilia is related to the love of mechanical processes over organic development, of order and control over spontaneity (since control "kills life"), and of possession over less definite relationships. Predictably, Fromm identified Hitler and Stalin as necrophilous types who, through their use of brutality, attracted other necrophiles—such as Adolf Eichmann—as followers (Fromm, 1964, pp. 38–58).

Narcissism

Adolf Hitler was also identified as narcissistic. Although Fromm accepted a kind of narcissism was normal and that it—even as an "element of insanity"—might protect leaders from self-doubts, he recognised the characteristic could become malignant (Fromm, 1964, p. 76). So, while it is acceptable to feel pride in what you achieve, Fromm believed malignant narcissism reflected solely who you are. This kind of narcissism ties the characteristic to nationalism, and certain social groups were deemed particularly vulnerable to it:

> For those who are economically and culturally poor, narcissistic pride in belonging to the group is the only—and often a very effective— source of satisfaction. Precisely because life is not "interesting" to them, and does not offer them possibilities for developing interests, they may develop an extreme form of narcissism. Good examples of this phenomenon in recent years are the racial narcissism which existed in Hitler's Germany, and which is found in the American South today. In both instances the core of the racial superiority feeling was, and still is, the lower middle class; this backward class, which in Germany as well as in the American South has been economically and culturally deprived, without any realistic hope of changing its situa- tion (because they are the remnants of an older and dying form of soci- ety) has only one satisfaction: the inflated image of itself as the most admirable group in the world, and of being superior to another racial group that is singled out as inferior. The member of such a backward group feels: "Even though I am poor and uncultured I am somebody important because I belong to the most admirable group in the world—I am white"; or "I am an Aryan." (Fromm, 1964, p. 79)

Since malignant narcissism lacks the relationship to reality affor- ded by actual personal achievement, it has no limits. If a susceptible group's narcissism is deeply wounded, the resulting collective rage can demand the offender's annihilation (Fromm, 1964, pp. 86–88).

Incest

Fromm regarded the desire for pre-genital incestuous symbiosis as a fundamental human passion, but he did not interpret it in a Freudian or sexual way, rather as a deep desire for protection, unconditional love, and the alleviation of all responsibilities as an infant experiences from its mother (Fromm, 1964, p. 97). As the person becomes older, the protective role is taken up differently:

> Genetically, mother is the first personification of the power that protects and guarantees certainty. But she is by no means the only one. Later on, when the child grows up, mother as a person is often replaced or complemented by the family, the clan, by all who share the same blood and have been born on the same soil. Later, when the size of the group increases, the race and the nation, religion or political parties become the "mothers", the guarantors of protection and love. (Fromm, 1964, p. 98)

Fromm believed a strong correlation exists between people fixated on their mother and those experiencing strong ties to "nation and race, soil and blood"—and once more he could have referred to Adolf Hitler. This allegiance to a substitute mother creates a separation from those owing allegiance to a different one. So, while Fromm believed incestuous fixation prevents an individual experiencing the freedom necessary to develop adequately, it also prevents the person experiencing as fully human anyone bound to another mother substitute (e.g., a different nation), hence the possibility arises of them being treated violently.

The syndrome in the nuclear age

Although necrophilia, narcissism, and the desire for incestuous symbiosis can exist independently, Fromm believed they blend together, forming a "syndrome of decay" (Fromm, 1964, p. 108). Rejoicing in destruction and prioritising one's own group over others are taken to explain the irrationality of "all national, racial, religious and political fanaticism" (Fromm, 1964, pp. 108–113). But Fromm felt the tragedy of modernity was not just that it rendered people susceptible to destructive nationalism, but also that they were armed with nuclear weapons:

> If man becomes indifferent to life there is no longer any hope that he can choose the good. Then, indeed, his heart will have so hardened that his "life" will be ended. If this should happen to the entire human race or to its most powerful members, then the life of mankind may be extinguished at the very moment of its greatest promise. (Fromm, 1964, p. 150)

Criticising modernity

Fromm believed modern society was institutionalising elements supportive of the "syndrome of decay". How, he asked, could people tolerate the existence of nuclear weapons and the remotest chance of nuclear war? It must mean too many people failed to love life and were attracted to death (Fromm, 1964, p. 56). Fromm maintained that modern society, particularly as realised in North America and Europe, was becoming increasingly mechanical (i.e., necrophilous), not least as reflected in the rise of bureaucracy. In an environment restricting individuality and spontaneity, there is a new kind of being: organisation man, or *homo mechanicus*. The person becomes merely an item, but:

> ... man is not meant to be a thing; he is destroyed if he becomes a thing ... Briefly, then, intellectualization, quantification, abstractification, bureaucratization, and reification—the very characteristics of modern industrial society, when applied to people rather than to things, are not the principles of life but those of mechanics. People living in such a system become indifferent to life and even attracted to death. (Fromm, 1964, pp. 58–61)

Here, life becomes alienated in multiple ways, and social character is affected accordingly. Modern capitalism expects production to increase relentlessly, consumption to increase incessantly. This society demands people who co-operate in groups without friction, who will consume more and more in ways that are standardised and easy to influence. It needs people who will conform to anonymous diktats, whether based on bureaucratic rule books, opinion polls, or balance sheets. People become components of a "gigantic machine", their behaviour controlled and predictable (Fromm, 1963a, p. 112). Consequently, they do not experience command of their own lives and feel slaves to impersonal forces they cannot influence. They become busy to an unprecedented degree and feel such uncertainty, that they crave to "fit in" without causing problems.

Before long, a person begins to feel just another commodity, since everyone uses everybody else: the employer, the employee; the salesman, the customer; and so on. Life becomes experienced as a kind of investment game, in which the person is the capital and a return is being expected constantly. Even love becomes ruled by commodity principles—a "favourable exchange" between individuals getting the most "they can expect, considering their value on the personality market" (Fromm, 1963a, p. 147).

Moreover, the very act of consumption is changed. It should provoke reflection and transformation in the individual. Constantly stimulated by sources beyond their control and constantly busy as part of the ever-producing, ever-consuming economic system, however, people are preoccupied and denied time for introspection. Under the circumstances, consumption becomes a shallow sensation leaving the person unchanged (Fromm, 1963a, pp. 133–136).

Unsurprisingly, Fromm believed prevailing democratic systems are shams in which voting is something superficial. Political choices are made in ways analogous to decisions to buy commodities, according to little more than marketing principles. Political parties function as if they are businesses, politicians advertise their manifestoes as if they are products, and voters are stimulated to buy. Mass politics becomes something trivial, with voting based on misleading information and impoverished thought, with real decisions taken by party elites behind closed doors (Fromm, 1963a, pp. 184–191). Fromm even feared the onset of *de facto* totalitarianism, or "technocratic fascism with a smiling face" (Fromm, 2009, p. 9).

Life under the Soviet system was also recognised as definitively tainted, particularly by "the executioner" who "watches behind the door" (Fromm, 1963a, p. 358), yet western politicians could never take the mental leap to appreciate how much capitalism and communism had in common. Arguing that Marx's ideas no longer motivated Moscow's agenda, Fromm identified both western and eastern societies as based on production and acquisition. Only paranoia, therefore, led western foreign policy "experts" to project their uncertainties on "the East", entrenching confrontation in international relations during the 1960s and 1970s (Fromm, 1961a,b,c, 1962, 1963a,b). It remained fateful that this polarisation of global politics happened as the most powerful weapons ever known were deployed.

With pessimism, Fromm maintained the psychological premises of modernity dictated that sooner or later society would fail (Fromm, 2009, p. 3). Routinisation and consumerism were increasing unlived life and promoting the likelihood of violent outbursts; they were supporting a "syndrome of decay" society-wide. So, although no one—not even politicians—actually wanted war, none the less it might become an unforeseen outcome of current trends. Hence, Fromm phrased a personal credo:

> I believe that today there is only one main concern: the question of war and peace. Man is likely to destroy all life on earth, or to destroy all civilized life and the values among those that remain, and to build a barbaric, totalitarian organization which will rule what is left of mankind. To wake up to this danger, to look through the double talk on all sides which is used to prevent men from seeing the abyss towards which they are moving is the one obligation, the one moral and intellectual command which man must respect today. If he does not, we all will be doomed. (Fromm, 1980, p. 172)

Solutions

People could be neither fully healthy nor happy under the prevailing circumstances. Satisfactory life demands that we live "intensively", that we are "fully born", "fully awake", experiencing reason and faith, respecting our own existence as well as that of others (Fromm, 1963a, pp. 203–204). Together, love of life, independence, freedom, and reason could produce the opposite to the syndrome of decay, a syndrome of growth (Fromm, 1980, p. 161), but how could you underpin it?

If Fromm feared automaton obedience might contribute to the end of humanity, he saw hope in disobedience and doubt. The rejection of commonly agreed "wisdom" should lay the foundations for a saner society, and to this end he quoted Goethe on nationalism: "At a time when everybody is busy erecting new Fatherlands, the Fatherland of the man who thinks without prejudice and can rise above his time is nowhere and everywhere" (Fromm, 1980, p. 161).

No one should be used as a means to an end; economic and political activities should serve the interests of human growth; greed, exploitation, and narcissism should be marginalised; conscience should become central; social and public affairs should be treated as if they are private ones; people should relate to each other lovingly; reason should be promoted; and people should express their inner needs through collective artistic experiences (Fromm, 1963a, p. 277). Fromm felt these aims were most likely to be achieved in societies offering the individual security, justice, and the freedom to become a responsible community member (Fromm, 1964, pp. 52–53).

The limitations of mass society and nationalism were to be side-lined in favour of: international development and wealth sharing; international government; disarmament (especially of atomic wea-pons); the separation of scientific priorities from economic and mili-tary ones; decentralisation of social responsibilities; worker partici-pation in enterprise; work to be given human proportions, not least by the breaking up of giant commercial and industrial enterprises; corre-sponding changes in systems of ownership; the application of capital and the economy to serve the interests of life; the replacement of consumerism with a new attitude; the lessening of the gap between rich and poor; greater meaningful popular engagement with political processes, specifically through the devolving of government functions to town meetings in which decisions could be taken by local groups of 500 people, all of whom had personal contact with each other; a Supreme Cultural Council to offer disinterested advice to government and to disseminate good quality information; bureaucratic adminis-tration to be replaced by active, responsible community action; the replacement of ties of "blood and soil" with those of brotherliness; as well as the strengthening of creativity through a cultural renaissance (Fromm, 1963a, pp. 360–363, 2009, pp. 152–160).

Finally, Fromm believed that young people should be surrounded by those who love life. Warmth and affection during infancy, freedom and absence of threats during education, teaching by example rather than "preaching"—all of these were desirable (Fromm, 1964, p. 51). Likewise, he looked to the day when education would not teach nationally particularistic syllabuses, but emphasise unifying achieve-ments relevant to all mankind, and here he specified the need to teach about the United Nations (Fromm, 1964, pp. 91–92). So, although Fromm's political suggestions for a future sane society—a system he called socialist humanism—lacked detail, they were coherent in their own terms and fitted both his psychoanalysis and critique of moder-nity (Fromm, 1967).

Discussion

So, in his quest for a mass audience, did Fromm's analyses become superficial? Is his voice still relevant today?

Although Fromm claimed his arguments were informed by psychoanalytical practice, there is little evidence of this, especially in his later writings (Fromm, 1980, p. 9). His texts lack the detail suggestive of close clinical engagement, yet it is hard to dispute many of the points he made. It is difficult to doubt that mental health is related to reason, security, and love. He was right to emphasise the importance of quality and reflection in life, not to say sensitivity, spontaneity, and personal growth. Given how intelligent, educated people can end up doing bizarre—even evil—things, he was correct to stress how unconscious processes and character help to cause world-shaping events. The point is true even if, as Fromm understood, it is difficult for someone born in one historical period to comprehend the emotional character of someone from a different time and place (Fromm, 1980, p. 153). Simply understanding that there were motivational factors operating in historical actors apart from conscious ones is always worth bearing in mind.

His insistence that study of the past should involve more than war, revolution, and trauma is also correct. We should not forget history's humanitarian triumphs. Many will still sympathise with Fromm's view of modernity, his warning about bureaucracy, conformism, consumerism, and the stifling of creative, sensitive living. The points were well made too, even if not completely original since, for example, Oscar Wilde denounced English bureaucracy as early as the 1890s and Fritz Lang's *Metropolis* provided memorable images of workers as automatons (Housden, 2006).

More important potential criticism is raised by Fromm's language describing Hitler:

> He was . . . deeply attracted to death and destruction; he was an extremely narcissistic person for whom the only reality was *his own* wishes and thoughts. Finally he was an extremely incestuous person. Whatever his relationship to his mother may have been, his incestuousness was mainly expressed in his fanatical devotion to the race, the people who shared the same blood. . . . Narcissism, death, and incest were the fatal blend which made a man like Hitler one of the enemies of mankind and life . . . (Fromm, 1964, pp. 108–109)

In the earlier *Fear of Freedom*, Fromm did not apply such language to Hitler, so why did he do so in the 1960s? Terms such as "incestuous" and "narcissistic" have valid analytical applications, but they are also insults. In his later writing, at least, was Fromm conducting objective psychoanalysis or was he issuing an educated slight—whether delivered consciously or subconsciously? Fromm's role as psychoanalyst speaks for the former, but his status as a German Jew might speak for the latter.

There are problems with his analysis of nationalism. The way necrophilia, narcissism, and incest unite in a "syndrome of decay" is so neat that it raises suspicion. Harsh phrases are applied to a political extreme, but does Fromm help us understand the actual lives of those who adopted it? It is easy to generalise about an "Eichmann", but harder to grapple with the loss, disappointment, and frustration suffered by many Germans between 1914 and 1945. People turned to Hitler based on all manner of personal narratives, and, although Fromm's ideas have a role to play in unravelling National Socialism, explanations couched disproportionately in terms of necrophilia, narcissism, and incest will not necessarily do full justice to all historical actors.

Then there is the positive role that national belonging can play. Although Fromm noted that in the past nationalism had been associated with constructive contributions to society (Fromm, 1963a, p. 58), in the context of recent history he was happier to recognise Edith Cavell's comment (1915) that patriotism was deficient (Fromm, 2009, p. 115). But if nationalism was associated with movements for liberation in Central and Eastern Europe in 1848, and Russia in 1905 and 1917, it also helped precipitate the more recent collapse of the Soviet Bloc. Some recent commentators have tried to identify a progressive concept: "liberal nationalism" (Auer, 2004; Tamir, 1993). In their view, national pride has proved a valuable asset in the gradual reconstruction of a democratic Central and Eastern Europe. Although destructive nationalism certainly accompanied some of the recent changes (e.g., in the former Yugoslavia), it might be an exaggeration to deny a sense of national belonging *all* positive qualities.

Take resistance to Nazism. Resisters acted for various reasons, but they included people who felt their national identity keenly. In the Baltic region, Paul Schiemann was an ethnic German politician who had good relations with Jewish groups (Hiden, 2004). From an early point he battled Hitler's politics, eventually experiencing house arrest during the Nazi occupation of Riga, yet he still saved a Jewish woman from the Holocaust. Schiemann prized his Baltic German heritage and believed it shaped his ethical view of the world. Likewise, within

Germany itself, patriotism helped motivate aristocratic resisters such as Helmut von Moltke and Peter Yorck von Wartenburg (Housden, 1997, Chapter Five).

Highlighting difficulties surrounding Fromm's treatment of national belonging, we should say that von Moltke developed a model of local democracy that bore comparison with Fromm's system of town meetings (Housden, 1997, pp. 113–114). Similarly, Fromm's insistence that an ideal society be "organic" was reminiscent of tradi-tional right-wing, conservative social critiques (Sontheimer, 1983). Finally, how could Fromm maintain that work as a small cog in a massive—maybe multi-national—corporation would never supply individuals with a sense of meaning, yet reject attempts to subdivide the dauntingly large category "humankind" into more manageable categories, including "nations"? *Although we understand only too well that nationalism can bring serious problems*, should Fromm not also have wondered about the possible dissatisfactions of living in a world scrubbed clean of ethnic variety?

Fromm's reading of post-war Germany was too negative. Writing in the early 1960s, he insisted significant forces for expansion remained within the Federal Republic. He said that German industry was as strong as ever and the German military class remained intact (Fromm, 1980, p. 23. Fromm, 1965). In fact, arguing that the next time Germany tried to expand eastwards, it would have the USA as an ally, he implicated Europe in a dire prospect:

> The New Europe, led by Germany, will be as expansionist as the Old Germany was; eager to recover the former German territories, it will be an even greater menace to peace. By this I do not imply that Germany wants war, and certainly not thermo-nuclear war. What I mean to say is that the New Germany hopes to attain its aims without war, by the very threat of an overwhelming force once this has been attained. But this calculation is most likely to lead to war, since the Soviet bloc will not stand by quietly while Germany gets stronger and stronger—just as little as Great Britain and France did in 1914 and in 1939. (Fromm, 1980, p. 23)

With hostile rhetoric, Fromm emphasised West Germany's contin-uity with the malign aspects of its past and warned about future threats:

> Motivated by its desire for nuclear weapons, West Germany seems to
> be preparing for the time when it will get them—and when it will have
> its own fingers on its own nuclear bomb triggers.

> Already there is talk of a new Fuehrer promising the German people
> nuclear weapons, just as Hitler promised the German people deliver-
> ance from the terms of the Versailles Treaty [a reference to comments
> by Franz Josef Strauss of the Christian Democratic Party]. (Fromm,
> 1966b)

Of course, West Germany's stables were not cleaned properly after
1945. For instance, judges, civil servants, and doctors tainted by
Nazism remained in post. Major industrial concerns which had prof-
ited from Hitler's years stayed in business. Still, Fromm demonised
rather than analysed post-war Germany. Although writing in a period
of swift social change (the 1960s), he failed to take account of his own
principles: context is dynamic and character can change over time.
Younger generations of Germans wanted to break with their parents'
heritage and prove that they had nothing to do with Nazism. This
partly explained their desire to identify with Europe rather than
Germany (which, in any case, was divided). So, although even today
we can trace a complexity in German society when it comes to
discussing nationhood and (say) citizenship (e.g., the Sarrazin con-
troversy), none the less, Fromm misread post-war Germany (Various,
2010).

There are also questions about Fromm's theoretical work and his
personal heritage. He set exacting standards for mental health. How
many people act rationally most of the time? His work implies not
that many; there is a long way to go until we can be healthy—but can
most people make the journey? Fromm equates healthy living with
spontaneous, original, creative, intellectual, cultural, and artistic
activity, but how many people actually have a chance of achieving
it? Perhaps Fromm was too ambitious, and the characteristic ties up
with his own life. As a middle class, international intellectual, and
as a member of an elite, he was suggesting that good health required everyone to become just like him. But is that either realistic or
desirable?

Equally, why did Fromm denigrate things that apparently did not
interest him? (Fromm, 2009, p. 117). While successful sportsmen and
women sometimes do have something of the pagan hero about them

(although that analogy is not entirely exact), sport is not all bad. What is wrong with maintaining that since we have reason, we should explore what it can achieve as much as possible, but also, since we have bodies, we should explore their capabilities, too?

Fromm's deprecation of natural beauty is also odd. He argued that ordinary people fail to understand beauty because they describe, say, a sunset as beautiful when, in fact, it is no more beautiful than fog or rain—although the latter can be less pleasant for the body (Fromm, 1968, p. 72). Fromm maintained that beauty should be found in truth, not a natural event; but why make that point at all? Is he not talking about two different things, each of which can be experienced as stunning in different ways? Perhaps people get a good feeling both when they recognise a truth and when exposed to something that appeals to their senses. We can appreciate both, and to try to prioritise one over the other involves creating a false dichotomy. Perhaps Fromm favoured beauty as truth because the quest for "truth" traditionally has been an elite, intellectual undertaking, while the appreciation of nature is something more sensuous, inclusive, and, therefore, too populist to appeal to him.

Given his background as born into a German Jewish business family in 1900, and his later place as an international "guru" of sorts, it is easy to see aspects of Fromm's biography reflected in his writing. In part, he was carrying out a personal debate with society. His German Jewishness even helps explain his more apocalyptic fears over the threat of nuclear war. After all, having witnessed the Holocaust, why doubt that any other man-made cataclysm will not happen eventually? But who does not include at least part of themselves in what they write? This is a more or less inevitable caveat to a massive body of work that provides many sensitive insights into the human condition and the impact society can have upon it.

References

Auer, S. (2004). *Liberal Nationalism in Central Europe*. New York: Routledge Curzon.

Fromm, E. (1951). *The Forgotten Language*. New York: Grove.

Fromm, E. (1960). *Fear of Freedom*. London: Routledge and Kegan Paul.

Fromm, E. (1961a). Sane thinking in foreign policy. In: *Sane Comment.* New York: National Committee for a Sane Policy). Available at: www. erich-fromm.de/e/index.htm (accessed 1 May 2011).

Fromm, E. (1961b). Communism and co-existence. The nature of the totalitarian threat today: an analysis of the 81-Party Manifesto. First published in *Socialist Call, 28*(4). Available at: www.erich-fromm.de/ e/index.htm (accessed 1 May 2011).

Fromm, E. (1961c). The future of the new Europe, typescript. Available at: www.erich-fromm.de/e/index.htm (accessed 1 May 2011).

Fromm, E. (1962). The Spiegel affair—an old pattern? Written in November to be published in the *Council of Correspondence Newsletter*, New York. Available at: www.erich-fromm.de/e/index.htm (accessed 1 May 2011).

Fromm, E. (1963a). *The Sane Society.* London: Routledge & Kegan Paul.

Fromm, E. (1963b). United States foreign policy after Cuba. *Council for Correspondence Newsletter, 23*(February): 8–21. Available a:t www. erich-fromm.de/e/index.htm (accessed 1 May 2011).

Fromm, E. (1964). *The Heart of Man. Its Genius for Good and Evil.* New York: Harper Colophon.

Fromm, E. (1965). The German question. Second part of a paper entitled Memo on Foreign Policy. Available at: www.erich-fromm.de/e/index. htm (accessed 1 May 2011).

Fromm, E. (1966a). The war in Vietnam and the brutalization of man. Speech at the SANE Garden Rally on 8 December. Available at: www. erich-fromm.de/e/index.htm (accessed 1 May 2011).

Fromm, E. (1966b). Is Germany on the March Again? In: *War/Peace Report*, 6(March): 3–4. Available at www.erich-fromm.de/e/index.htm (accessed 1 May 2011).

Fromm, E. (Ed.) (1967). *Socialist Humanism.* London: Allen Lane.

Fromm, E. (1968). *The Revolution of Hope. Toward a Humanized Technology.* New York: Harper and Row.

Fromm, E. (1980). *Beyond the Chains of Illusion. My Encounter with Marx and Freud.* London: Abacus.

Fromm, E. (2009). *To Have or to Be?* London: Continuum.

Hiden, J. (2004). *Defender of Minorities. Paul Schiemann, 1876–1944.* London: Hurst.

Housden, M. (1997). *Resistance and Conformity in the Third Reich.* London: Routledge.

Housden, M. (2006). Oscar Wilde's imprisonment and an early idea of "banal evil". *Forum Historiae Iuris* www.forhistiur.de/zitat/0610housden.htm (accessed 30 April 2011)

Internationale-Erich-Fromm-Gesellschaft e.V. (undated) www.erich-fromm.de/e/index.htm

Sontheimer, K. (1983). *Antidemokratisches Denken in der Weimarer Republik.* Munich: DTV.

Tamir, Y. (1993). *Liberal Nationalism.* Princeton, NJ: Princeton University Press.

Various (2010). *Sarrazin. Eine deutsche Debatte* (2010). Munich: Piper.

Editor's introduction to Chapter Ten

The chapter addresses how regulation of society by standardisation, using the concepts of registration, certification, and accred-
itation, is extended to ever new areas of human functioning,
and the requirements of this regulation are increasing in its demands.
Behind it all, argues the author, lie increasing demands for more
control, in larger areas of human activity. The chapter tries to pinpoint
how this is a result of the panoptic machinery. The panopticon, it is
argued, can serve as a concept for the understanding of these
processes in dialectical interaction with Freud's concept of the
uncanny. The word panopticon can be translated as the *all seeing*, or
total gaze. The idea was a building where each room could be monitored from any point and where everybody could see everybody. In
the 1980s and 1990s, it is argued, the ideology of "new public management" intensified the liberalisation of the free market and increased
the desire for standardisation. The author argues that it represents an
attempt to establish a uniform inter/national/social character, an ISO
character, one that is conformist and can be applied everywhere in the
world. The cultivation of the symbols, politics, and ideology of nationalism can be seen as a regressive step back to primary identification
to the local group in the face of the threats caused by globalisation.

The anger and anxiety created by new challenges, it is argued, brings forth extreme nationalism with the cultivation of clear, impenetrable boundaries between the in-group and those conceived of as "others".

CHAPTER TEN

The making of the isotype character in the panoptic system and its relation to globalised nationalism[1]

Svein Tjelta

Introduction

In today's seemingly confusing world, there are many processes in action. The major ones are globalisation and the efforts to uphold and maintain nation states within the different networks that have developed as part of globalisation. What is usually connected to globalisation is the increasing speed and efficiency in the flow of international capitalism and the urbanisation processes that follow, resulting in the building up of gigantic city centres as nodes in global networks of flow of information and capital. Living in densely populated areas mandates dependence on the behaviour of citizens acting rationally within the centres. Globalisation puts pressure on nation states to adapt to a certain standard in order to function within the networks it creates. Adaption to these standards, in many cases, threatens identity and specific cultural values. One reaction we have seen with the fall of the Soviet Union in the 1990s, and can observe in many nations of Europe today, is the cultivation of the symbols, politics, and ideology of nationalism. It is possible to see this as a regressive step back to primary identification with the local group—the nation—in the face of the threats caused by globalisation, which does not offer identification

and signifiers of power to many large groups within individual countries. In some cases, the anger and anxiety created by the new challenges that this brings, together with the reduction of traditional
society, brings forth extreme nationalism, involving the cultivation of
centripetal symbols and clear, impenetrable boundaries between the
in-group and the others, which might be migrant workers or refugees.
In the face of such perceived threats, a totalitarian ideology can easily
stimulate violent reactions and the scapegoating of other groups.
Ideology can function as a body politic, forming the minds of people
by indoctrination through mimesis, offering identificatory power to
its adherents as part of something bigger and stronger than themselves, which promises rescue and simple order in the maelstrom of
globalisation. As a result of the upheaval of many traditional identification signifiers, such as social class, family ties, and meaningful
work, unrest will follow, giving precedence for the development of
reactive, regressive, nationalistic movements.

Standardisation efforts as a panoptic supplicant for control and selection

Today, we can observe how nation states work with international
networks to establish some kind of compromise and control over the
dynamics that are created when the international meets the national.
One of these strategies is the body politic that is implemented on a
global scale, leading to increasing demands on people for uniform
behaviour in accordance with pre-programmed operational procedures and standards for acting instrumentally. Modern states need
standardisation to increase efficiency and rational behaviour. Across
nations, there are also many rational reasons for the importance of
standardisation. Standards for inanimate objects are a *sine qua non* for
exchange in modern societies. Also, in most productive sectors, standardisation is necessary. In the exchange of commodities, transport,
and traffic, it is, for example, mandatory to have signs that can be
universally understood and adapted to. This is the rationale for picto-
rial or sign language, based on pictogram systems used everywhere.
    Standardisation is also important in the human sphere. The elec-
tronic revolution, with its fantastic varieties of instruments for communication, registration, and possibilities for monitoring and control,

as well as the introduction of standards all over the world, is firmly based on compliance and conformity.

Standardisation has, therefore, become the *ultimo ratio* for the regulation of society, particularly from the 1970s onward. There are, however, excesses, and some of the ways in which it is imposed on the human domain are quite aggressive. Its development is everywhere: for example, in education and health services. The ideology of "new public management", a tentacle of global capitalism that appeared in the 1980s and 1990s, intensified the liberalisation of the so-called free market and also increased the desire for standardisation. What is happening, in my view, is an attempt to establish a uniform inter/national/social character, an ISO character, which is a character that is conformist and can be used everywhere in the world. However, there are some serious side effects to this development, which are being mystified as psychological problems of the individual, which need treatment. Many of those who come to me for treatment struggle in relation to their experience of not managing to live up to standards that are imposed on them. In this, there is some confusion of causes that is interesting, because it puts the burden of responsibility for the suffering it creates on the individual, defining him or her as being in the shameful position of being below standard. Professions such as psychology and psychiatry lend a helping hand in this confusion of causes, and, thus, uphold a kind of alienation in the containment of suffering. The dynamics are made up, on the one hand, of the processes that come with globalisation, which the increasing effort for standardisation is part of, together with international flow of capital, people, and information, urbanisation, and the development of giant cities (Giga polis) that function as centres or nodes in global networks and centres of power. On the other hand, there are the reactions that operate as a kind of resistance to this development. One of these resistance tendencies is the regression to primary identification with territorial borders and the development of the ideology of nationalism—sometimes ultra-nationalism.

Nationalism refers to nation. A nation is usually conceptualised as a territorial, geographically located area with clearly recognised borders and defined in relation to other nations. It usually has a distinct flag and other symbols that identify the nation. Larger nations have usually developed a state to control and serve its citizens. It is also usual that the members of a nation have been exposed to a

cultural influence of important values for a their particular nation and
that a national character is developed, which manifests the specific
values of the nation. The population plays along with the nation. We
can, therefore, assume that there is a form of politics at work here,
forming the values that are needed for compliance to the nation's
goals and strategies. Nationalism can be seen as an ideological tool
that is used to reach the emotions of the members of a nation in a
semi-religious way, to bind the members in a strong primary identity
that can be appealed to and sometimes be used, as when a state goes
to war under the premise "for God and the nation". When the Soviet
Union fell apart, there were essentially three foundations people fell
back on: religion, hedonism, and nationalism.

National and social character

The concept of national or social character and its roots can be traced
back to Weber, Durkheim, and others. How societies prescribed
norms and rules and ordered their practices in relation to cultural
fields of value, such as religious practice, production procedures, and
the exchange of trade, gifts, and marriage. More than 100 years ago,
Weber expressed his concern for the vulnerability of the autonomous
human being. He feared that the individual's originality and creativity would suffer from the emerging rationality and bureaucratic
developments. Humans are vulnerable in the face of forces that shape
them. Weber predicted that developments in modernity would lead
to increasing demands on conformity. The concept of social character
is sometimes used synonymously with national character. It is a
broader concept, and one must assume that every nation has a specific
national character, which has more facets than is stereotypically
depicted.

In particular, it was the Frankfurt school of social research, with
Theodor W. Adorno, Max Horkheimer, and Eric Fromm, later Herbert
Marcuse and David Riesman, who made the concept known in
psychoanalysis and sociology. Fromm defined the concept of social
character as follows:

> I refer in this concept to the nucleus of the character structure which
> is shared by most members of the same culture in contradistinction to

the individual character in which people belonging to the same culture differ from each other. (Fromm, 1963[1956], pp. 78–81)

The concept in this definition is related to culture, but people sharing a culture do not necessarily live within the same state. However, from the larger text, it becomes clear that, in saying "culture", Fromm is using social and national interchangeably. It also correlates closely with moral and ethical dimensions, and, as such, can be a tool in conjunction with some empirical research on the stability of norms and attitudes, and the possibilities for influencing these. For example, the Stanford group's investigations of the authoritarian character (Adorno, Frenkel-Brunswik, Levinson, & Sanford, 1950) and Milgram's experiment concerning social limits on inflicting pain (1963). Milgram wanted to find out how existential conditions such as order, rules norms, obedience, and duty affected the individual's freedom of choice, independence, conscience, and possible rebellion against an authority. The purpose was to find an answer to the question of why so many people in Germany during the Second World War could be instrumental in carrying out the greatest of atrocities and murdering millions of people. Could it be that Adolf Eichmann and millions of accomplices in the Holocaust just followed orders and were bound by obedience to an authority? Zimbardo's (1971) prison experiment showed how selected students, who were awarded the role of either prisoner or prison officer, soon forgot that it was an experiment, and got so deeply enmeshed into the roles that the experiment had to be called off because of ethical considerations. These classic experiments show how easily one can influence people through certain procedural contexts if they are given a "rational" explanation from an authority representing a system that supposedly stands for trust, the truth, justice, or the common good.

Europe has a long history of self-conscious awareness of national differences. National groups develop, over a period of time, certain stereotypical views of members of other national entities. While the perception of behavioural differences has led to a great deal of verbal expression and group prejudices, only since the 1940s have serious efforts been made to explore systematically the validity or precise nature of the perceived differences with respect to underlying personality configurations. One of the basic objectives of national character studies is to examine the tensions underlying the political and social structures of modern states. Social tensions are particularly apparent in societies that are rapidly changing. For example, one type of social tension that is frequently observed results from the systematic attempts of the establishment or an elite to inculcate particular patterns of directed social change.

The origin of the panopticon as a historical phenomenon

Jeremy Bentham, the co-founder with John Stuart Mill of utilitarianism, developed the concept; their philosophy provided the rationale for it. Utilitarianism is an empirically based moral philosophy. It is group focused. The good is only good when it results in the greatest possible well being for as many people as possible. It is a hedonistic, materialist, and pragmatic philosophy within a liberal capitalist framework. The word "panopticon" comes from Greek. It combines *pan*, which means *all*, and *opticon*, which concerns the optical domain. It can be translated as the *all seeing*, or total gaze. The idea was a building in which each room could be monitored from any point of view, and in which everybody could see everybody. This was aimed at factories and prisons in particular. It did not succeed very well as an architectural concept, but mentally, socially, and procedurally, as a way of ordering things in society, it has become widespread. Originally, what was implemented was the observing and surveying function. With the twenty-first century globalisation processes and urbanisation, together with an increase in crime and terrorist attacks, this element of the panopticon has escalated enormously, both privately and publicly, with cameras on every street corner in every city.

Surveillance and standardisation combined

The development of standardisation and subsequent procedure regimes as part of national and international politics in shaping and forcing whole populations to comply with certain standards of behaviour through intensive indoctrination and enforcement connected to the panoptic system is a relatively new strategy. It is today, to a large extent, left to commercial providers, such as the International Standards Organisation (ISO), the world's largest developer and publisher of International Standards. The ISO is a central node in the network of the national standards institutes of 162 countries. It is a non-governmental organisation that provides a bridge between the public and private sectors. On the one hand, many of its member institutes are part of the governmental structure of their countries, or are mandated by their government. On the other hand, other members are rooted uniquely in the private sector, having been set up by national partnerships of industry associations and networks.

ISO and its systems and networks, which operate and are implemented in our societies today, have a purpose that seems to be to develop standardisation into what they themselves call "harmonisation of the world". This vision will require an immense adaption to common standards, and the logical corollary is that it will influence national character to become what I have called the ISO-TYPE on an international level. This must be seen as part of the invasive globalisation processes into nations of the world.

Malign forms of resistance

There is, however, resistance to this, some forms of which are regressive and destructive, such as trying to establish an alternative in a totalitarian ideology. In extreme nationalism as an ideology, we often see the establishment and active use of myths of origin going back to ancient times, often connected to home and soil. If one adds blood and boundaries, this is the blueprint for nationalism. It is also common to find myths of "chosen people". Signs and symbols in customs and habits, conformity in clothing, and indoctrination procedures regarding behaviour are expressions of this. Historically, we can observe many examples of splitting into we–them, good–bad, Nazi–Jew, Soviet citizen–enemy of the people, and so on. The mythologies created usually stimulate nostalgia and idealise the group one belongs to while denigrating rivals or neighbouring groups, cultures, or societies. Nostalgia is a rebellion against the modern idea of time, the time of change and progress. The Norwegian author Knut Hamsun represents a long tradition of nostalgia as a reaction to modernity with all its confusions and changes. He earned the Nobel Prize for Literature for his book *Markens Gröde* [Growth of the Soil] (2009[1917]). The theme is nostalgic, harking back to some quiet agrarian existence in close connection with nature. Hatred, fear, and being predictable are components of this kind of nostalgia. However, there is the appreciation of modernity as a means to achieve a totalitarian goal and strong demands for conformity. There is firm regulation of society, uniformity, mass production of goods, and infrastructure, for instance, in this ideology.

Dissatisfaction with diversity and complexity and nostalgia for a clean and uncomplicated community was also part of the thinking of the totalitarian mind of Anders Behring Breivik, the thirty-two-year-old ethnic Norwegian, who, for nine years, planned a terror attack in Norway and cold-bloodedly carried it out on a Friday 22 July 2011. He wrote that Europe is infected with Marxism and Islamism and he set out on a course to become an example of how one is to stop this "disease". It is symptomatic that Islamic extremism has been given so much attention in the media after September 11, 2001. This stirs up anxiety and fantasies about the denigrated strange and destructive other who can harm us. Thus, the focus on one type of extremism can, by stirring up anxieties and hatred, stimulate another antagonistic kind of extremism, which, paradoxically, is very similar in its nostalgic longings for a "clean" paradise of true believers. In the pre-Second World War years, the Nazi mentality escalated and attracted many adherents because, at that time, Communism was perceived by many people as a huge threat to the culture of nations. Such beliefs created a regression to primitive fantasies of attack and annihilation anxiety, stirred up by propaganda, which made many feel they had to choose between the Nazis and the Communists. The same kind of anxiety could be stirred up again, I believe. Elias writes,

> Civilization is not 'reasonable'; not 'rational', any more than it is 'irrational'. It is set in motion blindly, and kept in motion by the autonomous dynamics of a web of relationships, by specific changes in the way people are bound and live together. (1998, p. 51)

Further on, he states,

> The web of actions grows so complex and extensive, the effort required to 'behave' within it becomes so great, that beside the individual's conscious self-control, an automatic, blindly functioning apparatus of self-control is firmly established. This seeks to prevent offences to socially acceptable behaviour by a wall of deep-rooted

fears, but just because it operates blindly and by habit, it frequently indirectly produces such collisions with social reality. (1998, p. 52)

However, Elias here avoids the question of the role of ideology, which can be more or less rational or irrational, and intentionally influence the course of events and developments. Ideology can be a steering wheel on history. Ideology is often the means by which politics stimulate and set in motion pattern and processes of idealisation and denigration. Often, rational calculation is used in the sought-after realisation of irrational ideas. Ideology is central in the recognition of identity. It is important in groups and cultures and evident in the signs and symbols by which identity is represented. It can be seen in the use of a nation's flag and special customs, as well as in certain habits, manners, fashions, restraints, constraints, and facilitations.

The ISO as a node in the global network

So, the ISO development could be conceptualised as part of the globalisation process that aims for the total similarity or identity of behaviour and thinking according to preconstructed procedures in the productive and reproductive sectors of society. It is an important node in a network, influencing nations to conform to standardisation regimens. This is in accordance with the simple digital defining principle of inside–outside. Inside is equal and in compliance with the standards. Outside means deviation, and that would mean not good enough. Harmonisation processes also seek to make nation states more similar. The ambition of the ISO is nothing less than standardisation throughout the world, called, possibly euphemistically, harmonisation. The instrumental logic of capitalist organisations and businesses is, of course, expansion and growth. According to the authors below,

There is an intrinsic connection between cognitive totalism and political totalitarianism: the mind that can only tolerate *one* approach to reality is the same kind of mind that must impose *one* all embracing structure of power if it ever gets into the position of doing so. (Berger, Berger, & Keller, 1974, p. 208)

*Standardisation as a driving principle
in a panopticon as a system for control*

In the panoptic system, distributions, deviations, series, and combinations are analysed. Instruments that visualise, formalise procedures of reporting, and draw correlations (e.g., national statistics and controls, the reporting of deviations from standards, the imposing of manuals in teaching and healthcare) are used. It is a model of a society that is completely permeated and controlled by disciplinary mechanisms. Foucault writes,

> There are superficial notions about the society, but under the surface there is a profound influence on the human bodies . . . The signs that are in circulation, define domination. The Individual is not amputated or alienated from our social order. On the contrary, the individual is carefully fabricated in a tactical use of the body and its powers . . . we are in the panoptic machinery exposed to the effects of a power which we ourselves forward by being cogs in the machinery. (Foucault, 1977[1975], p. 193)

According to de Certau, "The exceptional, even cancerous growth of panoptic procedures seems to be indissociable from the historical role to which they have been assigned; that of being a weapon to be used in combating and controlling of heterogeneous practices" (1984, p. 48).

What has been mostly focused on in the panoptic machinery is the principle of monitoring and surveillance. To this, I think it is also necessary to add the principle of control and regulation through standardisation procedures, of which ISO is an example. Its purpose is twofold: (1) the upbringing and education of friction-free manufacturers and workers that fully conform to the society; (2) the rational prevention and control of all possible dangers represented by all possible deviations from standard norms which are becoming more and more fixated and narrow. In short, all that is not registered, or perceived, as being under control.

The development of procedural efforts is not new, however. It is the speed, efficiency, and the focus and concentration on humans and human–machine systems and processes that have increased immensely.

The dynamics of the panopticon

What are the dialectical dynamics that seem to make the panoptic machinery work so smoothly? In his work "The uncanny" (1919h), Freud conducts an analysis of the origin of the phenomenon. He comes to the conclusion that the uncanny is the opposite of the friendly, homely, safe, and familiar known—the canny. But it has its origin in just this kind of atmosphere. With Freud, the origin of the uncanny is to be found in castration anxiety that, in essence, is annihilation anxiety. It is the "unthought known" (Bollas, 1987), because of unconscious recognition of danger—the return of the repressed. First, castration means loss of potency, power, and control. Freud connects, in this paper, potency to the gaze or vision. The power and potency lie in the optic ability for control. *Loss of the ocular is like a symbolic castration.* This is a less frequently acknowledged point of the oedipal myth. Oedipus's self-blinding when he discovers that his wife is his mother is, symbolically, castration.

Power resides in the optic possibility for overview and control—the panoptic ideal. If we extend castration anxiety as an expression of the fear of loss of power and control applied to society, we can assume the dynamics behind the desire for panoptic control. There is a dialectical interaction of internal and external threats (imagined or real), chaos anxiety, and demands for control. Inside individuals, there is evolving adjustment and impulse control. On the outside, a framework of restrictions and constrictions is generated, and requirements in line with the establishment of standards and procedure development are laid down. These are more or less incorporated into the social character.

The dynamic influence from the external to the internal world

The projective, introjective, and identificatory manifestations of the uncanny which serve as representations of the phenomenon vary. They influence, however, the idea that fuels the desire for panoptic development, which is establishing security buffers against unsettling discrepancies in ever-larger areas of society. The panoptic efforts work in harmony with the uncanny. Particularly, the press thrives on emphasising all kinds of crime and deviations, whether from Islamic or right-wing extremists, corruption, mismanagement, or deviance in vital fields of society, and contributes to a dynamic that increases the demand for more transparency, predictability, and efficient control. Living in a society where procedures are working to make everything equal, as in the ISO, it follows logically that it spreads to every corner of human activity. What is communicated is that evil is in our midst, within our pleasant daily living, and must be revealed and neutralised through increased surveillance and establishment of procedures in order to prevent harm and disorder at all costs. Anxiety is increasing, and less and less deviation is allowed to occur. We can observe ever-increasing demands regarding this in all productive sectors of society. This is internalised in the superego as standards of what it takes to be regarded as a successful, responsible citizen, etc. This also fuels competition and rivalry, and, as we know, the superego can be very sadistic. Lacan, in his work on ethics in psychoanalysis, has given a description of this:

> It is rather something that introduces itself immediately as possessed of a very special quality of malice, of bad influence. Freud isolates it increasingly in the course of his work up to Civilization and Its Discontents. . . . What is this paradox? It is that the moral conscience, as he says, shows itself to be the more demanding the more refined it becomes, crueller and crueller even as we offend it less and less, more and more fastidious as we force it, by abstaining from acts, to go and seek us out at the most intimate levels of our impulses or desires. In short the insatiable character of this moral conscience, its paradoxical cruelty, transforms it within the individual into a parasite that is fed by the satisfactions accorded it. (Lacan, 1992[1986] p. 89)

Paranoid–schizoid defences that are stimulated by anxiety have a powerful effect on thinking and symbol formation. Projective identification leads to confusion between self and object, and this results in confusion between the symbol and the thing symbolised (Broch, Lossius, & Tjelta, 1987). The concrete thinking which arises when symbolisation is interfered with leads to an increase in anxiety and in rigidity. Rigidity can easily develop into obsessions, as can be seen in the demand for repetition that is contained in the tyranny of standardisation and procedural efforts. Behind obsession lies annihilation anxiety, and behind this lies a profound lack of trust in one's fellow human.

Two potential and different polarised
mind-sets in the national character

The depressive position, which, theoretically, is closer to the oedipal location, could be regarded as a mental space where there is more room for thought and concern about destruction, love, and reparation than the paranoid–schizoid position. That is a very sketchy description, intended to lead up to what I want to present (with some speculative imagination) about two kinds of mind-set, or, perhaps, mentalities, in persons and groups which could be stimulated to produce the kind of social character a society aims to produce. The first I will call the dialogical, heteroglossical (Bakhtin, 2008), diversity mind-set. The other can be termed the totalitarian, adulterant (false) mind-set. I shall assume that they are both present in every human being as potential patterns and they could be primed or stimulated towards relative domination in the national character. In the first, which could be linked by analogy to the depressive position (Klein, 1921–1945), one connects with the world through representation, reflection, and reason, and, thus, gains a feeling of control from within by means of critical questioning of influential processes. The other works more in the direction of conformity mimesis. The world is taken in by imitation, autoplastic adoption, and conformity. This belongs to the visual, superficial, surface and behavioural domain, easily observed by changes in fashion and political correctness, hypocritical mimicry, and so on. This kind of mentality is going with the mainstream and is what is coerced, manipulated, or primed in groups and in society. This mind-set is prone to admire power and megalomania and follow what, at a given time, is presented as the right thing to do. Freud (1921c) connects the individual to the group and the leader by way of two kinds of identification within an organisation; the vertical and the horizontal dimension. In the vertical dimension, the leader is accorded the idealised position as the divine (Christ) or the visionary omniscient leader with the means and the way to achieve the goal, be it world rule or the kingdom of heaven. The horizontal identification is established with expressed conformity and uniformity in the group, that is, by means of the symbols, uniforms, and myths of the group. Identification by way of representation or by mimesis, respectively, is very different.

In the time of the Moscow processes, people became victims of arbitrary arrests; they were jailed, tortured, sent to gulags, or killed.

This terror came after a long period of indoctrination, where people were made to believe in, and identify with, the party and its leaders—especially Stalin. They were idealised as infallible. When the terror began, people could not believe that the party or Stalin could be blamed for anything. So, when, say, a father was arrested, the rest of the family and the neighbours assumed that (1) it must be a mistake, or (2) that he was actually guilty of something. They could not even consider the premise that the Party and its leaders were corrupted, rotten, and/or insane (Figes, 2009). We also see this in our evidence-based world of today. People seem to believe that what emanates from the authorities as instructions and regulations is sane and for the common good. However, there are good reasons to suspect that something is very wrong and even insane, as in the saying that "the road to hell is paved with good intentions". An important question is why individuals and groups are so easily susceptible to indoctrination and manipulation. Historically, the regimes of Hitler and Stalin give us many clues about totalitarian leader-worship and how power and terror can force people into coercion. But there is also what seems to be a human need for guidance and leadership. In addition, there is a growing interdependence between man and machines. There also is the fast growing closure of the traditional split between man and nature, subject and object. By way of procedures, it is now mandatory to adapt to prescribed conformity standards in society. The enormous possibilities for control and expanding displacements of boundaries that we experience today lead to relative changes in ethical standards concerning the structuring and regulation of man and society. If something is possible to do, it seems likely, sooner or later, that it will be done. We can see some subcultures trying to establish a kind of resistance, due mainly to religious values and ignorance, going back to pre-modernity: for example, regressive Islamic groups. On the other hand, there are the extremists, for example, Islamophobic groups experiencing themselves as under attack by migrant Muslims, both having a perverted nostalgia for some imaginary paradise past. There are, of course, also some sane action groups, such as the environmentalists and the Occupy movement. On the whole, however, people resign themselves and do not put up much resistance to what seems unavoidable, and politicians seem to pay lip service to what is going on. We can also see idealisation of everything representing a promise of the fast resolving of collective or individual problems, and the denigration of complexities. There is intense pressure to conform, as well as defocusing of reflection, representation, and symbol formation. We see increased use of pictogrammatic sign language for orientation in the outer world.

While evolution shows us that diversity and pluralism are good in nature, the development of standardised nations in the globalised world seems to go in the other direction, that of uniformity and homogeneity. A problem with too much conformity, uniform activity, or ISO-typing processes is the locus and focus of control. It is taken away from individuals as something belonging to the domain of autonomous thinking and reflection, as a self-regulating process, and returns as demands for adaption and conformity to whatever standard is being imposed from the state or some outside power agency. Traditional humanistic duties and rights are redefined by the state and transferred to state agencies, and often private actors, like the ISO, to be imposed again on society as very concrete standards to be adapted to. Currently, for example, there is a standard developed in the ISO-connected institutes in Sweden and Brazil concerning "Social Responsibility". The Swedish Standards Institute (SIS) and the Brazilian ABNT (Brazilian Association of Technical Standards) are responsible for the generation of this standard. Instead of this being something evolving from culture by way of precedence over the years, a group of specialists are setting up a standard to which everybody will have to adhere. That is top down instead of bottom up; those who do not comply, become deviants, perhaps in need of treatment, as was perpetrated in the former Soviet Union against dissidents who did not comply with the demands of the system and spoke out and demonstrated against it.

We end up with a procedural society with strict norms and rules for prescribed behaviour. It becomes more difficult for individuals to regulate themselves from inner-derived autonomous compasses, and to stand up for themselves when they experience something as wrong.

Some of the side effects of the standardisation mentality

The intentionality within the structural violence (Žižek, 2009) that unfolds in the desire for standardisation is, of course, to control people in modern society. However, treating humans as cogs in the

202 NATIONALISM AND THE BODY POLITIC

panoptic machinery can have some serious side effects: it locks genuine human acting into repetitive conditioned procedures (conformity mimesis). It empowers language and creates empty terminology without vitality—Newspeak. Inner commitment to duty is exchanged for outer controlled practices and procedures. The continual focus on performance and conformity measurement creates and upholds anxiety and doubt. It undermines genuine motivation and creates reluctance and resistance. Totalitarian tendencies in people are stimulated. The result is reduced autonomous self-regulation, which reduces vitality and lust for life. A great deal of time is spent on the compulsive filling out of forms to keep abreast of new regulations and to document activity, combined with fear of making mistakes and being exposed to shame and guilt. The balance between reflection and regulatory adaptive control is skewed in favour of the latter. There is little room left for idiosyncratic development, play, and exploration. This could eventually reduce creative imagination and innovation. People experience fatigue and exhaustion, and perhaps this could be a reason for the increased incidence of depression we experience. We seem to move from Homo Ludens (the playful man) to Homo Coactus (the compulsive man).

Concluding remarks

In the advanced industrial societies, nations have become globalised, urbanised states influenced by giant networks with nodes that I call Giga polis linked together across national boundaries. The ISO's function lies in developing and certifying standards that can further this development into what they call "harmonisation of the world". This demands the creation of a functional national character, which, at the same time, is global in the sense that it complies with standards that are globalised. Marcuse somehow had a premonition of this:

> The enchained possibilities of advanced industrial societies are: Development of the productive forces on an enlarged scale, extension of the conquest of nature, growing satisfaction of needs and faculties. *But these possibilities are gradually being realized through means and institutions which cancel their liberating potential, and this process affects not only the means but also the ends. The instruments of productivity and*

progress, organized into a totalitarian system, determine not only the actual
but also the possible utilizations. (Marcuse, 1972[1964], p. 198, my italics)

He considered rationality to be ideological, as something that could turn out to be rather irrational and become ideological power tactics. According to Adorno (1980[1966]), the social world is ruled by instrumental values. In the wake of the historical development of the Enlightenment, rationality has degenerated to instrumental reason, to the calculation of the most effective means to achieve the fulfilment of certain goals. Marcuse points out that rational development tends to view all thinking and generation of information as knowledge with which to master the outer world. This is what he calls thinking in the category of identity to control nature and also people as part of nature. Einstein's fundamental creed was that freedom was the lifeblood of creativity (Isaacson, 2008). Creativity requires independence of thought from authoritarian restriction and constriction. Creativity requires an attitude of non-conformity. This presupposes the nurturing of free minds and spirits. This, in turn, requires tolerance for otherness. Uniformity is not a way to further tolerance. If everything is to be structured according to the ISO's "harmonisation" principles, we will develop the perfect panopticon and be in serious trouble.

Note

1. I would like to thank the editor of this work for her patient help with my bad English in expressing my thoughts.

References

Adorno, T. W. (1980)[1966]. *Negative Dialektik.* Frankfurt: Suhrkamp.

Adorno, T. W., Frenkel-Brunswik, E., Levinson, D. J., & Sanford, R. N. (1950). *The Authoritarian Personality.* New York: Harper Bros.

Bakhtin, M. M. (2008). *The Dialogic Imagination,* M. Holquist (Ed.), C. Emerson & M. Holquist (Trans.) Austin, TX: University of Texas Press.

Berger, P. L., Berger, B., & Kellner, H. (1973). *The Homeless Mind.* London: Penguin.

Bollas, C. (1987). *The Shadow of the Object.* London: Free Association Books.
Broch, H. P., Lossius, K., & Tjelta, S. (1987). *Unconscious Interplays; A Book on Projective Identification.* Oslo: Cappelen Professional.
De Certeau, M. (1988). *The Practice of Everyday Life.* Berkeley, CA: University of California Press.
Elias, N. (1998). *On Civilization, Power, and Knowledge. Seclected Writings,* S. Mennell & J. Goudsblom (Eds.). Chicago, IL: University of Chicago Press.
Figes, O. (2009). *The Whisperers.* Oslo: Cappelen Damm.
Foucault, M. (1977)[1975]. *Crime and Punishment.* København: Rhodos Radius.
Freud, S. (1919h). The "uncanny". *S.E., 17:* 219–256. London: Hogarth.
Freud, S. (1921c). *Group Psychology and the Analysis of the Ego. S.E., 18:* 67–143. London: Hogarth.
Fromm, E. (1963)[1956]. *The Sane Society.* New York: Routlegde & Keegan Paul.
Hamsun, K. (2009)[1917]. *Markens Gröde.* Oslo: Gyldendal
Isaacson, W. (2008). *Einstein: His Life and Universe.* New York: Simon & Schuster.
Klein, M. (1921–1945). *Love, Guilt and Reparation and Other Works, Vol. One.* London: Hogarth Press.
Lacan, J. (1992)[1986]. *The Ethics of Psycho-Analysis 1959–1960. The Seminar of Jacques Lacan Book VII,* J.-A. Miller (Ed.). New York: Routledge.
Marcuse, H. (1972)[1964]. *One Dimensional Man.* New York: Sphere Books.
Milgram, S. (1963). Behavioral study of obedience. *Journal of Abnormal and Social Psychology, 67*(4): 371–378.
Zimbardo, P. G. (1971). The power and pathology of imprisonment. *Congressional Record, 15:* 10–25.
Žižek, S. (2009). *Violence.* London: Verso.

PART IV
THE "I" AND MOURNING

Editor's introduction to
Chapter Eleven

Nationalism, argues the author in this chapter, is always problematic; its basic operation is such that its apparently benign form is better understood as a latent moment of its more malign manifestation. Nationalism is intimately bound up with an idea of identification, and identification is a process; identity is not a given. In Seminar VII, *The Ethics of Psychoanalysis*, Lacan discusses the figure of the other under the term "neighbour" (referring to the biblical directive to love one's neighbour and Freud's critique of the realism of this directive), commenting that "my neighbor possesses all the evil Freud speaks about, but it is no different from the evil I retreat from in myself. To love him, to love him as myself, is necessarily to move towards some cruelty". The encounter with the other, it is argued, can be understood as consisting in three moments: the symbolic, the imaginary, and the real. In other words, there is that in the other which can be grasped on the basis of identification, that which can be grasped on the basis of comprehension, and that which escapes our grasp. The term given to this latter, ungraspable "component" is *das Ding*. While, in itself, *das Ding* must be without value, it tends to have an extreme negative value assigned to it: the evil referred to above. The author considers this gravitation towards assigning an evil character to the unknown in the other and the assigning of evil to the other, the neighbour, on the basis of this unknown. This is considered in light of the first dimension of encounter, that of identification and, specifically, national identity. Each of us enters the planet within the boundaries of a space called a nation. To refuse the slippage into an identification, into nationalism, concludes the author, is the point where the hard work starts.

The evil I retreat from in myself: nationalism and *das Ding*

Calum Neill

When it comes to nationalism we might ask, to paraphrase Edwin Starr, what is it good for? And if you know your Edwin Starr, you will understand the direction the argument of this chapter will take. Against the assumption, which is commonplace enough, that there are good nationalisms and bad nationalisms and that one is worth preserving while the other should be opposed, I shall argue that nationalism is always problematic, that the basic operation of nationalism is such that its apparently benign form is better understood as a latent moment of its more malign manifestation.

Nationalism is intimately bound up with an idea of identification. We gaze into the mirror of national identity and we find a version of what we might become. The mirror image, the projection of national identity, appears alluring in that it offers an image of completion, a sense of belonging, a suture for the lack we experience. Which is, then, necessarily to say that that which we come to internalise, that with which we choose, however unconsciously, to identify, is never what was there before. Identification is a process. Which is to say that identity is not a given.

This, of course, is the lesson of the mirror stage and, as Lacan insists, we should keep in mind that the mirror stage is not simply a moment of infanthood, a stage that is passed through and left behind (Lacan, 1949, p. 76). The *stade* in *stade du miroir* should be understood with all its polysemic variety. *Stade* is also stadium, connoting spectacle and performance as well as enclosure and, as Lacan explicitly draws our attention to in the paper itself, a stadium is a divided space and a space of contest (Lacan, 1949, p. 78). It is also a space that is empty at its core.

So, the mirror stage is something that is with us always. It is a perpetual mode of identification and what is crucial in the mirror stage is that we identify with something outside of ourselves. The mirror stage concerns the other, what is other to the one who would identify. It is the story of how we confront something external to ourselves and through this confrontation we develop an imaginary idea of what we might become ourselves. Which is to say, we come to identify with something that appears, that has the image of being, more cohesive than we are ourselves. What this sets up from infanthood, then, is a constant longing to be that which is more coherent. What is at the heart of the experience of the mirror stage, as well as the essay and the theory, is the fact that we are not coherent. This, then, means that identity is but a fantasy of coherence. We want to assume a coherence we do not have. We experience ourselves in an immediate bodily sense as incoherent, we experience ourselves in life as incoherent, and yet we want to be coherent.

So, life is a pulsion. It is a push forward towards this idea of coherence that is always a fantasy. We can see this in Lacan's formula of fantasy, which encapsulates very neatly the idea that what I fantasise is my divided self in conjunction with something that would make me complete. What Lacan calls *objet petit a*; $ \diamond a$.

This is not to say that the mirror stage entails something like a straightforward becoming other. The infant confronting the other of its own mirror image also sees, for example, its own hand as it reaches out to the image it would take to be itself. It sees its own arm and it does not know what it is, does not know how it links up with the rest of its body, and it is only through seeing the external image that it gets something like a blueprint, an idea of what it would become, an idea of the coherence it does not experience itself as having. What Lacan is arguing, then, is that the idea of a coherent self is an after-effect; it is not something we have originally or essentially. This is, then, to say that what you encounter in the mirror is never what you are. We could say that the key point in the mirror stage is that what you see in front of you is not you; it is an image of you, which is to say that it is, quite literally, not you. We all know ourselves, all have an idea of ourselves from looking in the mirror. You look in the bathroom mirror every morning as you shave, put on make-up, brush your teeth, but what you see is only a frontal figure of yourself, and perhaps only your face. But this is what you come to imagine yourself as and it is not what everyone else sees. They will see the back of your head, your profile, other angles.

We have an idea of ourselves that is formed through this mirror image, this image which is also literally a mirror image, in that it is an inverted image. What you see in the mirror in the morning is not yourself. It does not even look like you. Everything is the wrong way round. So, you have this division. You have this idea of yourself, which is taken from what is external and is internalised, and this comes to be what is at the heart of you. From the beginning we are split, divided from ourselves. "The subject is no one. It is decomposed, in pieces. And it is jammed, sucked in by the image, the deceiving and realised image, of the other, or equally by its own specular image. That is where it finds its unity" (Lacan, 1978, p. 54).

We should keep in mind, too, that, in addition to the other of the virtual self reflected in the mirror, essential to the mirror stage, even in its developmental sense, is the presence of someone else (Lacan, 1975, p. 146). So, there is always not just oneself as an Other, but also always other others in the mirror stage.

In terms of the Lacanian triad of Imaginary, Symbolic, and Real, identification is imaginary, but it is always conjoined with the symbolic. For identification, you need the other. In the developmental sense of the mirror stage, the mOther holds the baby in front of the mirror and says, "Look, that's you." Imaginary identification is always wrapped in some kind of symbolic explanation. There is never a complete separation of the two. In the same sense, there is always an other, as identification does not occur if we are not already born into a society and a language that precede us. In the simplest sense, you cannot identify yourself without recourse to the terms of the other: a name, a description, an association, a commonality. To identify oneself is necessarily to appeal to an outside of oneself. Even in this simplest sense, to identify is already to declare oneself divided.

We can understand this problematic of identification further by turning to Lacan's seminar on ethics. Here, he develops his notion of *das Ding*, which, although it could be understood as a precursor to his notion of *objet petit a*, stands as a distinct concept with its own nuance. In discussing *das Ding* in Seminar VII, Lacan is drawing our attention to the fact that the process of identification, although seemingly dominated by the imaginary, always involves all three components. This point comes to the fore later when he develops the full blown theory of the Imaginary, Symbolic, and the Real and uses the symbol of the Borromean knot, the knot of three circles which are linked in such a way that breaking one of the circles will result in the other two falling apart, suggesting, quite simply, that you cannot separate them. Identity, while always imaginary, is never simply imaginary. We never, that is, simply have an image of who we are, but always also have an idea of who we are. You can answer the question "Who are you?", but you can also feel who you are and want to feel a certain cohesion in this idea. This seems to be a fairly normal disorder, to have this attachment to these identification processes. The point Lacan is trying to make in *The Ethics of Psychoanalysis* (1986) is that there is also this third component, and this is what he calls *das Ding*. Whenever we look at ourselves, whether physically looking at ourselves or conceptually looking at ourselves, whether we imagine ourselves or we try to symbolise ourselves, there is always something that escapes. There is always something of us that is beyond symbolisation and beyond imagination, something that cannot be captured within those two realms. This is what Lacan calls *das Ding*.

Lacan brings in his discussion of *das Ding* while engaging with a moment in Freud's *Civilisation and Its Discontents* (1930a), where Freud ruminates on the idea of loving thy neighbour, the great commandment to love thy neighbour as thyself. Evoking this discussion in the context of a seminar on ethics, Lacan's point clearly concerns the question of how we relate to the other. His point is that identification always implies the other and so is always already a step towards this relation to the other. In identifying ourselves, we cannot help but identify something in the other and, as we identify something in the other, we cannot help but identify something in ourselves.

Drawing on Freud, Lacan goes on to make the point, which has been much repeated by Žižek, that there is always something horrific in the neighbour. Freud initially reacts to the injunction to love one's neighbour with "surprise and bewilderment" (Freud, 1930a, p. 109) but this soon turns to what Lacan characterises as "horror" (Lacan, 1986, p. 186) as he describes man's aggression to his own type; *homo homini lupus* (Freud, 1930a, p. 111). Freud's concern is twofold. He questions not only why we would want to love our neighbour as ourselves, but, moreover, how this will even be possible. How can I actually love my neighbour as I love myself? Love, Freud argues, is something special. It is something I should keep for those who are closest to me, for my family, my friends. I cannot go around loving any old neighbour. That would be to cheapen my love, to give it away, to squander it. Lacan disagrees with Freud on this point and suggests that we can use Freud's consternation here to get to the heart of what is going on in this Biblical and Talmudic injunction.

For Lacan, the commandment to love thy neighbour draws our attention to the persistence of *das Ding*. When I encounter the neighbour there is something in the neighbour that I cannot comprehend but that there is something in the neighbour that I cannot comprehend is also to point to the fact that there is something in myself that I cannot comprehend. This, for Lacan, opens up a space for breaking down the absolute border between self and other, between the closest, the familial, and the neighbourly, the enemy (Neill, 2011, p. 168).

> Every time that Freud stops short in horror at the consequences of the commandment to love one's neighbour we see evoked the presence of the Fundamental evil which dwells within this neighbour but if this is the case then it also dwells within me. (Lacan, 1986, p. 186)

Lacan draws our attention to a peculiar disjunction that appears to be denied in Freud: that that which is at the heart of me is also outside of me (Lacan, 1986, p. 87). This extimacy, as Lacan terms it, this exterior intimacy, this intimate exteriority, lies at the conceptual core of identification. Identification always entails this complex wherein the most intimate is always already predicated on the internalisation of what was (mis)taken from outside and what is seen to be outside is always already comprehended in terms of its fit with what is assumed to be inside. Inside and outside cannot be broken down. The evil I take to be in the other is also, then, the evil I retreat from in myself.

This complex of identification is at the core of the question of loving one's neighbour and the question of loving one's neighbour emerges when we begin to speak of nationalism. For Freud, the experience of the nationalisms of the First World War, as well as the identifications evident in historic invasions such as those of the Huns or Mongols and the religious identifications of the Crusades, all point to a confrontation with this injunction to love thy neighbour. Identifications such as nationalism are predicated on an exclusion that is never far from aggressivity. There is no nationalism without an other. Whether in a grand sense or a smaller sense, whether it is a forceful sense or a quiet sense, there is always a sense of the other. It simply makes no sense to have a nationalism that does not, at some level, imply some otherness, whether that is an otherness that has crept inside the nation or an otherness that sits on the other side of a boundary that marks the nation.

There is another reference to the commandment to love thy neighbour in Freud, in addition to the famous passage in *Civilization and its Discontents*. It is a much earlier and less direct reference. It comes from 1892, in one of the early drafts, Draft H, in the *Standard Edition*, where he is discussing paranoia. "They, the paranoiacs," he says, in conclusion, "love their delusion as they love themselves" (Freud, 1892, p. 212). There is clearly a parallelism at work here: neighbours and delusions. But what exactly is Freud saying here? Is this something peculiar to paranoiacs, that they love their delusions as they love themselves? It is certainly not the case that only paranoiacs have delusions. Perhaps, then, what Freud is saying is that we all love our delusions as we love ourselves or, to flip that around, we love ourselves as a delusion, which is to say that all identification is already a delusion which then, when we conjoin that with the idea of the neighbour, seems to suggest that we love the neighbour as we love the delusion of ourselves. This brings us to the Lacanian point. We need to go a little bit further and, rather than simply follow the letter of the injunction, we need to problematise the injunction and problematise the very notion of identification itself.

Identification is always in danger of becoming a solidification, is always in danger of becoming something absolute, something of which we feel we can be certain. Linked to this, part of the problem with identification, or part of the hidden dimension of identification, is those elements of identification which constitute the framework through which we try to comprehend identification, the very way we start to think identification, the very way we start to think of what the self is. A crucial contemporary instance of this is the dominance of psychology and the way it has come to determine how we see things in the twentieth and twenty-first centuries. Our time is a time of psychologisation.

Our time is a time of psychologisation, but psychology itself, in terms of its idea of the self, often unwittingly, builds on the work of René Descartes. The *cogito* encapsulates the modern sense of what the self is. It is so prevalent that it has almost become something that is impossible to argue against. It has become a common sense. It has become the sense of ourselves that we have in common. For many, this is simply something which would not be questioned. The Cartesian sense of the self is a very absolute sense of the self, an atomised self. What Descartes engages in is a process of doubt to find something of which he can be certain, and what he finds eventually is that what he can be certain of is himself. So, identity in Descartes, in a sense, is the first thing, it is the prime mover. But Descartes is also then symbolic of a certain sense of the very framework of how we understand personal identity. He is symbolic of the fact that we already understand identity as something separated, isolated, that we understand identity in terms of, and as synonymous with, individualism. Descartes, in this sense, is the marker of the turn to modernity, with the notion of identity as core to this turn.

If we conceive of the turn to modernity as the time of the dissolution of certainty, Descartes, as its metonymic marker, stands as a paradoxical figure. After centuries of Aristotelianism, Europe is forced to confront the failure of this system and, consequently, must seek a new philosophy. Rhetorically, in embarking on this task, Descartes sets out with his method of universal doubt. He is, or at least he dresses himself as, the very embodiment of uncertainty, but what he arrives at, and what he always sought, was a new, post-Aristotelian, certainty. We might understand the pillars of pre-modern life as the church and the monarchy. These are not only the institutions, but also the frameworks of understanding that could give sense to the world. These were the things in which one could be certain and, thus, the things that could provide certainty to the world. With Descartes, these pillars start to crumble, but the mission becomes not one of embracing uncertainty. Rather, the mission becomes the solidification of a new certainty. It is this that places Descartes at the centre. Through his process of universal doubt, he is able to erect a new certainty: a certainty in the self.

The certainty Descartes erects is the certainty contemporary psychology clings to and promulgates. Where the guarantors of certainty found in religion and a divinely ordained monarch fade, what emerges in their place is the self-identical, self-knowing subject of psychology. The mistake at the heart of Descartes *cogito* is, however, carried over here, and what we end up with is a faux certainty which can be no more certain than the outmoded certainties it replaced.

When Descartes deduces his core being as the thinking thing that persists as the one thing of which he can be certain, what he misses is that he necessarily already embarks from another certainty. From the outset, Descartes forgets to question the language through which he formulates and fashions his deductions and, ultimately, his self. The issue here is not simply that Descartes unwittingly imports the logic and rules of Latin grammar into his supposed pure thinking of the possibility of existence, but also that he bases his conclusion that the first thing of which he can be certain is his own solitary self on the prior, but unacknowledged, assumption of a social medium. Before the individualism that Descartes posits as primary, there is necessarily an other.

The self is social, if unconsciously so.

Nationalism itself arises around this same time. With the advent of modernity, we see the displacement of religion by science, the demise of feudalism, the revolts against monarchy in much of Europe, the invention of the printing press, the development of capitalism, and the emergence of the nation state. Amid this cacophony of social upheaval, modernity quietly establishes identity as the last pillar. This allows the flattening of religious hierarchies that, in turn, facilitates the conception of liberal democracies. This required some corralling, a process made possible by the popularisation of the printing press and the subsequent uniformisation of languages. The resultant nation states come then to rely upon a certain identificatory mode: nationalism. Just like the certainty of self we inherit from Descartes, so, too, the nation state comes to be seen as a timeless, irreducible, and natural phenomenon. The modern atomistic individual lives in a modern atomistic state and, unsurprisingly, comes to identify with this entity as though it were real.

In his *Critique of Hegel's 'Philosophy of Right'*, Marx makes the claim that "democracy is the essence of every political constitution" (1843, p. 30). On a first reading, such a notion might be understood to point to a historical inevitability, that democracy is somehow the essential form of governance that will, under the correct conditions, emerge from the flawed backdrop of monarchy. Marx aside, this seems a common enough presentation of what democracy is and stands for. In such a conception, what sits unquestioned in the background is the nation state itself.

What Marx's text allows us to discern, however, is an indication of that which monarchy would suture. In claiming that democracy is necessarily already "the truth of monarchy" (1943, p. 29), Marx should not necessarily be understood to be claiming a substantiality for democracy; rather, he should be understood as describing the complex conditions of uncertainty, which necessarily unpin any subjective engagement in the political. Democracy is the truth of monarchy in so far as even monarchies only function because we believe in them. Absolute monarchies function because we believe in them in an absolute sense. We do not decide in any conventional sense to believe in them. There is no conscious moment in which we endorse the monarchy. Retrospectively, however, we can understand that there was always a decision at work. The point at which we chop the monarch's head off is the point at which the monarch no longer functions for us and we no longer believe in them.

The logic here is the logic espoused by Lacan in his theory of the four discourses. Lacan argues that social relations operate on the basis of four fixed and relative positions. Each discourse implies an agent from which the message is seen to emanate. This message will be conveyed towards another, but never entirely successfully, as each moment of discourse entails failure on various levels; it is simply not possible to say it all, words cannot capture everything, there is always more to be said. This failure results in an excess, a product which is both creative and uncontainable. The agent itself, however, should not be understood as the instigator of its own discourse or as a certainty in itself. The agent is supported and, thus, the very discursive position from which it would be seen to speak is made possible by virtue of a truth which underpins it.

$$\frac{\text{agent} \rightarrow \text{other}}{\text{truth} \; // \; \text{product}}$$

These four functions constitute, in Lacan's schema, four unchanging positions into which four elements fit. The elements then rotate between these positions, creating different discourses depending on the positions occupied. The elements Lacan delimits are the subject, the master signifier, the chain of signifiers, and *objet petit a*. The subject is key here, for without subjective implication, discourse is not discourse, it is mere code. But the subject can occupy any of the four positions in the schema. The configuration that concerns us here, with regard to the nation, is what Lacan terms the discourse of the master.

$$\frac{S_1 \rightarrow S_2}{\$ \,//\, a}$$

The discourse of the master captures neatly the point Marx wants to make with regard to democracy being the truth of monarchy. A master signifier for Lacan is that which confers sense, that which provides the possibility of some sense accruing around a combination of words. It is the guarantor that halts the otherwise never ending questioning of what is said. The master signifier is the authority behind the *because I said so*. In our context here, the master signifier can be understood to be the signifier of the monarch.

$$\frac{\text{Monarch} \rightarrow S_2}{\$ \,//\, a}$$

By so placing the monarch, it becomes clear that it, the monarchy, functions because it is underpinned by subjective belief. The subject endorses the monarchy and keeps it in place. The monarch, as master signifier, addresses the political field, the law, but in doing so, it always produces an excess, a remainder. This remainder, however, is never commensurate with the subjective underpinning of the monarch's agency and, consequently, the configuration cannot hold. The discourse of the master cannot be maintained for the simple reason that it is fragile, and it is fragile because it is always reliant for its authority on subjective endorsement.

Of course, monarchy here does not need to be a traditional monarchy. Contemporary monarchies rarely name themselves as such. Take, for example, the events of the Arab Spring. An absolute ruler like Muammar al-Qadafi could maintain power for forty-two years, his removal from his position seemingly unthinkable, and yet protests against his regime began in February 2011. Within days a National Transitional Council had been established and within a month this council had declared itself the legitimate representative of the people.

Within nine months the unopposable leader had been executed. Forty-two years of subjective endorsement turned. This turn is figured in our schema with a clockwise rotation of the elements: a revolution.

$$\frac{\$ \rightarrow S_1}{a \; / / \; S_2}$$

The subject comes to occupy the position of agency

Essentially, what we have at work here is the gist of Hans Christian Andersen's "The Emperor's New Clothes" (1837). The Emperor parades around town wearing his fine new robes and everyone applauds. Everyone is thoroughly satisfied with the situation, until one young boy points out the fact that the Emperor is not actually wearing any clothes and suddenly the crowd turns on the Emperor and his position becomes untenable at that point: the people see him as naked.

Historically, we have a shift away from monarchy, away from this absolutism. The common name for this shift is democracy. This is Marx's point. But we should remember that this democracy is very fragile. We can easily become self-congratulatory, but democracy as truth is not something that is easily maintained. We might well have done away with absolutes, in the sense of absolute monarchs, but we are perpetually in danger of assuming the particular mechanism of what we call democracy itself as an absolute.

With the advent of modernity, we have dispensed with the notion of an absolute master or monarch and we have replaced it with a system that purports to maintain an open space as the location of power. Into this open space, figures will step, but they are not, or are not supposed to be, commensurate with the seat of power itself. Each president or prime minister occupies a position, but it is the position that is authorised to rule on behalf of the people, the elected representative is but a temporary occupant.

This idea of democracy is, however, only one side of the story. The other side of the story is nationalism. With the dissolution of traditional monarchies, the rule of the people is only one dimension of what emerges in its place. For there to be a rule of the people, there must be a people. *A* people. Implying, then, an identity. Historically, the most evident means of attaining such an identity is through the supposition of the nation as identifiable entity. Which is to say, where democracy is one side of the story, nationalism is the other.

Nationalism is the reoccupation of this position of the master. We no longer have the monarchy, we no longer have this pre-rationalistic belief in a political absolute. But, apparently, our gravitation towards, our reliance upon, such absolutes is strong. Thus, we replace this with the idea of nationalism. Here, the flag becomes the ultimate symbol, the new master signifier.

Put very simply, there is something wrong with nationalism. There is something wrong with nationalism in a structural sense. It is not that there is something wrong with certain forms of nationalism which are malignant, as opposed to those forms of nationalism which are benign. The problem is the construct of nationalism itself, the erection of the nation as a point of identification, for the simple, structural fact is that this is never more than a misidentification.

In one of the seemingly less controversial moments in his 2006 performance at the White House Correspondents' Association Dinner, the comedian Stephen Colbert declares,

> I'm a simple man with a simple mind. I hold a simple set of beliefs that I live by. Number one, I believe in America. I believe it exists. My gut tells me I live there. I feel that it extends from the Atlantic to the Pacific, and I strongly believe it has 50 states. (Colbert, 2006, p. 220)

The humour here obviously relies on the ambiguous usage of the word "believe". To believe is both to acknowledge the existence of and to deeply endorse or support something. This play on "believe" draws our attention to a common enough slippage from nation to nationalism. That there are nations does not necessarily imply a need for nationalism. Colbert's joke rests on the unusual separation of these two notions, the separating out of what are properly two distinct discourses; the discourse of the nation and the discourse of nationalism. Each of us, through dint of the political conditions of our time in history, can be understood to enter the planet within the boundaries of a certain juridical space. We call such a space a nation. Through certain legal processes, we can come to gain membership of other bounded spaces. To slip from such contingencies into an identification is, to return to Freud, to start to love our delusion as we love ourselves.

To refuse this slippage, however, to refuse the call of the delusion, is not an easy thing. This, then, is the ethical point here. This is the point where the hard work starts.

References

Andersen, H. C. (1837). The Emperor's New Clothes. In: *Fairy Tales*, J. Wullschlager (Ed.), T. Nunnalli (Trans.). London: Penguin, 2004.

Colbert, S. (2006). The White House correspondents' dinner. In: *I Am America (And So Can You)* (pp. 218–227). New York: Grand Central, 2007.

Freud, S. (1895). Draft H: Paranoia (Extracts From The Fliess Papers). *S.E.*, 1: 206–212. London: Hogarth.

Freud, S. (1930a). *Civilization and its Discontents. S.E., 21*: 59–145. London: Hogarth.

Lacan, J. (1949). The mirror stage as formative of the function of the I as revealed in psychoanalytic experience. In: *Écrits: The First Complete Edition in English* (pp. 75–81), B. Fink (Trans.). London: Norton.

Lacan, J. (1975). *Freud's Paper on Technique: The Seminar of Jacques Lacan, Book I, 1953–1954*, J. Forrester (Trans.). New York: Norton, 1988.

Lacan, J. (1978). *The Ego in Freud's Theory and in the Technique of Psychoanalysis: The Seminar of Jacques Lacan, Book II, 1954–1955*, S. Tomaselli (Trans.). New York: Norton, 1988.

Lacan, J. (1986). *The Ethics of Psychoanalysis: The Seminar of Jacques Lacan, Book VII, 1959–1960*, D. Porter (Trans.). New York: Norton, 1992.

Marx, K. (1843). *Critique of Hegel's 'Philosophy of Right'*, J. O'Malley (Ed.). Cambridge: Cambridge University Press, 1970.

Neill, C. (2011). *Lacanian Ethics and the Assumption of Subjectivity*. Basingstoke: Palgrave MacMillan.

Editor's introduction to Chapter Twelve

The chapter explores fantasy and melancholia in relation to political and social violence. The author argues that violence is either "put" outside an identity (through projection) and/or inside it (through introjection), depending on how identities deal with lack. In fantasy that accompanies episodes of political violence and nationalist hatreds, it is argued, there is an overproduction of meaning and enjoyment of exclusion of the feminised other who appears as a threat to the possibility of "fullness" of the national identity. Violence is here related to a constitutive lack (or impossibility of representation) in every social identity and to the dynamics of covering up such lack, which include the creation of scapegoats. Melancholia, on the other hand, is related to a type of violence that is neither heroic nor sacrificial (as most cases of political violence which involve fantasy); it is characterised by the fact that lack is neither covered nor projected, but introjected instead. Not having a clear scapegoat for their own failure, melancholic subjects introject blame and hatred. If melancholia is no longer thought of as the right to recover the lost object, but as the mourning of the (lacking) Thing, both fantasy and melancholia could be seen as mechanisms for dealing with the impossibility of the real: its covering up would be constitutive of ideological fantasy, the attitude of exposing the space of lack characteristic of melancholia. Thus formulated, melancholia not only no longer informs struggles for political justice, but even produces violence—violence of a kind where the self and the other die together, or where self and other are together "only in death".

CHAPTER TWELVE

Between fantasy and melancholia: lack, otherness, and violence

Margarita Palacios

Introduction

Psychoanalytic theory has demonstrated that it is able to help in the conceptual analysis of processes of social exclusion and violence (i.e., nationalism, ethnic hatred, totalitarianism) and the libidinal dynamics involved in otherwise regarded to be exclusively social and political processes (Glynos & Stavrakakis, 2008; Palacios, 2004, 2009; Palacios & Posocco, 2011; Yegenoglu, 1998; Žižek, 1997). This conceptual "success", particularly of the use of the notion of fantasy, in my view has not been paralleled by the use of the notion of emancipatory melancholia. Indeed, it is quite interesting to see that while the concept of fantasy has been used to understand processes of othering, exclusion, and political violence, the concept of melancholia has inspired a variety of research on militant resistance precisely to those acts of exclusion and violence (Butler, 1997; Cheng, 2000; Eng & Kazanjian, 2003; Khanna, 2003). In particular, works on gender, sexuality, race, and ethnicity have stated that the "impossibility of finishing processes of mourning" informs political struggles against a variety of violences and exclusions that marginal subjectivities have suffered; that is, the lost object will not be let go.

My argument is that the possibility of this conceptual distinction (between, so to say, being able to differentiate "non-democratic and democratic political struggles") is based on the fact that the first approach (on fantasy) theorises violence as related to a constitutive lack (or impossibility of representation) in every social identity and to the dynamics of covering up of such lack, which include the creation of scapegoats, who are blamed for every failure of society, and their consequent exclusion from social life. The second approach, on emancipatory melancholia, on the other hand, does not theorise lack, but loss. This allows theorists of racial and gender melancholia to state that a "certain object was possessed", then lost and not mourned. The recovery of the lost object is what appears as a (legitimate) struggle for justice and some form of reparation. I want to argue here that this appears as a conceptual fallacy in so far as the theorisation of loss (as opposed to lack) and the political agency that such claim (of unjust loss) provides in many ways resemble the very logic of fantasy itself, which is precisely characterised by the denial of lack in the first place, and the illusion of recovering what was never possessed. To quote Žižek,

> insofar as the object-cause of desire is originally, in a constitutive way, lacking, melancholy interprets this lack as a loss, as if the lacking object was once possessed and then lost. In short, what melancholy obfuscates is that the object is lacking from the very beginning, that its emergence coincides with its lack, that this object is nothing but the positivization of a void or lack of a purely anamorphic entity that does not exist in itself. The paradox, of course, is that this deceitful translation of lack into loss enables us to assert our possession of the object. What we never possessed can also never be lost, so the melancholic, in his unconditional fixation on the lost object, in a way possesses it in its very loss . . . .. For this reason, melancholy is not simply the attachment to the lost object but the attachment to the very original gesture of its loss. (Žižek, 2000, pp. 659–660)

In an attempt to differentiate expressions of violence that clearly spring from phallic fantasy logics from other expressions of violence (which are commonly perceived as "anomic" forms of social violence or related to "narcissism"), I would like to explore the notion of melancholia. Broadly defined, this logic would be characterised by the severity of the introjected super-egoic-cultural mandate (i.e., "you have to succeed no matter what") and, at the same time, by the fragility or incapacity of the "signifier" to provide a mediating fantasy—which acts as an ideological protective mechanism—that could secure a subjective position regarding meaning and desire, while evacuating enjoyment or the death drive. That is to say, in this symbolic constellation, the subject and "a" would not be—or, at least, not entirely—separated by fantasy or the signifier, but in much closer proximity to each other. As with every identity formation, this logic of melancholic inclusion challenges us with new paradoxes. Although, in this case, a clear friend–enemy line is not constituted (and, therefore, there seems to be more space for inclusion of otherness and less political antagonism), aggression towards the self and any other (not necessarily an ideological enemy) seems to emerge without a particular "ideological" motive, but informed by a variety of locally established or spontaneous struggles or disputes. I would argue that this is so because, instead of processes of "projective identification" (on to the excluded other as the cause of the failure of the symbolic mandate and failure to enjoy), this symbolic constellation of "failed fantasy" seems to be characterised by the introjection of the death drive and the lack of covering of the abject-Thing. Although this would result in what is commonly perceived as "weakened" social ties, in my view this would not spring from lack of the establishment of symbolic order and, therefore, from the reign of imaginary aggression (i.e., narcissism), but from the logics of a melancholic symbolic space which hides a deeper nihilistic and defiant approach towards the self, others, desire, and the possibilities of satisfaction.[1] Not having a clear scapegoat for its own failure, melancholic subjects introject the blame—and hatred—which has not been projected outwards as in the case of fantasy.

In order to further explore these ideas, it will be necessary to displace the notion of melancholia from its current privileged status, where it is primarily understood as reflecting forms of political emancipation. In what follows, I shall start by looking at the genealogy of the relation between melancholia and criticality, and then elaborate on the conceptual distinction between lack and loss. I will argue that once melancholia is theorised as a particular way of dealing with lack, it could also illuminate the analysis of forms of violence against self and others which are not necessarily politically emancipatory.

Melancholia and criticality

The study of melancholy has a long trajectory. It was the Greeks who developed the "humoral" theories, and first described melancholia as a particular temperament resulting from excessive black bile in the body (a theory that offered a cosmology which related the body to transpersonal forces, such as the seasons); in the Middle Ages, melancholia was perceived as a sin, the sin of *acedia*, expressed in lack of interest for the "glory of god", and in the Renaissance, melancholics were no longer sinners but geniuses: melancholy was the necessary temperament for philosophers and thinkers, who are inclined to think of difficult and absent things, and implied the notion of heightened self-awareness. Although not elaborated openly, at this point melancholia became associated with heroic action, essentially referring to the capacity of dwelling on *acedia* as a way of fighting against it. To put it differently, writing on melancholia was seen as a way of combating melancholia.

Particularly in the context of contemporary critical theory, the name of Walter Benjamin is crucial here, as he revived the notion of "heroic melancholia". As several of Benjamin's commentators have argued, for Benjamin, the notion of melancholia had a paradoxical and central status in his notion of criticality. Although Benjamin despised the melancholic lament of his contemporaries (as expressed in his *Linke Melancholie*, (Benjamin, 2005) where he accused the Left of not being rebellious enough, but, rather, of just being sad for what they had lost), the status of melancholia as a method is remarkable in his notion of criticality. The question for Benjamin was, then, how melancholia's political dimension could be activated, that is, how the passivity associated with melancholia could be superseded. As Pensky has argued,

> Benjamin in the last years of the Weimar Republic, understood a critique of melancholia as a demand for decisiveness and thus a victory over, rather than a redemption of, the object of critique. Critique is a strategic act in a politics of intervention, directed toward the heard of the present, against a politics of melancholia. (Pensky, 1993, p. 12)

Melancholia, in Benjamin's writing, is related to the process of distanciation, that is, it relates to the moment of separation between subject and object, and the possibility of emergence of meaning (or, in the case of Benjamin, the destruction of the "myth"). In his theory of allegory (or allegorical transformation) Benjamin argues,

> the deadening of emotions, and the ebbing away of which are the source of these emotions in the body, can increase the distance between the self and the surrounding world to the point of alienation from the body. (Cited in Flatley, 2008, p. 37)

This (melancholic) state, where the objects lack meaning according to Benjamin, prepares and facilitates allegorical transformation. So, if Benjamin opposes the inaction that might be associated with melancholic sadness, he believes that melancholy—dwelling on loss, the past, and political failures—enables insights in the logic of history and changes in the present world.

Decline and loss, in Benjamin and others, are associated with the experience of modernity. In his *Affective Mapping, Melancholia and the Politics of Modernism* (2008), Flatley argues that modernity and loss are inextricably linked, starting from the loss of the past:

> In fact it may be that modernity signals nothing more or less than the impulse to declare the difference of a present moment in respect to moments that preceded it, to perceive the specificity and difference of one's own historical moment. (Flatley, 2008, p. 29)

However, it was not only temporality, but a whole array of transformations—from urbanisation to industrialisation, secularism, bureaucracy, science, and technology—that created a new environment which, while offering promise and hope, also meant the facing of the failures and even horrors that derived from some of the modern interventions in the world.

According to Benjamin, modernity triggered protective mechanisms, or "shields", which insulate individuals from disruptive emotional experiences. He argued that this shielding results in a lack of affective contact with the material world, a change in temporality and fewer memory experiences associated with objects and places. In this context, Benjamin proposes historical materialism as a practice of melancholic remembrance:

> wherein what has been comes together in a flash with the now to form a constellation . . . a combination of surprising historico-political

insight that brings with it a joltingly electric sense of emotional investment in the possibility of transformation. (2008, p. 72)

Seizing images from the past is central in revolutionary action; that is,
for Benjamin, revolutionary consciousness is necessarily melancholic,
and, as Flatley puts it, "conversely, melancholia contains within it a
revolutionary kernel" (2008, p. 74).

It is this relation between melancholia and criticality that I think
has informed the current use of melancholia in gender and racial studies. Before we turn to them, let us look briefly at the account that is
given to us by Freud, whose own writings on melancholia took place
during the First World War, a moment of history that was openly
marked by decline and loss.

Freud's essay "Mourning and melancholia" (1917e) starts by differ-
entiating "normal mourning" from melancholia. Mourning, Freud
writes, "is regularly the reaction to the loss of a loved person, or to the
loss of some abstraction which has taken the place of one, such as one's
country, liberty, an ideal, and so on" (Freud, 1917e, p. 243). In this
context, mourning involves a process of detaching "each one of the
memories and expectations in which the libido is bound to the object"
(1917e, p. 245). During this process, the mourner pretends the object is
still there by almost obsessively recollecting memories of it, a process
which imaginarily extends the life of what has been lost, although not
indefinitely. Once the mourner establishes that the object is no longer
there, and once the process of mourning is done, the mourner can
make other libidinal attachments. Melancholia is of a different nature.
Although mourning and melancholia are psychic strategies in
response to the absence of the libidinal object, melancholics, instead of
projecting feelings of anger or withdrawal into compensatory objects,
turn those feelings upon themselves. As Freud writes,

> The distinguishing mental features of melancholia are a profoundly
> painful dejection, cessation of interest in the outside world, loss of the
> capacity to love, inhibition of all activity, and the lowering of the self-
> regarding feelings to a degree that finds utterance in self-reproaches
> and self-revilings, and culminates in a delusional expectation of
> punishment. (Freud, 1917e, p. 244)

Different from mourning, cathexis is no longer attached to external objects, but to the ego itself. This "introjected emotional tie, to

reiterate, introduces a particular relationality into the ego, producing a 'cleavage' (as Freud writes) in which one part of the ego (the critical agency) 'rages' against the other" (Flatley, 2008, p. 47). According to Freud, this critical raging responds to the ambivalent presence of the emotional tie. That is, although ambivalence is characteristic of any emotional tie, for Freud this ambivalence in the context of loss is expressed in the open. Freud writes,

> If love for the object – a love which cannot be given up though the object itself is given up takes refuge in narcissistic identification, then the hate comes into operation on this substitute object, abusing it, debasing it, making it suffer and deriving sadistic satisfaction from its suffering. (Freud, 1917e, p. 251)

Interestingly, although not exactly "Benjaminian", Freud also assigns to melancholia a critical, active agency. In his *The Ego and the Id* (1923b), Freud revises his previous opposition between mourning and melancholia, and argues that all losses require some type of incor- poration or introjection. In other words, "there is no melancholic loss, no mourning that leaves the ego unchanged. Indeed, he (Freud) goes even further to argue that the very character of the ego is *formed* by its lost objects" (Flatley, 2008, p. 49). As Flatley explains, according to Freud, all losses of sexual objects are dealt with melancholically through the establishment of the object inside the ego:

> When it happens that a person has to give up a sexual object, there quite often ensues an alternation of his ego which can only be described as a setting up of the object inside the ego, as it occurs in melancholia . . . It may be that this identification is the sole condition under which the id can give up its objects. . . . it makes it possible to suppose that the character of the ego is a precipitate of abandoned object cathexes and that it contains the history of those object choices. (Flatley, 2008, p. 49).

The work of sociologist Wolf Lepenis, and, in particular, his *Melancholy and Society* (1992), to a certain extent also continues with this presupposition of the link between melancholia and criticism while arguing that melancholia is a cultural phenomenon charac- terised by the rejection of means and ends of "sanctioned social behaviour". According to Lepenis, the melancholic rebel recedes into a "resigned interiority", characterised by homesickness for the past, and apathy for the present. This is expressed in pessimist ideologies and the belief in the futility of action and indecisiveness.

It is in this very long trajectory that links loss and criticism, or melancholia and critique, that the work of postcolonial and gender melancholia can be situated. Let us look, for instance, at the way David Eng formulates the problem:

> As Freud's premier theory of unspeakable loss and inexorable suffer-ing, melancholia serves as a powerful tool for analyzing the psychic production, condition, and limits of marginalized subjectivities predi-cated on states of injury. In this regard, melancholia as a theory of unresolved grief is useful for investigating the formation of not only gendered subjects but also a host of other minoritarian group identi-ties mobilized through identity-politics movements of the last quarter-century. (Eng, 2000, p. 1276)

Moreover, it is this condition of marginalised subjectivity which acts as a political transformative force:

> As a psychic paradigm in which the lost object holds pride of place, melancholia's tenacious attachment to objects of loss convinces us, finally, of something we might otherwise doubt: our enduring attach-ment to (disparaged) others. . . . In this formulation lies a nascent polit-ical protest. (Eng, 2000, p. 1280)

Quoting Butler's notion of "ungrievable loss" (Butler, 1997, p. 185), Eng argues that if

> the proliferation of melancholia in the late twentieth century insists that gender is not the only or the primary guarantor of loss that orga-nizes our psychic and social lives, an expansion of melancholia as nascent political protest allows us to resituate gender and feminisms at the millennium as crucial sites of progressive politics in their renewed configurations on the global stage. (Eng, 2000, p. 1280)

Lack or loss? Melancholia or fantasy?

The eclectic work of Sanchez-Pardo seems to be able to contribute to a different way of thinking about melancholia. Although she situates her work in the context of "emancipatory" politics (that is, melancholia being primarily the affect of racial and gender minorities or those who suffered diaspora between the two World Wars), she does not have the political investment of Eng and other racial and gender melancholia theorists; by basing her account on Melanie Klein—that is, by giving first importance to the death drive—she is able to dwell on aspects of melancholia which are interesting for the argument I want to develop here. Sanchez-Pardo argues that the feelings at the beginning of the twentieth century—which was characterised by anxiety, insecurity, and transformation—were explored in modernist texts which are "riven with the horror of the war and haunted by the unprecedented spectre of anxiety neurosis, the effects of shell shock, manic depression and melancholia" (Sanchez-Pardo, 2003, p. 10). As she shows in her analysis, modernism in art opens up a space within modernist culture, a space that, according to the author, is characterised by the "traumatic relationship with exteriority". Interestingly, she argues that in melancholia, "*a fantasy* of dispossession of both a social and psychic space is at work" (2003, p. 195), that reality is perceived as an "object-destructive space" (2003, p. 195), and that, therefore, one could speak of "cultures of the death drive". This notion of cultures of the death drive, from my perspective, speaks of the fact of death as part of—and not excluded from—life, that is, as co-habiting with meaning.

It is this tracing of the death drive which will allow me to rethink melancholia as linked primarily to lack (the trace of the drive), and subsequently move the orientation of melancholia from emancipation to a logic that informs a different type of identity, and a different type of violence. Lacan's reading of Freud allows him to claim that language will always be "the other", as different and separated from the "sameness" of the subject. That is, different from a purely culturalist or interpretative approach, the use of psychoanalytic theory assumes the incompleteness (or failure) of the process of representation and, therefore, also the breakdown of the intersubjective process. According to this theoretical approach, there is something beyond language that constitutes the space of lack in the subject, a part of it which cannot find representation, and this is the condition of the subject's desire. "Desire is neither the appetite for satisfaction, nor the demand for love, but the difference that results from the subtraction of the first from the second, their phenomenon of their splitting"

(Lacan, 1977, p. 287). Furthermore, the subject is defined as "lacking" in the sense that it depends on the signifier, and this signifier is primarily in the field of the other. Lacan states that it seems as if the subject could eventually choose between being represented by language (and being part of the world of meaning) *or* simply being. This "or", however, demonstrates the essential alienation of the subject, for if it chooses meaning, being is left out, and if it chooses being, there is no way of saying so.

If we choose being, the subject disappears, it eludes us, it falls into non-meaning. If we choose meaning, the meaning survives only deprived of the part of non-meaning, that is ". . . that which constitutes in the realization of the subject, the unconscious" (Lacan, 1978, p. 211).

Although the Lacanian understanding of the signifier (in particular his notion of "master signifier", or Phallus) has been rightly criticised by feminists (Irigaray, 1985; Mitchell & Rose, 1982) and by deconstruction theorists (as is well known, Derrida has offered his notion of *differance* instead, which means that no signifier has the privilege of transcendence; see Derrida's *Resistances to Psychoanalysis*, 1993), still Lacan is able to address failure, opacity, exclusion, and desire as constitutive of any social formation. The split/barred subject of the unconscious will always find inadequate representation in language, and the real will always emerge as a symptom, a disruption. As Freud taught us,

> If you take up a theoretical point of view and disregard the matter of quantity, you may quite well say that *we are all ill*, that is neurotic— since the preconditions for the formation of symptoms (that is repression) can also be observed in normal people (Cited in Fink, 2000, p. 77)

This same statement applies for any social formation which will always entail some form of exclusion or misrecognition, and, as we shall see, also some form of unconscious enjoyment.

Now, in order to understand the difference between loss and lack, it is necessary to remember the Lacanian distinction between "Thing" and "object", and between the "object" and the "object-cause of desire". Let us look at the way Heidegger puts this idea forward: "Language, by naming beings for the first time, first brings to word and to appearance. Only this naming nominates beings to their being *from out* of their being" (Heidegger, 2011[1977], p. 128). In Schwenger's interpretation, this "being from out" does not mean recreation of beings, but that things become objects:

> Language, according to Heidegger, is an inherent part of the human subject; but there is no language in the being of a stone, plant, or animal. When such a being is named, then, it is also changed. . . . All of our knowledge of the object is only knowledge of its modes of representation. The object "is thus first of all the represented". What is not, in Kantian terms, is the thing-in-itself [*Ding an Sich*], which Heidegger specifically opposes to the human act of representing it. "In a paradoxical way, beyond the knowledge we always know something more, namely, that there is an unknowable otherness to the thing. . . . And beyond that appearance, which represents the thing to us as subject, there is an ineluctable presence—the thingness of the thing—that we can never grasp. (Schwenger, 2001, pp. 101, 201)

From a Lacanian psychoanalytic perspective, it is argued, the thing-itself is related to the death drive in so far as it is "the other within us", which neither finds representation in language nor satisfaction: "The symbol manifests itself first of all as the murder of the thing, and this death constitutes in the subject the eternalization of his desire" (Lacan, 1977, p. 104). In relation to the differentiation between "object" and "object-cause of desire", we learn from Žižek that

> while the object of desire is simply the desired object, the cause of desire is the feature on account of which we desire the desired object. . . . From this perspective, the melancholic is not primarily the subject fixated on the lost object, unable to perform the work of mourning, but rather the subject who possesses the object but has lost his desire for it because the cause that made him desire this object has withdrawn, lost its efficiency. . . . Melancholy occurs when we finally get the desired object, but are disappointed in it. (Žižek, 2000, p. 662)

A very different operation is the operation of fantasy, which attempts to cover up lack and, as such, is the necessary counterpart of the real:

> Fantasy conceals the fact that the other, the symbolic order, is structured around some traumatic impossibility, around something, which cannot be symbolized—i.e. the real of *jouissance*: through fantasy, *jouissance* is domesticated, gentrified . . . (Žižek, 1997, p. 123)

As such, fantasy frames our desire (our own space of failed interpel-lation). It teaches us *how to desire*, and, because of the metonymic structure of desire, the excluded other remains a "spectral object which does not have positive ontological consistency but that fills the gap of the constitutive impossibility" (Žižek, 1997, p. 76). The stated features of language, desire, and subjectivity are expressed intersub-jectively in the impossibility of full recognition between the self and the other. Fantasy plays the role of concealing this inconsistency. It gives a framework through which we experience the world as con-sistent and meaningful. The nature of this narrative is still more complex than it appears at first sight: the transcendental narrative not only establishes the law, it also frames desire: "what the law prohibits, (unconscious) desire seeks" (Fink, 2000, p. 207). Fantasy not only gives a sense of wholeness to the identity, but it also involves enjoyment while transgressing, so the "expressed" discourse about the excluded other is always accompanied by a hidden experience of enjoyment.

The other, according to this perspective, not only threatens the possibility of meaning, but also the possibility of enjoyment. The excluded other is guilty of preventing the self from fulfilling its desire, of stealing the self's enjoyment. The self–other relation, then, is one of aggressive jealousy. The self cannot satisfy its desire, because the other is "enjoying too much". Thus, what characterises aggressive jealousy is that, on the one hand, the subject feels deprived of some-thing which he considers his due and which has been taken away by his rival, and, on the other, that he not only "sickens at the sight of enjoyment . . . but he is easy only at the misery of others" (Klein, 1975[1957], p. 181).

If melancholia is no longer theorised as the right to recover the lost object, but as the mourning of the (lacking) Thing, it could be said that both fantasy and melancholia are mechanisms for dealing with the impossibility of the real: whereas its covering up is constitutive of ideological fantasy, the attitude of exposing the very space of lack would be characteristic of melancholia. This conceptual distinction is quite significant, since, formulated this way, melancholia not only no longer informs struggles for political justice, but even produces violence—a type of violence where the self is equally exposed to death as the other or, to put it differently, a type of violence where the self and the other die together, or where self and other are together "only in death". Much of current social (particularly youth) violence seems to exhibit this logic.

Freud provides the key elements for making this Lacanian interpretation of melancholia by explaining that (different from mourning) melancholia relates to unconscious processes, emotional ambivalence, and feelings of hate towards the self and others: whereas mourning is the reaction to the loss of a loved person or ideal, in the case of melancholia, there seems to be a loss more of an ideal kind to the extent that

> one feels justified in maintaining the belief that a loss of this kind has occurred, but one cannot see clearly what it is that has been lost, and it is all the more reasonable to suppose that the patient cannot consciously perceive what he has lost either. ... This would suggest that melancholia is in some way related to an object-loss which is withdrawn from consciousness in contradistinction to mourning in which there is nothing about the loss that is unconscious. (Freud, 1917e, p. 245)

Quite different from the case of fantasy, where the self projects into the other the responsibility for its own failure, and excludes him in order to save itself, in the case of melancholia, the relation self–other is much more complicated. As we can see in the following two extracts, the self itself is diminished or depleted:

> The analysis of melancholia now shows that the ego can kill itself only if, owing to return of the object-cathexis, it can treat itself as an object – if it is able to direct against itself the hostility which relates to an object and which represents the ego's original reaction to objects in the external world. (1917e, p. 252)

> The melancholic displays something else besides which is lacking in mourning – an extraordinary diminution in his self regard, an impoverishment of his ego on a grand scale. In mourning it is the world which has become poor and empty, in melancholia it is the ego itself. (1917e, pp. 245–246)

But, as Freud explains, self-hatred expresses hate for the internalised lost other:

> The melancholic erotic cathexis in regard to his object has thus undergone a double vicissitude: part of it has regressed to identification, but the other part, under the influence of the conflict due to "ambivalence" has been carried back to the stage of sadism which is nearer to

that conflict. It is this sadism alone that solves the riddle of the tendency to suicide which makes melancholia so interesting—and so dangerous. . . . We have long known, it is true, that no neurotic harbours thoughts of suicide which he has not turned back upon himself from murderous impulses against others. (1917e, pp. 251–252)

Now, as Kristeva argues, although initially the melancholic's discourse of self-reproach was seen as hiding aggression towards the other, modern theory has theorised melancholia differently. In her words, the melancholic "mourns not an Object but the Thing . . . as the real that does not lend itself to signification" (Kristeva, 1989, p. 13). "Glued to the Thing (Res), they (melancholics) are *without* objects. That total and unsignifiable Thing is insignificant – it is a mere Nothing, their Nothing, Death" (1989, p. 51). For Kristeva, melancholia is related to the failure of the signifying process, as she states: "intolerance for object loss and the signifier's failure to ensure a compensating way out of the states of withdrawal in which the subject takes refuge to the point of inaction (pretending to be dead) or even suicide" (Kristeva, 1989, p. 10).

The (sexual) logics of violence: exclusion and inclusion

In order to discuss the logics of exclusion and inclusion that fantasy and melancholia, respectively, involve, I would like to take a short detour through the psychoanalytic concepts of introjection and projection that will offer a model for understanding different ways of dealing with lack and otherness. Without going into great conceptual detail here, it could be said that the defence mechanisms of introjection and projection are related to the phenomenon of splitting, and that they emerge in order to avoid anxiety or pain. Splitting refers to the process by which "parts of the mind (affects, cognition, memories, wishes, intentions) or even functions (e.g., understanding, perception) may become split off from consciousness and (usually temporarily) obliterated" (Hinshelwood, 1995, p. 187). As Hinshelwood explains,

in essence, [the full theory of internalized objects] is concerned with the way in which, initially in the course of development but also throughout our lives, our experiences with the people with whom we develop close relationships can become assimilated into the self, thus contributing to our sense of identity or remain unassimilated as alien objects internal to, but jeopardizing, the sense of self. (Hinshelwood, 1995, p. 186)

Although it is mostly via Klein that the notions of introjections and projection became widely known, Freud had already discussed them in his work. In *Beyond the Pleasure Principle* (1920g), for example, when analysing the delicate balance between pleasure and unpleasure, and the difficulty of the body in dealing with high amounts of stimuli and the need of a "protective shield", Freud gives us a definition of the mechanism of projection. He states,

> a particular way is adopted in dealing with any internal excitations which produce too great an increase of unpleasure: there is a tendency to treat them as though they were acting not from the inside, but from the outside so that might be possible to bring the shield against stimuli into operation as a means of defence against them. This is the origin of projection, which is destined to play such a large part in the causation of pathological processes. (Freud, 1920g, p. 33)

Although here Freud is talking about internal stimuli, projection was theorised by Klein as belonging to the relation between mother and child. In Klein's words,

> The primal processes of projection and introjections, being inextricably linked with the infant's emotions and anxieties, initiate object-relations; by projecting, i.e. deflecting libido and aggression on to the mother's breast, the basis for object-relations is established; by introjecting the object, first of all the breast, relations to internal objects come into being. . . . The core of the superego is thus the mother's breast, both good and bad. Owing to the simultaneous operation of introjections and projection, relations to external and internal objects interact. (Klein, 1952, p. 433)

Although these concepts originally attempt to describe individual psychological mechanisms, it seems they can greatly contribute to the understanding of the social dynamics of identity formation and othering in so far as they describe mechanisms of exclusion and inclusion as constitutive of identity formation. In light of the argument I have presented so far, I would like to state that violence is either "put" outside the identity (through projection) and/or inside it (through introjection), depending on how identities deal with lack: whereas the first movement loosely describes the logic of fantasy and political violence, the second resembles the logic of forms of social violence—such as youth violence—and the emotional ambivalence (of detached love and aggression) that characterises the melancholic culture that surrounds it. Regarding political violence, one could argue that an antagonistic relationship is established in the process of identity formation between the identity and what needs to be excluded from it for the identity to exist. This first foundational act of exclusion is cast in positive terms by a transcendental narrative about the identity, which Castoriadis (1998) called "the social imaginary". Since the stability of the identity relies on such exclusion, any threat to the boundary of the identity, from within or without, enacts a (probably violent) response from the identity against the apparent cause of its instability. Moreover, the transcendental narrative provides the identity with the moral legitimacy to attack whatever threatens it and so restore social order. The transcendental narrative about the identity is also a narrative about the apparent cause of its instability; a narrative about a pernicious other is also constructed and its exclusion—through transgressive violence—provides not only the possibility of meaning but also a surplus enjoyment.

From this perspective, one could rethink Sanchez-Pardo's "cultures of the death drive", and look at how current forms of social violence do not entail transgression of the sacred boundary of society (paradoxically, to save society from a perceived threat). Instead, violence takes place "within" the symbolic order (the realm of the profane) while still entailing enjoyment. Within the melancholic symbolic space, the other is no longer a mortal threat to the identity of the self but an introjected and "ambivalent object", neither of love nor of hate, with whom there is little attachment and poor identification. From the perspective presented here, it could be said that some forms of social violence (in particular some forms of current youth violence) would be the acting out of the melancholic mandate of not giving up desire. The acting out of fantasy, in this case, does not need the construction of an enemy and the enjoyment of its exclusion. On the contrary, it is the own self that is given up to the enjoyment of death *through* the death of the objectified (friend) other. As Kristeva has argued, adolescents—as true believers in the Thing (the Thing must exist!)—enjoy without limits: "*jouir a mort*" (Kristeva, 2007). This form of violence would, then, be the expression of an encounter with the other that takes place within a particular melancholic symbolic space characterised by inclusion without recognition and by the non-sacrificial character of death.

The distinction between narcissism and melancholia is, thus, quite significant. Far from being challenged by *infantile subjects* turned "into themselves" in para-political, fetishistic, and deviant ways which (as is argued by Hall, Winlow, & Crun, 2008) result from the fact that consumerism prevents the constitution of the symbolic order making our society remain in a state of narcissism, we face instead a different symbolic constellation which exhibits the paradoxes of its own logics of exclusion and exclusion. That is, from a narcissistic perspective, what needs to be done is to reinstall the paternal law and its prohibitions (to let society "mature"). According to my analysis, this would only increase the punitive and exclusionary logics of fantasy (in this particular case of those that represent such "narcissistic" tendencies as the racialised–feminised youth), and also the nihilistic and defiant logics of melancholia. Society and its institutions would show, once more, their failure to *signify* by simply increasing their punitive logics.

In other words, the restitution of meaning does not appear to be a challenge only on the "melancholic side", but also and even more importantly (as power and severe means of violence are located at this side of the equation) on the "fantasy side". Now, as every form of meaning involves its exclusion and paradoxes, maybe one can again think of the space that *disobedience*, as a form of distanciation, dis-identification, or separation, can have in this identity formation process.

Final remarks

I have presented the concepts of fantasy and melancholia as two possible ways of dealing with lack, or the failure of the process of symbolisation. In both cases, I have stated, there is meaning and there is enjoyment. In the case of fantasy that accompanies episodes of political violence and of nationalist hatreds, it is possible to perceive an over-production of meaning and the enjoyment of the exclusion of the feminised other, who appears as a threat to the possibility of "fullness" of the national identity. Actually, in this sense, it could be argued that fantasy fosters identification processes whereby the incompleteness of the subject finds—even if imaginarily—some sense of fullness, of "identity" mechanisms, or the identification with the promise of fullness. As Glynos and Stavrakakis argue,

> Typically, nationalist narratives are rooted in the desire of each gener-ation to try and heal this (metaphoric) castration, and give back to the nation its lost full enjoyment. The identity of the evil 'Other' who prevents the nation from recouping the enjoyment it has lost shifts as a function of historical context. It may be a foreign occupier, those who 'always plot to rule the world', some dark powers and their local sympathizers 'who want to enslave our proud nation', immigrants 'who steal our jobs', etc. (Glynos & Stavrakakis, 2008, p. 8)

In the case of melancholia that accompanies some expressions of current social violence, on the other hand, it is possible to perceive the inclusion without recognition of the other. "Being", so to say, seems to be faced, in this case, without the effective mediation of the signi-fier (i.e., without the above mentioned identification), and what is encountered is the death drive, which has not been projected into an exterior other, but on to the self (or community). Different from fantasy, melancholic "acts" are neither heroic (they are not under-taken in order to save the self or the national identity), nor are they acts of transgression (as death is not the other of meaning but co-habits meaning). That is to say, melancholic acts and the violence that results from them do not need to transgress the (masculine) sacred boundary of society as political violence does (paradoxically, to save society from a perceived threat). In the case of melancholia, there is an experience of non-wholeness, as language has not entirely succeeded in the evacuation of enjoyment. To finish, I would like to suggest the similarity of this paradoxical figure of inclusion and violence and Lacan's idea of the feminine position regarding language: "when any speaking being whatsoever situates itself under the banner 'woman', it is on the basis of the following—that it grounds itself as a being not-whole in situating itself in the phallic function". And Lacan goes on,

> There is no such thing as a Woman, Woman with the capital W indi-cating the universal. . . . [T]he fact remains that if she is excluded by the nature of things, it is precisely in the following respect: being not-whole, she has supplementary jouissance compared to what the phallic function designates by way of jouissance. (Lacan, 1998, pp. 72–73)

Since the logic of exclusion that characterises political violence can be said to resemble male–phallic enjoyment, I would like to venture the idea of the logics of inclusion without recognition as linked to the female way of failing within language. Although this Lacanian feminine logic (as the space of separation from the symbolic order) has often been theorised as a source for ethics and sublimation, social change, disruption, and democratisation, one could also wonder whether the social *acting* of melancholia and embracement of death— as different from the purely "theoretical space of separation"—are also constitutive of feminine identity and enjoyment.

Note

1.   Part of this material has been published in my recent book, *Radical Sociality: Studies on Disobedience, Violence and Belonging* (Basingstoke, Palgrave, 2013), where I expand and fully develop the distinction between narcissism, melacholia, and fantasy.

References

Benjamin, W. (2005). *Selected Writings Vol. 2, Part 1: 1927–1930*. Cambridge, MA: Belknap Press of Harvard University Press.

Butler, J. (1997). *The Psychic Life of Power: Theories on Subjection*. Palo Alto, CA: Stanford University Press.

Castoriadis, C. (1998). *The Imaginary Institution of Society*. Cambridge, MA: MIT Press.

Cheng, A. (2000). *The Melancholy of Race*. Oxford: Oxford University Press.

Derrida, J. (1993). *Resistances to Psychoanalysis*. Palo Alto, CA: Stanford University Press.

Eng, D. (2000). Melancholia in the late twentieth century. *Signs*, 25(4): 1275–1281.

Eng, D., & Kazanjian, D. (2003). *Loss: The Politics of Mourning*. Berkeley, CA: University of California Press.

Fink, B. (2000). *A Clinical Introduction to Lacanian Psychoanalysis. Theory and Technique*. Cambridge, MA: Harvard University Press.

Flatley, J. (2008). *Affective Mapping: Melancholia and the Politics of Modernism*. Cambridge, MA: Harvard University Press.

Freud, S. (1917e). Mourning and melancholia. *S.E.*, *14*: 239–258. London: Hogarth.

Freud, S. (1920g). *Beyond the Pleasure Principle*. *S.E.*, *18*: 7–64. London: Hogarth.

Freud, S. (1923b). *The Ego and the Id*. *S.E.*, *19*: 3–66. London: Hogarth.

Glynos, J., & Stavrakakis, J. (2008). Lacan and political subjectivity: fantasy and enjoyment in psychoanalysis and political theory. *Subjectivities*, *24*: 256–274.

Hall, S., Winlow, S., & Crun, C. (2008). *Criminal Identities and Consumer Culture: Crime, Exclusion and the New Culture of Narcissism*. Cullompton, Devon: Willan.

Heidegger, M. (1977). The origin of the work of art. In: *Martin Heidegger Basic Writings*, D. F. Krell (Ed.). London: Routledge, 2011.

Hinshelwood, R. D. (1995). The social relocation of personal identity as shown by psychoanalytic observations of splitting, projection and introjection. *Philosophy, Psychiatry and Psychology*, *2*: 185–204.

Irigaray, L. (1985). *This Sex which is not One*. Ithaca, NY: Cornell University Press.

Khanna, R. (2003). *Dark Continents: Psychoanalysis and Colonialism*. Durham, NC: Duke University Press.

Klein, M. (1952). The origins of transference. *International Journal of Psychoanalysis*, *33*: 433–438.

Klein, M. (1957). Envy and gratitude. In: *Envy and Gratitude and Other Works 1946–1963* (pp. 176–236). New York: Free Press, 1975.

Kristeva, J. (1989). *Black Sun: Depression and Melancholia*. New York: Columbia University Press.

Kristeva, J. (2007). Adolescence, a syndrome of ideality. *Psychoanalytic Review*, *94*: 715–725.

Lacan, J. (1977). The function and field of speech and language in psychoanalysis. In: *Ecrits: A Selection* (pp. 23–87). New York: Norton.

Lacan, J. (1978). *Four Fundamental Concepts of Psychoanalysis: Seminar XI*. New York: Norton.

Lacan, J. (1998). *Seminar X: On Feminine Sexuality, The Limits of Love and Knowledge*. New York: Norton, 1972–1973.

Lepenis, W. (1992). *Melancholie and Society*. Cambridge, MA: Harvard University Press.

Mitchell, J., & Rose, J. (1982). *Feminine Sexuality. Jacques Lacan and the Ecole Freudienne*. London: Macmillan.

Palacios, M. (2004). On sacredness and transgression: understanding social antagonism. *Psychoanalysis, Culture and Society*, *9*: 284–297.

Palacios, M. (2009). *Fantasy and Political Violence*. Wiesbaden: VS Verlag für Sozialwissenschaften.

Palacios, M., & Posocco, S. (2011). War and the politics of sexual violence. In: S. Seidman, N. Fischer, & C. Meeks (Eds.), *The New Sexuality Studies*. London: Routledge

Pensky, M. (1993). *Melancholy Dialectics: Walter Benjamin and the Play of Mourning*. Amherst, MA: University of Massachusetts Press.

Sanchez-Pardo, E. (2003). *Cultures of the Death Drive: Melanie Klein and Modernist Melancholia*, Durham, NC: Duke University Press.

Schwenger, P. (2001). Words and the murder of the thing. *Critical Inquiry*, 28(1): 99–113.

Yegenoglu, M. (1998). *Colonial Fantasies. Towards a Feminist Reading of Orientalism*. Cambridge: Cambridge University Press.

Žižek, S. (1997). *The Plague of Fantasies*. New York: Verso.

Žižek, S. (2000). Melancholy and the act. *Critical Enquiry, 26*: 657–681.

Introducing Psychoanalysis and Politics: a conversation with Lene Auestad and Jonathan Davidoff

Conducted and edited by Steffen Krüger

E ven though the Psychoanalysis and Politics group has existed for only four years so far, it has already become a veritable institution within psychoanalytic and psychosocial studies. True to its straightforward title, the group is engaged in the border regions of the two disciplines. With its two organisers, the Norwegian philosopher Lene Auestad and the Mexican psychologist Jonathan Davidoff (both living in London), Psychoanalysis and Politics has reached far beyond national and cultural borders—a trick not easily pulled off within an interdisciplinary field that is relatively little known outside Britain. A member of the Nordic Summer University (NSU), an open access, democratic forum for intellectual debate, Auestad was invited to organise her own group under the forum's auspices. This invitation resulted in the birth of the group and its first three-day conference in Copenhagen in March 2010. "Reflecting my research interest in the theme of prejudice, this conference bore the title: Exclusion and the Politics of Representation,"[1] says Lene Auestad in recapitulating the first steps in establishing the project.

Jonathan Davidoff, who presented a paper at this first symposium, subsequently joined Auestad as co-organiser. Since then, the plan has been for the Psychoanalysis and Politics group to convene biannually, but, in 2012, a third date had to be added, because of the many responses to its calls for papers. Additionally, the publication of the first conference volume (Auestad, 2012) has marked the beginning of the Psychoanalysis and Politics book series; and a special issue of the *American Imago*, forthcoming in 2014, will further solidify the group's position within the field of the psychoanalytic study of socio-political conflict.

In light of this positive reception and the fast pace at which the group is outgrowing its original setting,[2] the time seems ripe for a first round of stock taking and thorough reflection on Psychoanalysis and Politics. What are the project's roots and whereabouts; what are its further aims and objectives, its inner dynamics and—yes—politics?

By way of producing such a statement, Lene Auestad, Jonathan Davidoff, and I, Steffen Krüger, a member of the group since early 2011, agreed on the interview format as a vehicle well-suited to transmit the open, dialogical form that we thought characteristic of both the group's cultural–political outlook and the overall feel of its symposia. It is in this sense that I can surrender my editorial authority at this point and round off my introduction with a substantial outtake from the interview, the rest of which readers will find below. Thus, Auestad writes about the group's work so far,

> There is a thread running through our conferences in the sense that the questions which each of them raises are derived from discussions we have had at previous conferences. For example, while the first symposium discussed acts of denigration and demonisation, the following one was about the reverse side of such acts, specifically: idealisation and the idealised, pure object. This latter conference, Nationalism and the Body Politic, (Norwegian Psychoanalytic Institute, Oslo, March 2011), addressed the revival of neo-nationalist policies in different countries, as well as the fantasies connected with them. In the autumn of 2010, when we developed the outline of this symposium, there were frightening signs of such developments in many countries, and there was strong resistance to raising these issues. Curiously, as we now know, the terrorist attacks in Oslo by Anders Behring Breivik took place a few months after that; the situation, with hostile debates around immigration and multiculturalism, has now exploded in Norway. The following conference, Narrativities and Political Imaginaries, held in Sweden in summer 2011, continued exploring this theme, with a special focus on the use of literature and film.

In the course of these initial conferences, it occurred to us that there is a link between neo-nationalist revivals and a lack, or failure, of mourning. In particular, the paper that Margarita Palacio gave in Oslo, "Between fantasy and melancholia: lack, otherness and violence", raised the question of what it means in a political context to say that someone needs to work through their losses. That again inspired us to think further about these issues. The conferences on "Shared Traumas, Silent Loss, Public and Private Mourning", at the Swedish Psychoanalytic Society, Stockholm, in March 2012, then at Brandbjerg College, Denmark, in August 2012, and, finally, at the British Psychoanalytic Society, London, October 2012, approached that subject from a wide range of different cultural settings and political contexts. In turn, the conference, "Eruptions, Disruptions and Returns of the Repressed", at the Finnish Psychoanalytic Society in Helsinki in March 2013, took The Arab Spring, the UK Riots and the Occupy movement, as well as the recent violent right-wing attacks in Europe, as its point of departure. Here, we questioned how to evaluate and think about these phenomena, and also to what extent these events challenge the limits of psychoanalytic conceptualisation. So, looking at the way our symposia have developed, one can say that there is an inner logic to the development of the themes as well as an outward-directed one; a need to think about what is happening now. (Auestad, 2012–2013, interview with the author)

In closing my introduction, let me briefly emphasise some of the aspects that Auestad listed as central concerns of Psychoanalysis and Politics. These are: the attentiveness to inner and outer, mental and cultural mechanisms and their interplays (mechanisms of exclusion and elevation, repression and idealisation), to the dynamics of narrative lines, contexts, associations, to processes of working upon the various layers of meanings and their investments, the anxieties with which they are protected and defended, as well as the intensities with which these meanings are often threatened, transformed, and sometimes shattered. While each of us pieces these aspects together in unique ways, shaping the peculiar dynamics of each of our psychic realities, the manifold framings and interplays of these interior dynamics, in turn, form the social realities against which, in a dialectical loop, our psychic ones are made and remade. I would like to think that, to a substantial degree, the psychosocial as well as cultural-analytical sensitivity which goes into the planning of the conferences of Psychoanalysis and Politics can be taken as representative of the group's orientation as a whole. Having thus jumped head-on into the interview, here is the rest.

Steffen Krüger (SK):   Lene, you are a research fellow both at the philosophy department and at the Centre for Studies of the Holocaust and Religious Minorities in your home town, Oslo, Norway; you are living in London. And Jonathan, you are a psychologist and honorary psychotherapist at the West Middlesex Hospital, doing your PhD in psychoanalysis at University College London; you are from Mexico City. Actually, it is only now, in presenting the two of you in such compressed form, that I realise how poignantly the two of you, as the organisers of the Psychoanalysis and Politics group, represent the combination of psychoanalysis and politics through your interests. Could you tell me more about your academic and personal paths that led you to an interest in the combination of psychoanalysis and politics?

Lene Auestad (LA):   At first I could say that these interests, to my past disappointment, do not really combine in the institutions I am affiliated with. I found philosophy to a large extent turned inwards, focused on technical matters rather than being engaged with the outside world, scholars who study the Holocaust to be mostly adverse to explanations that take the unconscious into account; and psychoanalysts often seem reluctant or afraid to take a stand in political and social issues—such a stand perhaps being seen as a retreat from a "safe" objectivity.

To me, psychoanalysis and philosophy were always parallel interests; I picked up *The Interpretation of Dreams* and Sartre's *Le Mur* at fourteen, and later thought I would start to study philosophy, because I was rather sick of school, which was mostly about passively learning "facts". I saw philosophy as a discipline that was about actively taking a stand, as containing a self-critical reflectivity I found lacking elsewhere. What I missed in philosophy, and continued to look to psychoanalysis to find, was what you might call a phenomenologically accurate, highly developed sensitivity for describing concrete situations, situated—conscious and unconscious—subjectivity.

I might add that, since my mother was an analyst in Norway who led a clinic working with children, adolescents and their families, serving parts of Oslo in the public health system,[3] I took political engagement as part of psychoanalysis for granted. From time to time, local politicians wanted to cut down on the services, and my mother and her colleagues would regularly turn up to lecture them on how these cuts would affect their patients, and persuade them to change their minds. Therefore, this link between individual suffering, public policies, as well as small and large scale social systems—how there is a shared responsibility for symptoms or pain that may just look individual—is something I think of as self-evident.

SK: Did your mother also inspire your reading? That is, did she suggest things you should dig into and discuss them with you?

LA: As I remember it, she did not really tell me what to read; it was more the case that I hungrily went through the bookshelves at home and asked what the books were about, though she did talk about her reading, and I enjoyed discussing with her. Actually, she was inspired to become a psychoanalyst because of her aunt, my great aunt, Nic Waal, who founded child analysis in Norway, and combined her interest with a strong political engagement. Trained in Berlin, Nic's story goes back to the early days of psychoanalysis, illuminating how there were conflicts from early on as to whether psychoanalysis should engage with social and political reality or attempting to be more *salonfähig* by remaining aloof, detached and "neutral".

Jonathan Davidoff (JD): I first encountered psychoanalysis as a psychology student. I believe I studied psychology in the first place because I wanted to help people; I had in mind clinical psychology from the outset. I also relied on an intuition: wanting to understand how people are and the reasons for it. Later on I was to discover—through psychoanalysis—that the answer to the question "why did you study what you studied" could get complicated.

The tradition of psychology as a discipline in Mexico, where I come from, is deeply rooted in psychoanalysis. Therefore, psychoanalysis was almost a natural discipline to engage with. I found psychoanalysis to be a fountainhead of knowledge and inspiration for me. Having studied in Argentina as well meant that the psychoanalytic heritage of psychology was further emphasised for me. Indeed, the Lacanian psychoanalytic tradition is inextricably linked to philosophy, and I guess that was my gateway into it. That, and, of course, a personal interest or disposition, if you will. Sociology and politics, being social sciences in a constant dialogue with psychology, thus came in dialogue with psychoanalysis in a quite natural form in my personal path. In Britain, I studied Philosophy and Psychoanalysis at the University of Essex and trained as a psychodynamic psycho-therapist at the Tavistock Centre. These further enriched my psycho-analytic knowledge and experience and contributed to my belief in the fruitfulness of the dialogue between social sciences and philoso-phy. Currently I'm a PhD candidate at UCL, where I believe this dialogue between psychoanalysis, philosophy, and the social sciences can be further explored.

I think I have always been interested in exploring different perspectives; "otherness" has always been quite magnetic for me. Per-haps that is one of the reasons I have moved to different places at different times. Intellectually, it has been interesting to go and "meet the stereotypes": the Lacanian and rationalist Argentineans and the Object Relations and empiricist Brits. Of course, only to find out that the stereotypes are nothing more than that and that such a "meeting" is always postponed; yet a difference between these "stereotypes" confirms them, none the less.

SK: What seems to be prevalent in both your career paths is your involvement with socially produced suffering on micro and macro scales, with otherness, as well as processes of othering. Clearly, it is on these themes that the social–therapeutic focus, if you will, of our symposia lies. How, do you think, can a psychoanalytical perspective contribute to these themes, or, even more pragmatically put, how can it contribute to remedying these shortcomings and injustices? And how might this involvement feed back into our understanding of psychoanalysis?

JD: Overall, my personal view is that psychoanalytic theory, the method of psychoanalysis, and the psychoanalytic mind-set can contribute to the enrichment of the disciplines with which these come into dialogue. The focus of psychoanalysis on the unconscious, the discontent, the repressed, and the non-commonsensical, in my view, broadens the scope of any object of study. The reason for this is that while other disciplines situate themselves in the realm of the logical, the self-assertive, and the sort of discourse that posits itself as ratio-nal, psychoanalysis brings into consideration that which escapes this realm. This, in my view, pushes further the self-set boundaries estab-lished by social sciences and, in many cases, philosophy.

However, when it comes to suffering, I believe things can get a bit thorny. If one were to understand social or political injustice as part of *civilisation's discontents*, then I would say that the remedy, if we were to speak of remedies, is to learn to accept it as part of existence. This is not to say that social and political action should disappear or that they lack purpose. Nevertheless, if through psychoanalysis we have learnt anything about civilisation and its discontents, it is that we are bound to remain discontent, because civilisation implies relinquishment, which we dislike. Furthermore, civilisation entails disillusionment too, for instance, that of civilisation (society, or social justice if you will) not being perfect. The question that remains open for me is: does it follow from this knowledge that the revolutionary spirit should disappear? Does accepting discontent mean that changing reality is pointless?

When it comes to individual suffering, the story is also different in a way. I would say psychoanalysis works very well in transforming neurotic suffering into real suffering. Psychoanalysis can deal with other kinds of individual sufferings as well, such as trauma for example, and can definitely help the individual to work through, mourn, or reposition him/herself differently in the face of suffering. On the other hand, I believe that the desire for mental health and happiness that a subject might have at the beginning of the analytic process is bound to be disappointed. This is part of the analytic process as well. So, I would say that coming to terms with this and working through disillusionment in this sense is part of the process. Again, the question that remains open is the extent to which one as a person can or should aim for self-improvement or self-realisation, knowing that this process will intrinsically entail disillusionment and disappointment.

SK: Both of you point to philosophy and psychoanalysis as parallel, sometimes even tautological, interests. Lene, you mention reading Freud's *Interpretation of Dreams* and Sartre's *Le Mur* at an early age. Was it already then that you began criss-crossing the borders of their respective ways of reflection? And then you mention phenomenology in connection with psychoanalysis, a combination that seems to be very much alive in your two recent book publications: an essay collection on Hannah Arendt (in Norwegian with Helgard Mahrdt: *Handling, Frihet, Humanitet*, 2011) and the first collection of contributions from the Psychoanalysis and Politics group (*Exclusion and the Politics of Representation,* 2012). Where do you see the connection between the two and how do you combine them in your thinking?

LA: In philosophy, I became interested in ethics/political theory, the branches that are more concerned with real life, and then often found that these lines of thought were in need of an adequate psychology—which psychoanalysis can supply—to consider what actually motivates human beings. Part of my fascination with Arendt is that she is a thinker who is motivated by political experiences, takes them very seriously, and then re-evaluates, rethinks the Western tradition on the basis of that. In fact, this is the opposite of the "top-down" approach which is characteristic of most philosophy. I see psychoanalysis as providing very accurate and sensitive phenomenological descriptions of situations, interactions, emotions, and unconscious intentions, thus offering a concrete point of access to human reality that philosophy often lacks. If we think, for example, of Freud's description of his grandson's *fort-da* game:

> The child had a wooden reel with a piece of string tied round it. It never occurred to him to pull it along the floor behind him, for instance, and play at its being a carriage. What he did was to hold the reel by the string and very skilfully throw it over the edge of his curtained cot, so that it disappeared into it, at the same time uttering his expressive 'o-o-o-o'. He then pulled the reel out of the cot again by the string and hailed its reappearance with a joyful 'da' ['there']. This, then, was the complete game – disappearance and return." (Freud, 1920g, p. 15)

It gives an accurate account of a detailed situation, and questions what is going on here, so it offers careful attention to the nuances of something very concrete, taking place before Freud's eyes. At the same time, you could say, it is concerned with something much more mysterious, absent, and invisible, with unconscious fantasies and affects against the background of which these actions make sense. So, I find psychoanalytic thinking very valuable in so far as it offers descriptions that expand what we think of as the domain of human experience—conscious and unconscious. In that sense, it is an empathic discipline concerned with enlarging the humanly meaningful, and I think it is far less so when it offers concepts that remain very remote from experience that you could say are at once unphenomenological and unempathic in the sense that they would not add anything meaningful if you were to try to apply them to yourself.

As I see it, psychoanalysis has the virtue of a situated sensitivity and imagination as a fruitful basis for thinking, though I have become more critical of its frequent tendency to think of itself as taking up a "view from nowhere". Coming to Essex to take courses in psychoanalytic studies[4] made me realise how a lack of cultural and social sensitivity can be a crucial flaw. In a course about groups with observations analogous to infant observations, we were three participants, one from Italy, one from the Congo, and myself from Oslo, and the group leader said that studying the university there would be ruled out as it would be far too familiar. In fact we had all just arrived and felt very alienated; I think we shared a sense of that, and the group leader did not understand what we tried to express or where we came from at all. Based on some of that, I have, in recent years, started to think much more about how socially engaged psychoanalytic thinking needs to reflect to a greater degree about how one reflects a particular cultural and social position. In a Gadamerian formulation: to think about one's situation as that which limits one's possibility of vision in order to be able to, by listening, see some more.

SK: And you, Jonathan, what was your first encounter with psychoanalysis outside the consulting room?

JD: I guess the first time I ever understood anything psychoanalytically, or at least so I thought at the time, was when I was in high school and looked into a psychoanalytic reading of children's fairy tales. It was a simple and youthful task, but I believe that the interpretation of fairy tales such as "The Sleeping Beauty" really woke my curiosity about psychoanalysis. It was not until much later that I began to develop a stronger interest in understanding different phenomena psychoanalytically. Although now that I think of it, one could say that little has changed since my first attempt: a devotion to an alternative reading of things.

Nevertheless, I believe the first text I read that engaged psychoanalytically with social, political, and historical phenomena was *The Labyrinth of Solitude*, by Mexican writer Octavio Paz. That book was my first encounter with a psychoanalytically minded analysis of Mexican identity. It made so much sense to me at the time that I suppose my own intellectual interests were somehow attracted to it.

I first read this book at university while studying psychology, and it described what someone, as a Mexican, knows intuitively about things in general, in an explicit and succinct way. It made so much sense, and it opened a possible avenue for thought. Later on, I began studying philosophy as well, and having had a background in psychoanalysis already meant that I would engage with philosophy through a psycho-analytic lens. So, for instance, when studying the notion of myth in philosophy, its logic, structure, etc., I remember finally understanding why Lacan called that version of our childhood and familial history "family myth". Making connections like this one felt like revelations to me. In the case of the myth, the understanding of how a speech act like a myth constitutes the past, yet at the same time the past constitutes it, felt like a discovery of something important.

SK: At our 2012 symposium in Denmark, you said you have been part of the Psychoanalysis and Politics group since the first sympo-sium. I can remember you saying "it was a lucky call for papers". Does that mean that Lene developed the idea and you joined later? How did the group come together?

JD: Yes, that's right, Lene developed the idea along with others. I sent an abstract to the first symposium in Copenhagen in 2010 and presented a paper. Then, after the symposium, I was invited by Lene to become a co-ordinator. The group came together precisely like that: people who knew about the Nordic Summer University or who had an interest in psychoanalysis or in its relation with other disciplines answered the call for papers or simply attended the symposium. From then on, it has been the case of people simply attending the symposia, and that alone makes them part of the group.

But Lene and I had actually already met, at the University of Essex, although each of us was involved in his/her own studies then. I was studying Philosophy and Psychoanalysis at the Centre for Psycho-analytic Studies.

LA: I had set up a Bion reading group, where we read through his books from *Learning from Experience* to *Attention and Interpretation*, and this is where Jonathan turned up for the first time, bringing with him an article by Abraham and Torok, which I thought was interesting. He came and presented to the first conference in Copenhagen in 2010 and I invited him to become a co-organiser from the second one in Oslo in 2011.

SK: How did you first conceive of the group; how did it come together? Was there a particular moment when you thought: all right, I will do it myself then?

LA: I had participated in a previous group in the Nordic Summer University (NSU), about Cornelius Castoriadis. One of the co-ordinators, Ingerid Straume, a Norwegian pedagogue, suggested to me that I start a new group. That's when I came up with Psychoanalysis and Politics, in which I wanted to encourage and include contributions from different psychoanalytic directions. I also wanted it to be a meeting place for clinicians and non-clinicians; in fact, our participants come from a wide range of academic, creative, and clinical backgrounds.

The central aim of the NSU is to further academic collaboration within the Nordic countries, with a view to introducing and developing new subjects that lack an established university seat in Scandinavia. The Nordic Ministerial Council, which finances it, is aiming for a closer collaboration with the Baltic States. About half of our participants have been from Scandinavian countries and half from other parts of the world.

SK: Apropos the group's international character and orientation: both of you are from outside the UK but have (more or less) settled in London. Was it because of the psychoanalytic/psychosocial scene that you went to England? The popularity of psychosocial studies, I think, says something about the relative strength and currency of psychoanalytic concepts in Great Britain.

LA: It was the Centre for Psychoanalytic Studies at Essex University that brought me to the UK in the first place. And it was only gradually, after having been in the UK for a while, that I discovered that other institutions also did research in psychosocial studies. I discovered and started subscribing to the journal *Psychoanalysis, Culture and Society*. Via a special issue on British psychosocial studies, I discovered and joined the UK psychosocial network and presented papers at two of their conferences (in 2010 and 2011); the first time I was very nervous as a foreigner/outsider coming to present. So, the field of psychosocial studies is important (although not all of it is psychoanalytic) as a site for psychoanalysis as a non-clinical, but, rather, cultural, social, and political interpretative resource. Also, I do think of British psychoanalysis as being special—I thought of that when we had our symposium in the rooms of the British Society (19–20 Oct 2012). Of course, the Scandinavian societies look up to the British Society—and I do so as well. Although the British Society is not specifically British, in the sense that it became a fertile soil for refugees from the European continent, when the centre of gravity shifted from central Europe to Britain. Another cultural reason is that British analysts come from many different professional backgrounds—there is no monopoly of "the health professions", which posed a limitation in the USA, although they also received central European refugees from Nazism.

Politically, in Norway (and some other countries), they originally managed to include psychoanalysis in the public health service by arguing that mental health is as important as physical health, and that therefore everyone ought to have access to good enough service, which I think is praiseworthy in itself. But then the matter of "marketisation" and government control enters in. A Norwegian analyst told me that they are required to hand in reports on how efficiently they work—and to exaggerate that efficiency. And as Svein Tjelta, the Norwegian training and group analyst, told us at the Psychoanalysis in the Age of Totalitarianism conference (London, 2012), psychotherapists are now also forced to give up on confidentiality—to hand in data about patients and diagnoses, which I think is even worse, since confidentiality is a cornerstone of psychoanalysis—indeed, the whole of psychoanalysis is undermined without confidentiality. So, in Britain, you have a situation where psychoanalysis is wholly private, and therefore does not have to answer to the government's demands, but then it is accessible only to the upper and middle classes, whereas in Norway psychoanalysis is accessible to everyone, but seems forced to sacrifice central parts of its essence, which is very serious. The third (the state) intervenes in the conversation of two consenting adults in analysis.

SK: In terms of theoretical orientation, would you position yourself mostly within the British tradition of object relations, then, or are you happily eclectic, so to speak? And, excuse a very childish question: do you have a favourite psychoanalytic writer?

LA: I have several favourites, and not only from Britain. It may be counter-productive to start "name-dropping", as it might give the impression that I do not appreciate others than the theorists I name.

Rather, I could say that I am probably somewhat eclectic, although when I reach for new theoretical contributions it would be because of a sense that what you can say using this particular theorist has come to an end, that you are faced with a problem that he/she does not succeed in addressing (and not just for the sake of being eclectic). So, I believe that each theorist should be given his/her due, while I also find that you sometimes need new or different thoughts for new or different situations or problems.

JD: I very much agree. I am interested in the differences between psychoanalytic schools of thought, too. I find it fascinating that different schools of thought have emerged and thrived in different places of the world, each under particular social and political circumstances. The directions that psychoanalytic schools have taken in each part of the world is, I believe, related to the idiosyncrasy of the people that live in each of these places. This is true, to a degree, for every discipline. However, in the case of psychoanalysis, this is even more interesting, given the close, almost inextricable relation between the theoretician's thought and his clinical work. What I mean by this is that the way that patients and analysts think and situate themselves as subjects is quite different in different parts of the world, and the psychoanalytic theory that develops therefrom takes very different directions in each case. This never ceases to amaze me.

To my mind, every psychoanalytic school of thought has strengths and weaknesses, elements of genius, dark and cryptic claims, as well as embedded metaphysical stands. It is difficult to really categorise them without making overly generalised claims. In any case, I believe that being eclectic is important; different theoretical questions, patients, and clinical settings may call for different theories to operate.

SK: I agree with you on the importance of eclecticism. It was brought home to me when I read Mitchell and Black's *Freud and Beyond* (1995), which seems to have become a standard here in Norway, where I live. In the book, the authors introduce the most prevalent psychoanalytic traditions today, not only by explaining the central theoretical pillars, but also by discussing a clinical case study for each of the approaches that can be seen to call for the respective theoretical/methodological approach to treatment.

However—and this one is particularly for Lene—in spite of appreciating the emphasis you put on openness and respect for the range of psychoanalytic approaches, which I find all the more important in a field that has been ridden by schisms, I wouldn't think that your naming a couple of major inspirations would imply a lack of appreciation of other writers. Rather, it would point to a certain profile of/in your thinking and feeling, which, from a psychoanalytic perspective, can hardly be avoided. To my mind, even the schisms can be read productively in that they point to the personal involvement and strong reverberations of particular explanations of the workings of the mind and, ultimately, individual suffering. In this respect, I hope you won't mind me pushing you a bit for your favourites as well as your greatest hurdles, and of course the ambivalent middle ground, if you wish.

LA: Well, thanks for your provocation, Steffen. I appreciate Melanie Klein for her empathic manner of writing, in the sense that she is very phenomenological, describes unconscious phantasy from within. She could be thought of as a representative of German expressionism, which I appreciate. Freud himself, of course, has a wonderful style of writing, analytical and also literary. Winnicott also remains a favourite, with his emphasis on the centrality of paradox and his careful descriptions of environmental nuances. It strikes me that all of these have a rather different style of writing. Another favourite, Bion, is different again, with his compact, partially frustrating style, while also being funny and clever, with an appreciation of the absurd. So, from these it is clear that I am focused on Britain, though Ferenczi is yet another favourite, with his very sensitive clinical descriptions, his philosophical insights, and his theories of trauma. Karl Abraham, with his stunning descriptions of part-object relationships, is another. Among the French, I think of Kristeva as being among the greatest living theorists. Other favourites are Abraham and Torok, and Jean Laplanche. Among Americans, I like Bruno Bettelheim very much, also for his cultural reflections. A living American analyst I enjoy reading is Thomas Ogden, a very creative writer in a provocative way, who sometimes makes the reader think "he is far out at sea" but then pulls the threads back together again in a brilliant way, so he pushes the boundaries and does so successfully.

I would like to add that a major source of inspiration to me is the Frankfurt School tradition, writers who are not themselves analysts, but philosophers using psychoanalytic thinking in a socially critical and fruitful way—above all Adorno, who is very much alive to me. Perhaps the greatest living philosopher, Judith Butler, also deservers mention here—a thinker who combines a very serious ethical engagement with psychoanalytically informed reflections.

SK: And Jonathan, going by what you said about travelling and "meeting the stereotypes", it appears as though you try to keep an arm's length distance between you and much of the theory that you use—an attitude which fascinates and puzzles me. None the less, from your references, it also becomes clear that you have a favourite.

JD: Yes, my favourite is undoubtedly Freud. I am fascinated by his kind of genius. I believe geniuses have existed in maths for a long time, or physics, or biology. But Freud was a genius in an area that did not properly exist before him. It is as if knowledge needed to grow to fit him, and usually it is one that needs to grow to understand knowledge—see what I mean? I also admire him as a man, I think he was brave. I can only imagine what it meant for him to present his theory of infantile sexuality to the Viennese Victorian medical society. And also, I admire how he positioned himself as "a man of culture", like a "true intellectual", without necessarily being employed as an academic. A true intellectual outside academia, I think that is remarkable. It is, I believe, one of the legacies of Freud to the psychoanalytic community, and the world: a model for an independent intellectual and academic profession that stems from an honest devotion to knowledge.

Nevertheless, I think that you meant that my favourite is Lacan, right?

SK: Yes, that's right.

JD: I find Lacanian theory astonishing regarding its deep engagement with Freud's thought. I believe Lacan was very much on to Freud's thinking. Of course, then he developed his own ideas, some of which I find more useful clinically as well as theoretically than others. But I do think that, like Freud, Lacan was a genius. Having read quite a big part of Lacan's writings and seminars, I believe that most post-structuralist authors have really built a philosophical career by unpacking what Lacan had already theorised in a very condensed form. I think Lacan is really the thinker that inspired all post-structuralist philosophy.

In terms of the influences that I have encountered, I believe that a very Freudian and Kleinian milieu at my university in Mexico and a very Lacanian environment in Argentina really set the co-ordinates of my compass. Essex University, as well as the Tavistock, have a strong Kleinian and post-Kleinian tradition, which, of course, influenced me greatly.

My engagement with Kleinian theory is the one that troubles me more, and, therefore, also makes me passionate. I came to understand Klein more deeply after having studied Lacanian theory, so I became biased there. However, it is becoming ever clearer to me that she is a great thinker and theorist, on a par with Freud and Lacan. Lacan criticised Klein's (and others') engagement with what he called "the imaginary" (i.e., fantasy). However, Klein's *phantasy* is not exactly Lacan's imaginary *fantasy*; it is, I think, more than that. Furthermore, as a clinician, engaging with the patient's phantasy is crucial. It is as if Klein's phantasies were a very detailed description of the script of Lacan's fantasies. In fact, I doubt that Lacan ever said that the analyst should do without primitive phantasies like the ones Klein described. The point I would like to make here is: how can one, as a clinician or a theoretician, do without any of these schools of thoughts without really missing something important? It is in this spirit that I believe the more eclectic the understanding of psychoanalysis, the better understanding of the patient and the social, political, or historical phenomena one can achieve.

SK: It is striking how much you, Jonathan, argue from the perspective of the therapist/analyst and you, Lene, from that of the cultural critic. Again, the combination of the two of you seems to make a lot of sense within the frame of the Psychoanalysis and Politics group. Yet, what crossed my mind, Lene, is that, seeing that you come from a real psychoanalytic pedigree (you mentioned your great aunt, Nic Waal), it is all the more interesting that you have chosen to get so close to psychoanalysis but not to become a psychoanalyst yourself. What kept you from it?

LA: When I was in Norway, aiming to become an analyst would have meant studying either medicine or psychology, since the training is not open to others, and I was more attracted to philosophy. In London (where the training is open to people from different backgrounds, from the humanities, social sciences, and other fields), I have explored more clinical thinking by taking first the Introductory Lectures series and then the Foundation Course at the Institute of Psychoanalysis. I liked the former more than the latter because there were more engaging intellectual discussions. So, I very much enjoy intellectual exchange, and felt that there might not be enough of that for me in clinical training. Having said this, my own analysis in London has, of course, been very important to me, personally, and it also has an impact on my thinking. So, I do not see myself as advocating theory without practice, so to say, although I think it is important that the debates are open to "pure theorists" as well as clinicians and that there are exchanges between them.

JD: In Psychoanalysis and Politics, we have aimed to create an environment for dialogue and exchange, not only between psychoanalytic schools of thought, but also across disciplines. I believe that multi-disciplinarity is one of our most important principles. It is motivated by a true conviction of democracy, egalitarianism, and the unyielding need to challenge our intellectual and personal comfort zones. I believe that multi-disciplinary fora can be really enriching, by preventing each of the disciplines from adopting an approach of closure of meaning, rather than one that would aim to unsettle established truths. This is why, when Lene and I collaborate in writing calls for papers, we are careful not to skew it too much to any school of thought or discipline. Yet, we strive to keep it multi-disciplinary as well, and include possible questionings that might come into play from different perspectives.

LA: Yes, to continue on from what Jonathan says about multi-disciplinarity and egalitarianism, I believe this is something that sets this forum apart from many other fora and that makes it worth doing. Hannah Arendt puts the point thus:

> If someone wants to see and experience the world as it "really" is, he can do so only by understanding it as something that is shared by many people, lies between them, separates and links them, showing itself differently to each and comprehensible only to the extent that many people can talk about it and exchange their opinions and perspectives with one another, over against one another. (Arendt, 2005, p. 128)

And, to my mind, the space we have created has given me an experience of what this means—a sense that there is a real openness and a desire to pose new questions together. She describes this situation's opposite in *Men in Dark Times* as

> the result that all men would suddenly unite in a single opinion, so that out of many opinions one would emerge, as though not men in their infinite plurality but man in the singular, one species and its exemplars, were to inhabit the earth. (1983, p. 31).

I should think this is a well known situation from many fora. Christopher Bollas describes this situation in an article in relation to psychoanalytic supervisory groups where the "right" interpretations are rewarded and the "wrong" ones silenced or unappreciated—though you could see this happening in all kinds of groups, that there is a pull towards conformity. By having symposia composed of people who differ quite a lot intellectually, in terms of disciplines and directions and in being clinically or more theoretically orientated, and also geographically, I think we have managed to avoid this, which is a very refreshing experience.

Freud's characterisation of the "I" as not being "master in its own house" is and remains provocative on a personal as well as on a political level. In so far as they do not remain theoretical items, when they become current and concrete, and when they are close up, such things as saying or doing something other than the "I" intended, the opening up of a territory of intentions and motivations beyond the surface ones, is indeed frightening and shocking. Psychoanalytic thinking, furthermore, carries the message that there is no "quick fix" for personal or social problems, which is out of line with both the current political wish for short-term psychotherapy designed to solve problems quickly and efficiently without thinking about the larger context within which they occur, and politicians' desires for "social engineering", for implementing solutions from above, thus desiring to forcefully reshape human beings. Human beings are willing to do a lot not to deal with pain, by attacking or stifling both self and other, and psychoanalytic thinking is concerned with pain, whether in a larger or a smaller way, more or less directly. Thus, it can be provocative and unwelcome both in its perceived "destructive" mode, of questioning the intentions or integrity of the "I" or seemingly attacking a good or idealised object such as the nation-state and also in what you might call its "non-destructive" aspects; in its implicit stance against instrumentalisation and manipulation, in favouring a long, slow, painful, and difficult process of dialogical discovery from within. Thus, psychoanalysis's respect for otherness is an enduring legacy that needs to be defended.

SK: It being the task of the Psychoanalysis and Politics group to defend this legacy means that the "process of dialogical discovery" (Auestad) has to be kept intact also for the project of the group itself. In this respect, it is instructive to return to a passage in the interview. Davidoff asks there, "Does accepting discontent mean that changing reality is pointless?" (see above) and, somewhat irritatingly, he leaves the question hanging in mid-air—unanswered, discontent provoking. Yet, the first call for papers issued by Auestad and Davidoff after this interview was conducted bears the title: "Action—a Limit to Psychoanalysis?", inviting "contributions that discuss the potential political role of psychoanalytic thinking and reflections on psycho-analytic understandings of action, activism, 'engagement' and 'neutrality'", as it reads in the description of the call.[5] To my mind, this is quite a powerful demonstration of the dialogical sensitivity with which the organisers approach their "discoveries from within", as well as the vitality with which they challenge their comfort zones. One can only wish for this legacy to endure, and readers are heartily invited to join in the effort:

psychoanalysis.politics@gmail.com
www.facebook.com/psApol
www.psa-pol.org

Notes

1. This is also the title of the first group publication, edited by Auestad (2012).
2. The organizers are planning for the group to become a fully independent organisation. For this purpose, Psychoanalysis and Politics was registered as an association, a non-profit organisation, in Norway in 2012, with the organisation no. 998 503 221.
3. Mentalhygienisk Rådgivningskontor, Drammensveien, Oslo.
4. Centre for Psychoanalytic Studies, University of Essex, UK.
5. www.psa-pol.org/?p=222 (last accessed: 03/07/2013).

References

Arendt, H. (1983). *Men in Dark Times*. San Diego, New York, London: Harcourt Brace.

Arendt, H. (2005). Introduction *into* politics. In: H. Arendt & J. Kohn (Eds.), *The Promise of Politics* (pp. 93–200). New York: Schocken Books.

Auestad, L. (Ed.) (2012). *Psychoanalysis and Politics. Exclusion and the Politics of Representation*. London: Karnac.

Auestad, L., & Mahrdt, H. (Eds.) (2011). *Handling, frihet, humanitet. Møter med Hannah Arendt*. Trondheim: Tapir Akademisk.

Bion, W. R. (1962). *Learning from Experience*. London: Tavistock.

Bion, W. R. (1970). *Attention and Interpretation: A Scientific Approach to Insight in Psycho-Analysis and Groups*. London: Tavistock.

Freud, S. (1900a). *The Interpretation of Dreams*. S.E., 4. London: Hogarth.

Freud, S. (1920g). *Beyond the Pleasure Principle*. S.E., 18: London: Hogarth.

Mitchell, S. A., & Black, M. J. (1995). *Freud and Beyond. A History of Modern Psychoanalytic Thought*. New York: Basic Books.

Sartre, J.-P. (1939). *Le Mur*. Paris: Gallimard.

INDEX

Adler, A., 127–128, 134–137
Adorno, T. W., 29, 56, 190–191, 203, 261
aggression/aggressive, xxii, 57, 97, 137, 139, 152, 189, 213–214, 227, 236, 238–240
  feelings, 97
Alford, C. F., 96
ambivalence, 9, 124, 144, 151, 231, 237, 240, 260
amoeboid, 86, 93, 95, 97
Andersen, H. C., 219
Anderson, B., xvii–xviii
antiproduction, 111, 117–118, 120
anti-Semitism, 15–17, 22, 28, 30, 32–33, 66
  propaganda, xxv, 14, 21, 26, 39, 51
anxiety/anxious, 5, 10, 12, 18, 27, 85, 88, 94, 98, 101, 137, 186, 188, 194, 198, 202, 233, 238–239, 249
  see also: castration
annihilation, 194, 197–198

chaos, 197
fantasy, 11
painful, xvii
psychotic, 92–93
social, xxv
Anzieu, D., 11–12, 21, 27
Arendt, H., xxiii, 104, 253–254, 263
Armstrong, D., 88
Auer, S., 178
Auestad, L., xii–xiii, xxiv, 23, 247–251, 253–254, 256–258, 260, 262–263, 265
Aztecs, 148–150

Bain, A., 91
Bakhtin, M. M., 199
Bandehy, L., 56
Barthes, R., 154–155
basic assumptions (ba), xxv, 85, 87–90, 93–94, 97–102
  dependency, 85, 88, 92, 98, 102–103
  fight/flight, 85, 88

Incohesion:
  Aggregation/Massification
    (I:A/M), xxv, 85, 87, 89–90, 93,
    97, 100–101
  pairing, 85, 88–89
Bauman, Z., 73
Baur, S., 6
behaviour(al), 10, 28, 47, 51, 135, 148,
    151–152, 166, 173, 187–188,
    191–195, 199, 201
  acceptable, 194
  human, 168
  patterns, 135, 138
  social, 147, 153, 231
Benjamin, W., 153, 228–231
Berger, B., 95
Berger, P. L., 195
Betz, H.-G., 65
Bible, The, 76, 127, 130–132
Bielik-Robson, A., 79
Bion, W. R., 85, 87–89, 95, 256, 260
Bjånesøy, K. B., 44
Bjurvald, L., 54
Black, M. J., 259
Blut und Boden (blood and soil), 25
body see also: mother
  as foreign, xxv, 3, 13
  foreign, xxi–xxii, xxv, 3, 13, 21, 24
  of a nation, 143, 147
  politic, xxi, 23, 41, 188
  social, 13–14, 120
  without organs, 111, 113, 117–118,
    120–122
Bogue, R., 119
Bollas, C., 197, 264
Borchgrevink, A. S., 49, 51–52, 54
Bowman, G., 15
Breivik, A. B., xxiv, 23, 41, 49–54, 56,
    58, 194, 248
Brenner, I., 104
British Nationalist Party (BNP), xvi
Broch, H. P., 198
Brown, A., 54
Bruntland, G. H., 47, 51
Buber, M., 103
Butler, J., xxii, 225, 232, 261

Canovan, M., 66
capitalism/capitalist, 73, 107,
    109–111, 113–114, 116–119, 122,
    124–125, 166, 168, 173–174, 187,
    189, 192, 195, 216
  anti-, 66
Carrion, J., 146, 148
Castoriadis, C., 240, 257
castration, 51, 153, 197, 242
  anxiety, 197
  symbolic, 51, 197
Centre for Studies of the Holocaust
    and Religious Minorities, 250
character
  inter, 185, 189
  ISO, 185, 189
  national, 185, 189–191, 193, 199, 202
  social, 161, 166–167, 173, 185,
    189–190, 197, 199
Chasseguet-Smirgel, J., 25, 28–29,
    32
Cheng, A., 225
chingada, 149–150
chingadera, 151
Christ of Nations, 76–77, 79
Christian/Christianity, xxiii, 33, 44,
    46–47, 52, 76, 153
  faith, 127, 129–132
  fundamentalism, 127, 129–130
Christian Democrat (Union) Party,
    xv, 180
Civic Platform (Platforma Obywatelska)
    (CP), 71–72, 74–75, 79
clinging, 22, 28, 55, 86, 93, 158
Colbert, S., 220
Coleridge, S. T., 103–104
communism/communist, 69–70, 72,
    75, 174, 194
  anti-, 35, 69
  post-, xxv, 72–73
conscious(ness), 6, 28, 90, 92–93, 127,
    135–136, 146, 148, 166–167,
    177–178, 194, 217, 230, 237–238,
    250, 254 see also:
    pre-conscious(ness), self,
    unconscious(ness)

containment, 91, 97, 101, 143, 146,
    148, 189, 217
Copjec, J., 12
Corell, S., xx–xxi
Craighead, W. E., 135
Crun, C., 241
crustacean, 86, 93, 95, 97

Dalal, F., xxiii
Darré, R. W., 25
das Ding, 207, 212–213
Davidoff, J., xiii, 247–248, 251–252,
    255–256, 259, 261, 263, 265
De Certeau, M., 196
De Maré, P., 95
death, xviii, 6, 11, 27, 53, 82, 92, 113,
    122, 143, 153, 170, 173, 177, 224,
    233, 235–238, 240–243
    cult of, 153
    drive, xxvi, 227, 233, 235, 240, 242
    instinct, 89
    living, 17
    of politics, 72
Deleuze, G., xxv, 107, 109–118,
    120–124
Demand for Right-Wing Extremism
    Index (DEREX), 35–36
Derrida, J., 234
Descartes, R., 215–216
deterritorialization, 109, 113–115,
    117–119, 124 *see also*:
    reterritorialization
Dillon, B., 5–6, 13, 17
Dypvik, A. S., 47–48
Dzwończyk, J., 73

Edwards, D., 135
ego, xxii, 8–9, 12, 28, 43, 53, 78–79,
    81–82, 132, 135, 230–231, 237
    actual, 81
    body, 12
    ideal, 45, 81
    infantile, 81
    libido, 7
    loss, 78
    skin, 11, 21, 27

super, 3, 12, 198, 226, 239
Eichmann, A., 170, 178, 191
Elias, N., 194–195
Ellman, L., 9–11
Emin, T., 12–13
empathy, 5–7, 16, 254–255, 260
empty signifier, 68, 70–71, 78
enactment, xxiv, 92, 94, 98, 101, 117,
    210
Eng, D., 22, 232–233
envy, 83, 88–89, 102, 158
Eriksen, T. H., xviii, xx, xxii, 56
European Union (EU), 34, 73, 123

Fairbairn, W. R. D., 89
Fangen, K., 53
fantasy, xvi, xx–xxii, xxiv–xxvi, 17,
    26, 29–30, 32, 41, 51–52, 54, 98,
    112, 143, 145, 158, 194, 210, 223,
    225–227, 232–233, 235–238,
    240–243, 248–249, 254, 262
    see also: anxiety/anxious
fascism/fascist, 29–30, 35, 57, 86, 99,
    109, 115, 118, 123, 128, 137, 139,
    169, 174
    neo-, 123
    propaganda, 140
fear, xiv, 9, 11–14, 17, 29, 40, 51,
    57–58, 79, 86, 92–93, 137, 151,
    153, 174–175, 181, 190, 194–195,
    197, 202
    contagious, 12–14
    of abandonment, 86, 93
    of annihilation, 89, 92–94
    of contagion, 12–14, 50
    of disease, 4, 17
    of weakness, 128, 137, 139
Fekete, L., xvi
Fenichel, O., 31
Ferenczi, S., 3, 8, 18, 260
Figes, O., 200
Figlio, K., 51
Fink, B., 234, 236
Flatley, J., 229–231
Flemmen, H., 133, 138
Foucault, M., 196

Frenkel-Brunswik, E., 29, 191
Freud, A., 96
Freud, S., xii, xv, xix–xx, xxii, 7–8, 13,
    41, 45, 47, 63, 78, 81–82, 110, 132,
    134–136, 153, 161, 164–166, 171,
    185, 197–199, 207, 212–214, 220,
    230–234, 237, 239, 253–254,
    260–262, 264
  Wolf Man, xx, 153
Fromm, E., xii, xxv, 161–181, 190–191
  Internationale-Erich-Fromm-
      Gesellschaft e.V., 163
fundamentalism/fundamentalist,
    xxv, 34, 36, 47, 99, 127–136, 139
    see also: Christian

Genosko, G., 119
Germany see also: Nazi/Nazism
  Kaiserreich, 163
  Third Reich, 161, 163
  West, 56, 179–180
Gilman, S., 14–15
globalisation, xxvi, 71, 185, 187–189,
    192–193, 195, 201–202
Glynos, J., 225, 242
going-in-search, 22, 28
Gould, L. J., 91
Green, A., 53
group see also: hypochondria, racial,
    trauma
  actual, 88, 102
  identity, 97, 104, 232
  sub-, 90–91, 95, 97
  subject, 117, 119, 122
  subjugated, 117, 119, 123
  work, 87–88, 95, 101–102
Group of Independent
    Psychoanalysts, xii, 89
Group of Independent
    Psychoanalysts of the British
    Psychoanalytical Society, xii, 89
Guattari, F., xxv, 107, 109–118,
    120–124
guilt, 6, 43, 56, 150, 202, 236
Gullestad, M., xvi–xvii, xxi, 39, 42–43,
    46

Halbwachs, M., xvii–xviii
Hall, S., 241
Hamsun, K., 193
Hardt, M., 122
hate, xxvi, 9, 11, 33, 40, 43, 50–51,
    55–57, 82, 93, 144, 151, 161, 170,
    194, 223, 225, 227, 231, 237,
    240–241
Heidegger, M., 234–235
Hermann, I., xxv, 22, 28, 32–33
Hiden, J., 178
Hinshelwood, R. D., 152, 238–239
Hitler, A., 13, 25, 30–31, 170–172,
    177–178, 180, 200
Hoggett, P., 48
Holland, E. W., 116, 118–119, 124
Holocaust, 16, 178, 181, 191, 250
Hopper, E., xiii, xvii, 87, 89, 95–96,
    101, 103
Housden, M., 177, 179
Hume, D., xxiii
Hungarian(s)/Hungary, 21, 23–25,
    28–36
  citizens, 21, 24
  extreme right, xxv, 21, 23, 30–31
    see also: Jobbik
  Guard, 35
hypochondria/hypochondriac(s),
    3–13, 16–18
  fortress, 3, 6, 8
  group, xxi

idealisation, xxiv, 41, 43, 88, 94, 102,
    195, 200, 248–249
immigrant(s), xxii, 13, 40, 43–46, 53,
    55, 57, 242 see also: Muslim
  anti-, xvi
  hostility towards, xix
incest, 50, 161, 169–172, 177–178
inferiority, xxvi, 29, 115, 127,
    135–137, 139–140, 149–150, 171
instinct, 48, 73, 81, 135, 161, 165, 168
    see also: death
International Standards Organisation
    (ISO), 192–193, 195–196, 198,
    201–203 see also: character

Internationale-Erich-Fromm-
    Gesellschaft e.V. *see*: Fromm, E.
introjection/introjective, 197, 223,
    226–227, 230–231, 238–240
    identification, 93, 99
Irigaray, L., 234
Isaacson, W., 203
Islam/Islamist(s), 47, 52–54, 56, 129,
    194, 198, 200 *see also*: Muslim
Islamophobia, 40, 54, 200
Israel/Israeli, 15–16

Jacobs, M., 135
Janion, M., 75
Jegerstedt, K., 51, 53
Jensen, P. N., 54, 56
Jew(s)/Jewish, 14–17, 21, 24, 26,
    29–33, 104, 163, 178, 181, 193
    see also: Norwegian
    persecution of, xxv, 28
Jewish Voices for Peace, 16
Jobbik, xxv, 21–23, 25, 33–35
Jung, C. G., 7

Kaës, R., xx
Kaczyński, J., 70, 75, 79
Kaczyński, L., 74–77, 79
Katyń, 64, 74, 77
Kazanjian, D., 22
Kazin, M., 65
Kellner, H., 195
Khanna, R., 225
King Olav, 39, 43–44
Klein, M., xii, 29, 43, 88–89, 102, 199,
    233, 236, 239, 260, 262
Klimova, H., 99
Koenigsberg, R. A., xxi
Kövér, G., 30
Krasnodębski, Z., 70
Kreeger, L., 102
Kristeva, J., xii, 32, 238, 240, 260
Krüger, S., xiii, 248, 250–253, 255–259,
    261–262, 265

Lacan, J., xii, 69, 110, 112, 198, 207,
    210–214, 217–218, 233–235, 237,
242–243, 251–252, 256, 261–262
    object petit a, 69, 210, 212, 218
LaCapra, D., 156–157
Laclau, E., 63, 66–72, 75, 80
Law and Justice Party (*Prawo i
    Sprawiedliwość*) (L&J), 70–72,
    74–75, 79
Lawrence, W. G., 87, 91, 103
Le Bon, G., 67
Leader, D., 8
Lehet Más a Politika (LMP), 33, 36
Lepenis, W., 231
Levinson, D. J., 29, 191
Lien, M. E., 42
Lithuania/Lithuanian, 121,
    123–124
    parliament, 107, 121
    political scene, xxv, 107, 109, 120
Long, S., 99
Lossius, K., 198

Macho, 143, 150–152
Mahrdt, H., 253
Marcuse, H., 190, 202–203
Marczewska-Rytko, M., 73
Markowski, R., 73
Marx, K., 161, 164–166, 174, 216–219
Marxism/Marxist, 52, 120, 164, 194
masochism, 96, 150
    sado-, 99, 150, 152
McGrath, M., 12
melancholia, xxvi, 8–9, 18, 78, 81–82,
    157, 223–233, 235–238, 240–243,
    249 *see also*: racial
Melhuus, M., 42
Meltzer, D., 154
memory, xvii, xx, xxii, 12, 73, 76–78,
    135, 229–230, 238
    collective, 31, 77–78
Mény, Y., 66
Menzies-Lyth, I. E. P., 87
Mexican/Mexico, 143–154, 157–158,
    163, 250–251, 256, 262 *see also*:
    national identity
    conquest of, 143–144, 148, 150,
    154–155, 157–158

history, xxvi, 143–144, 146, 148,
153–154, 157–158
Mickiewicz, A., 76–77, 79
Miller, E., 103
Milne, S., 54
minorities, 56, 108, 232
ethnic, xxv, 121, 147, 233
gender, 233
sexual, xxv, 108, 121
mirror
image, 209–211
stage, 210–211
Mitchell, J., 234
Mitchell, S. A., 259
Mojovic, M., 99
monarch/monarchy, 215–220
Money-Kyrle, R., xxi
Monkey Trials *see*: Scopes, J. T.
Moran, J. P., 132
Moscovici, S., 143, 145, 147–148
mother, xxii, 28, 31–32, 49–52, 58,
148–150, 153–154, 157, 165, 167,
172, 177, 197, 211
breast, 239
body, 28–29, 32
–child, 157, 239
Nature, 25
motherland, 73, 150
mourning, xiii, xxvi, 9, 18, 55, 57, 63,
74, 78–79, 81–82, 99, 157–158,
223, 225–226, 230–231, 235–238,
249, 253 *see also*: populism
Mudde, C., 65, 80
Muslim(s), 40, 51–55, 57 *see also*: Islam
anti-, xvi
(im)migrants, xv, 200
Myhre, A. S., 55

narcissism, xix, 7–8, 10–11, 16, 28, 39,
41, 45, 48–49, 51, 53, 56, 79,
81–83, 93, 150, 161, 170–172, 175,
177–178, 226–227, 231, 241
see also: racial
Narcissus, 146
national identity, xvii, xxvi, 147–148,
158, 178, 208–209, 223, 241–242

Mexican, 143, 145–146, 148, 154,
255
Norwegian, 39, 46–47
National Socialism, 32, 127, 129,
137–138, 161, 178
nationalism (*passim*)
character of, xviii
destructive, 172, 178
ethno-, 21, 24, 31, 35
extreme, 186, 188, 193
ideology of, xxvi, 185, 187, 189
liberal, 178
ultra-, 189
Nazi/Nazism, xxv–xxvi, 14, 25, 29,
32–33, 128, 137–138, 169, 178,
180, 193–194, 258
Germany, 16
ideology, 29, 32
party, 14
propaganda, 32
necrophilia, 161, 170, 172–173, 178
Negri, A., 122
neighbour, love one's, 207, 213–214
Neill, C., 213
Nipen, K., 55
Nissen, I., xxvi, 127–129, 133–139
Nordic Summer University (NSU),
247, 256–257
Norway/Norwegian, xviii, xxi,
xxiv–xxv, 24, 39, 42–44, 46–49,
51, 53–57, 127, 129–131, 138, 194,
248, 250–251, 258–259 *see also*:
national identity
Church, 44
Jews, xxi
Progress Party, 54–55, 57
society, 46, 54–55
nostalgia, xxvi, 193–194, 200

object, 7–8, 28, 43, 45, 48, 53, 78–79,
81–82, 86, 90–93, 98–99, 134, 149,
150–153, 156, 188, 198, 200, 226,
228–240
alien, 28, 239
-cause, 226, 234–235
external, 152, 230, 239

female, 149–153
good, xxv, 264
ideal(ised), xxiv–xxv, 43, 248, 264
internal, 152, 238–239
libido, 7, 230
loss, 78, 81, 231, 237–238
lost, 223, 225–226, 231–232, 235–236
love(d), 18, 43, 45, 78, 81–82, 231
male, 143, 150–153, 158
new, 78, 82
part(ial), 111, 260
pure, xxiv, 248
relations, 43, 152, 239, 252, 258, 260
sexual, 231
objective/objectivity, 71, 112, 118,
    131, 134, 156, 158–159, 169, 178,
    191, 248, 250
Oedipus, 110, 197

Palacios, M., 225, 249
Palestinian, 15–16
Palikot, J., 75, 79
panopticon, 185, 188, 192, 196–197,
    202–203
paranoia/paranoiac/paranoid, xxv,
    3–4, 8–9, 13–16, 50, 107–109,
    114–121, 123–125, 169, 174, 214
    see also: unconscious(ness)
    investment(s), 122–123
paranoid–schizoid
    defences, 98
    position, 199
Parnet, C., 111–112
Paz, O., 143, 145–153, 155–157, 255
Pedersen, E., 56
Pensky, M., 228
phantasy, xx, 143–145, 148, 152–154,
    158, 260, 262
    primal scene, xxvi, 153–154,
        157–158
Phillips, C., xxiii
Phillips, M., 54
Poland/Polish, 64, 69–71, 73–79, 82
    Air Force, 73
    government, 74
    history, xxv, 64, 74–75

populism, 64, 70–74, 77
populism, xxv, 63–67, 69–75, 79–80
    see also: Poland/Polish
    bad, 71
    good, 71
    mourning, 63, 74, 80, 82
Posocco, S., 225
pre-conscious(ness), xvii, 110, 118,
    120–123 see also: conscious(ness),
    unconscious(ness)
projection, xxvi, 14, 43, 81, 99, 101,
    152, 174, 197, 209, 223, 227, 230,
    237–239, 242
projective identification, 93, 99, 152,
    198, 227
propaganda, 26, 33, 39, 51–52, 56,
    136, 139, 194 see also:
        anti-Semitism, fascist,
        Nazi/Nazism, racist
Psychoanalysis and Politics
    (www.psa-pol.org), xii, xxiv,
    247–250, 253, 256–257, 262–263,
    265
purity, xxi, 96
    of blood, 29

racial
    character, 14
    group, 171,
    melancholia, 226, 230, 233
    mixing, 31
    narcissism, 171
    superiority, 171
racially coded majority, 39, 42
racism/racist, xvi, xxv, 4, 13, 15–16,
    39, 49, 51, 56–57, 99, 169
    anti-, 69
    ideology, 25, 29
    imagery, 29, 33
    propaganda, 39, 51
rage, 43, 51, 138, 157, 171, 231
rape, 30–31, 52–53, 144, 149–152,
    154–155, 157–158 see also:
        chingada
Ravnaas, N. R., 56
refugee(s), xix, xxii, 40, 57, 188, 258

Reich, W., xxi–xxii, 29, 118
repression, xx, 108, 118, 121, 134–135,
    166–167, 197, 234, 249, 252
    sexual, 29
reterritorialization, 109, 115–119, 124
    see also: deterritorialization
Ricoeur, P., 155
right-wing
    activist(s), 33
    extremism, xvi, 16, 21, 23, 34, 53, 198
    parties, xvi, 21, 23, 34
    press, 138
    ultra-, 49, 51
    views, 21
ritual, 29–30, 35, 93, 99, 103
role(s), xx, xxvi, 14, 66, 68, 85, 88,
    95–96, 100, 113, 119, 168, 172,
    178, 191, 195–196, 236, 265
    of jester, 95–96
    of stable-cleaner, 95–96
    of whistleblower, 95–96, 103
Roma/Romani, 21, 24, 33, 35, 40, 57
Rose, J., 234
Rosenfeld, H. A., 93
Russia, 74–75, 77, 80, 178 *see also*:
    Soviet Union

sadism, 198, 231, 237–238
Sanchez-Pardo, E., 232–233, 240
Sanford, R. N., 29, 191
Sarrazin, T., xv, 180
Sartre, J.-P., 250, 253
scapegoat, 96–97, 101, 188, 223,
    226–227
schizoanalysis, 110–112, 114–117
schizoid
    isolation, 101
    movement, 117
    reaction, 86, 93
schizophrenia/schizophrenic, xxv,
    107, 109–110, 113–120, 122–125
Schreber, D. P., 8, 13–14, 18
Schwenger, P., 235
Scopes, J. T. (Monkey Trials), 130–131
self, xxvi, 3, 6, 9, 18, 43, 48, 92, 94,
    143, 151, 153, 215–216, 224, 227,
    229, 236–238, 240, 242
    -aware(ness), 191, 228
    -conscious(ness), 191
    -control, 194
    -esteem, 8, 82, 88, 132
    -identity, 21, 27, 216
    -images, 49
    -love, 3, 9, 47, 81
    -mutilation, 28, 52
    -other, 7, 236–237
    -reflection, xvi
    -regulation, 201–202
Seth, V., 14
sexism, 39, 51
sexual *see also*: minorities, object,
    repression
    abuse, 29
    allusions, 152
    incapability, 137
    insecurity, 138
    interest, 40, 51
    needs, 8
    partner, 8
    relation, 150
sexuality, 29, 88, 136, 158, 225
    homo-, 152
    infantile, 261
Shakespeare, W.
    Coriolanus, 96
    Hamlet, 78–79
    Julius Caesar, 96
    King Lear, 79
    Tempest, The, 96
Simonsen, M., 57
Skirbekk, G., 39, 46–47
Smoleńsk, 64, 77, 82
social representation, 143–145,
    147–152, 158
Solidarność, 69–70
Solnit, R., 100
Solymosi, E., 29–30
Sontheimer, K., 207
Soviet Union, 121, 174, 178–179, 187,
    190, 193, 201 *see also*: Russia,
    Stalin
Śpiewak, P., 70

splitting, 9, 43, 67, 99, 110, 150, 152,
    193, 200, 211, 233–234, 238
Stacey, R., 98
Stalin, J., 169–170, 200
standardisation, xviii, xxvi, 10, 173,
    185, 188–189, 192–193, 195–196,
    198, 201
State Centre for Child and Youth
    Psychiatry (SSBU), 50
Stavrakakis, J., 225, 242
Stavrakakis, Y., 79, 225, 242
Stepansky, P. E., 135
subjectivity, 8, 48, 68, 110, 144, 154,
    158–159, 217–219, 227, 236, 250
  account(s), 154–156, 159
  inter-, 233, 236
  marginal, 225, 232
  popular, 68–69
Surel, Y., 66
Svendsen, 56
symbol(-ism), xviii, xx, 21, 23, 30,
    32–33, 35, 46, 77, 82, 94, 102, 110,
    113, 155, 185, 187–189, 193, 195,
    198–199, 201, 207, 211–212, 215,
    220, 227, 235, 240–241, 243
  see also: castration
syndrome of decay, 161–162, 170,
    172–175, 178
Szacki, J., 66
Szasz, T., 16

Taggart, P., 65
Taine, H., 67
Tamir, Y., 178
Tavistock Centre, 252, 262
terrorist(s), xxiii–xxiv, 39, 49, 51,
    53–55, 97, 192, 248
Tiszaeszlái, 29–30
Tjelta, S., 198
transference, 9, 18, 156, 166
  counter-, 101
trauma/traumatic/traumatised
    (passim)
  experience(s), 85, 89, 92–94, 98,
    101–102, 156
  group, 85, 91–92

organisations, 100
patients, 101, 103
people, 93, 95–96
personal, 91–92
social, xviii, 97, 99, 104
society, xxv, 86, 96–97, 99–100,
    104
traumatogenic, xiv, 91, 93
Turquet, P., 91, 95, 102
TV 2, 57

unconscious(ness), xvii, xx, xxv, 7, 88,
    93, 103, 110–112, 115, 119–120,
    123, 132, 135–136, 146, 148,
    152–153, 161, 165–166, 177, 197,
    209, 216, 234, 236–237, 250, 252,
    254, 260 see also: conscious(ness),
    pre-conscious(ness)
  alliances, xx
  investment(s), 107, 110, 120–123
  libidinal, 120
  life, xxv, 85, 89, 91, 100
  paranoiac, 107, 120–121, 123
  revolution, 120–121
  social, xiii, 161, 166–167
Unknown Soldiers, xviii

Vaihinger, H., 128, 134–135
vermin, 4, 14–17, 21, 26, 29
Vettenranta, S., 55
victim(s), xxi, 33, 52, 55–58, 74, 76–77,
    80, 154–156, 199
violence, xxii, 33–35, 50, 52, 55, 57, 97,
    151, 170, 172, 174, 188, 201,
    223–227, 233, 236–242, 249
  political, xxvi, 223, 225, 240–243
  social, xxvi, 223, 226, 237, 240,
    242
Virno, P., 122
Vogt, R., 129–135, 139

war, 53, 64, 69, 74, 77, 103, 138, 154,
    157, 164, 174–175, 177, 179, 190,
    233
  Cold, xix, 163
  First World, 163–164, 169, 214, 230

inter-, 121, 233
Korean, 163
nuclear, 173, 179, 181
on terror, 13
post-, 56, 139, 179–180
pre-, 108, 121, 194
Second World, xix, 51, 53, 57, 163, 169, 191, 194
Yom Kippur, 43
Warsaw Uprising, 64, 77
weakness, 57, 66, 128, 137–140, 156, 259
Weinberg, H., xiii, xvii, 103
Weiner, I. B., 135
Weingart, L., 15–16
Welldon, E. V., 101
Winlow, S., 241
Winnicott, D. W., 89, 98, 103, 158–159, 260

world *see also*: war
external, 6, 27, 132, 197, 237
inner/internal, 18, 197
of Warcraft, 49
outer/outside, 6, 8–9, 18, 110, 150, 201, 203, 230, 250
real, 250
Western, 54
Wysocka, O., 73

xenophobia, xvi, xxv–xxvi, 40, 54, 57

Yegenoglu, M., 225
Young-Bruehl, E., xix–xx, 48

Zakaria, F., 65
Zimbardo, P. G., 191
Žižek, S., 70, 201, 212, 225–226, 235–236